GETTYSBURG
BATTLEFIELD

GETTYSBURG BATTLEFIELD

THE DEFINITIVE ILLUSTRATED HISTORY

DAVID J. EICHER

FOREWORD BY JAMES M. McPHERSON

THREE-DIMENSIONAL MAPS BY LEE VANDE VISSE

CHRONICLE BOOKS
SAN FRANCISCO

For Chris Eicher, with hope that he will grow up with a deep
appreciation of Gettysburg, the Civil War, and the American nation.

Library of Congress Cataloging-in-Publication Data available.

ISBN 0-8118-2868-9

Manufactured in the United Kingdom

Designed by ORG inc.
Typesetting by ORG inc.

Distributed in Canada by Raincoast Books
9050 Shaughnessy Street
Vancouver, BC V6P6E5

10 9 8 7 6 5 4 3 2 1

Chronicle Books LLC
85 Second Street
San Francisco, California 94105

www.chroniclebooks.com

Contents

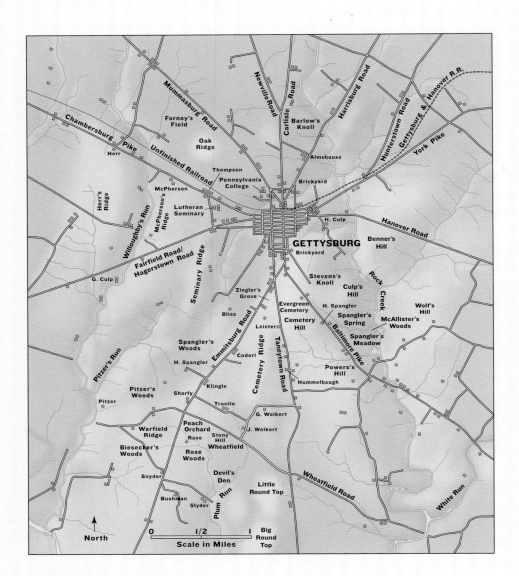

The Battlefield of Gettysburg
1863

The town and battlefield of Gettysburg
in 1863 comprised a borough of 2,390
citizens. The battle lines would
eventually form along Seminary Ridge
(Confederate) and Cemetery Ridge
(Union), giving the Federals the advanta-
geous high-elevation positions of Culp's
Hill, Cemetery Hill, and Little Round Top.

Foreword

by James M. McPherson

I have lost count of the number of times I have walked, bicycled, or driven over the Gettysburg battlefield. My first visit occurred in 1958, when I knew little more of this hallowed ground than the average tourist. My most recent visit occurred in November 2000, when I led a tour of about 40 Civil War enthusiasts. In between I have guided dozens of groups around the battlefield, ranging in size from 4 to more than 100 and ranging in age from 8 to 80.

One might think that, having traversed almost every acre of the nearly 5,000 acres of this battlefield, I would have become sated with seeing the same topography and monuments, explaining the same strategy and tactics, and telling the same stories over and over again. Not a bit of it. Every time I go to Gettysburg, I see and learn something new, because the time of day or of year is different, the sun strikes something at a different angle, or strikes nothing at all because it is obscured by clouds, or because someone on my tour asks a question I had not heard or thought of before. Even the things I have seen or heard dozens of times seem fresh on each occasion, for this is truly hallowed ground whose depth and power of meaning can never grow old. If the American Civil War is the crossroads of our being, as Shelby Foote has said, then Gettysburg stands at the very center of that crossroads. Unless we also stand at that spot and understand what happened there and why, we can never get our bearings, can never know whence we have come or where we are going.

A substantial percentage of the nearly two million people who tour the Gettysburg battlefield every year are foreign visitors. They too want to see the place where the greatest battle in the history of the Western Hemisphere was fought, and to walk the shaded grove of the national cemetery that is the final resting place of more than 4,000 Union soldiers who gave "the last full measure of devotion" so that "government of the people, by the people, for the people" would not perish from the earth. Even the adversaries of the United States in the Cold War considered Gettysburg a special place. In 1976 a delegation of historians from the Soviet Union visited this country to take part in events commemorating the bicentennial of the American Revolution. Their host, a historian of the Revolution and early republic, asked them which site they wanted to visit first — Independence Hall, perhaps, or Lexington and Concord, or Williamsburg and Yorktown?

Their answer: None of the above. They wanted to start with Gettysburg. Why? asked their surprised host. Because, replied these Russians who had lived through World War II, Gettysburg was the American Stalingrad — the battle in America's "Great Patriotic War" that turned the tide toward ultimate victory.

Just as more people visit Gettysburg than any other Civil War battlefield, more books have been written about this battle than any other — hundreds of books, perhaps thousands. Why, then, we might ask, why another book about Gettysburg? What could possibly be left to say that has not already been said many times? Just as every one of my visits to the battlefield reveals something new, *Gettysburg Battlefield: The Definitive Illustrated History* offers fresh perspectives and insights. This book is unique. David Eicher has put together a volume that combines a narrative of the campaign and battle with color two-dimensional and three-dimensional maps, plus photographs taken just after the battle and photographs of the same locales from the same camera angles taken 137 years later. These features make *Gettysburg Battlefield: The Definitive Illustrated History* a multidimensional history and image of the battle without parallel in the literature, and a superb guidebook for anyone touring Gettysburg.

But the most intriguing features of this book are the 15 mini-essays by experts on key aspects of the battle and battlefield. These essays evoke an empathy with the men who fought and suffered and died there. "In all great deeds, something abides," wrote Col. Joshua Lawrence Chamberlain of the 20th Maine Infantry. More than anywhere else, the greatness of deeds abides at Gettysburg. One need not be a mystic to sense the presence of ghosts on the battlefield. One needs only a little imagination to hear the hoarse yells of the exhausted survivors of Chamberlain's regiment as they launch their bayonet charge at Little Round Top, or to hear George Armstrong Custer shout, "Come on, you Wolverines!" as his Michigan troopers gallop toward Jeb Stuart's horsemen on the East Cavalry Battlefield, or to listen to Lincoln's immortal words as he speaks at the dedication of the soldiers' cemetery. These and other powerful and poignant events come alive again in the sidebar essays, which along with a total of 486 photographs — more than any other book on Gettysburg — make *Gettysburg Battlefield: The Definitive Illustrated History* more than a book. It is an experience not to be missed.

The author as a 10-year-old on the porch of the Leister House, Meade's Headquarters, 1971.

Preface

Gettysburg is one of my favorite places in the world. It may have been the result of considerable exposure to historical places in general and Gettysburg in particular when I was a kid. My father, a professor, took the family on long summer vacations that wound around through many sites of interest, historical and cultural. In those days we had one of those campers you pulled behind your car and set up as a glorified tent each night in some parklike setting. In 1971, when I was 10, one of those trips coincided with several convergences that created a magical, permanent impression. Between infanthood and the teenage years, not only was I getting old enough to understand complex historical events, but I was electrified by actual things historical (collecting Minié bullets, seeing cannon on the field, wondering over the uniforms in the park museum, and so forth) and still young enough to feel a mystical connection to the past. As we camped one night at the Drummer Boy campground, in a pouring rainstorm, we went to bed reading about the grandiose battle of Gettysburg by flashlight and then got up the next morning, tramped up Culp's Hill, and — with the rains continuing, thunder clapping, and slight fog permeating the air — we ran down from the summit toward our car, seeing only a lone, ghostly Confederate reenactor marching along as if nothing alarming were happening. It was the kind of ethereal event in a boy's summer that created a lasting memory.

I later became much attached to the story of Gettysburg and the battle, despite my own Civil War ancestor's having fought in the western theater under Grant and Sherman.

Gettysburg has such a powerful grip on the American psyche that it has overshadowed all other actions of the war, although its strategic significance was arguably not as great as quite a few other actions and campaigns. Yet Americans love Gettysburg, and historians and writers have produced a great quantity of books about it. So why write another?

Gettysburg Battlefield: The Definitive Illustrated History presents a unique visual remembrance of the battle and the place by including a range of materials. Two dozen color illustrations and maps have been created by illustrator and Civil War buff Lee Vande Visse, showing significant areas of action and movements during the campaign. They provide a bird's-eye view of certain celebrated phases of Gettysburg — action in the Devil's Den, in the Wheatfield, on Little Round Top, and more, showing the lay of the land and significant troop encounters during the battle. On them, Xs represent unit sizes as follows: X = brigade; XX = division; XXX = corps; and XXXX = army. These maps were carefully checked against the authoritative work of Tom Desjardin, who spent several years devising the topographical maps published in 1998 by the Friends of the National Parks at Gettysburg, the atlas that accompanies the *Official Records of the Union and Confederate Armies*, excellent maps in campaign studies by Harry W. Pfanz and David G. Martin, and other sources. Coupled with them are 486 photographs showing the battlefield and significant and unusual participants in the campaign.

In compiling the photographs for the book, I have attempted to include all historical images of the Gettysburg battlefield made during the Civil War years themselves, 1861–1865. I have included only a few postwar historical views of some significant places that are known not to have been photographed at close range during the war years, as with the field of the Pickett-Pettigrew-Trimble Charge. The collection comprises some 160 historical images of the battlefield. With homage to the pioneer of Gettysburg photographic studies, William A. Frassanito, I have employed his style of presenting matching, modern photographic views of many of the historical images, comprising 89 color frames taken in the late 1990s and 2000, which can be compared with the most important historical images. As Bill Frassanito has shown us, it's really quite striking to take the book to the field and match up the historical scene with the modern counterpart, to stand right on the trail of history. Moreover, I have included 117 color photographs of structures, monuments, and historically important portions of the field that were not covered by the contemporary Gettysburg photographers, and 113 images of participants in the battle. Thus, the work contains the most complete collection of Gettysburg imagery in a single volume.

I have presented a text of some 50,000 words about the

campaign and the battle, attempting to provide a good story of the tactics and strategy of the action in Pennsylvania, along with the most prominent individual struggles during the three days of fighting and the tales of the most interesting officers and men who fought the battle. Many controversies exist over interpreting the actions at Gettysburg, and I have written about a good many of them, hoping to provide a clear and entertaining overview of the battle. Additionally, captions provide a great amount of information on the historic images that early photographers created, as well as on the modern features of the field, such as restored houses and monuments.

Offering a fresh contrast to the story of the battle are 15 essays contributed by 14 prominent Gettysburg historians. I asked them to reflect on various portions of the battle or parts of the battlefield, and the fascinating collection of their thoughts formulates one of the greatest contributions of this work. The contributors include 4 principal historians of the Gettysburg National Military Park — Kathy Georg Harrison, Scott Hartwig, John Heiser, and Winona Peterson — as well as the distinguished authors Ted Alexander, Tom Desjardin, Lance Herdegen, Wayne Motts, Brian Pohanka, Rick Sauers, John Simon, Peter Sutter, Jeff Wert, and David Woodbury. I also offer a slimmed-down version of the order of battle compiled by my father, the guy who first took me to Gettysburg, appearing as an appendix. A fuller order of battle, with references to the officers and units mentioned in the text of this book, appears as an appendix. (For a comprehensive Gettysburg order of battle, see the Web site http://www.gdg.org/eicherorder.) The nation's leading Civil War historian, Jim McPherson, has graciously contributed a brilliant and inspiring foreword to this book.

I only hope that you will use this book to discover the joys of studying and walking over the battleground at Gettysburg, where so much of the memory of our great national struggle resides.

Gettysburg can be infectious: the author's son Christopher, age two and a half, at the North Carolina Monument, 1995.

Introduction

On a warm summer morning filled with blue sky only peppered with clouds, a young man hiked through tall grass and weeds in his trousers, boots, and jacket, leaving the grounds of Pennsylvania College and arriving at a long, flat ridge. After his journey of some 20 minutes, the 18-year-old boy met a large group of other boys and men assembled on a forested plat of the ridge known as "Railroad Woods," because an unfinished railroad cut through eastward toward the town. It was early on the morning of July 1, 1863, and Dan Skelly, a civilian who had just failed entrance to the military academy at West Point, was anxious to watch a brush with the Confederates, "not dreaming of the terrible conflict that was to occur," and "not having the slightest conception of the proximity of the two armies."

Skelly and the other boys and men from Gettysburg got their wish on that sunny morning. As the troops found each other, the civilians made a hasty retreat for the town. On his way back, Skelly noted, "a cannon ball struck the earth about fifteen or twenty feet from me, scattering the ground somewhat about me and quickening my pace considerably." During the next three days, civilians spread into the country, hid in houses inside town, and lived through what is still the largest battle ever fought in the Western Hemisphere. When it was over, Skelly and the other townsfolk of Gettysburg emerged from the shadows and slowly began to explore the unthinkable.

Young Skelly walked across the battlefield at great length on July 6, two days after Robert E. Lee's army began its south-ward retreat. Not only was the danger apparently reduced, but the heavy rains that followed the battle had subsided, replaced by the hot July sun. What Skelly saw shocked and transformed his view of civilization for the rest of his life. The debris of battle lay everywhere; broken cannons, wrecked limbers, dead horses, scattered shells, haversacks, canteens, tents, and clothes were strewn across the landscape. More than 23,000 longarms (muskets, carbines, and rifles) had been abandoned on the field. Dead men and hideously wounded horses lay in seemingly meaningless disorder, and it appeared that nearly every vacant structure had become a field hospital. Piles of amputated arms and legs could be spied chaotically stacked at aid stations. On the Emmitsburg Road, across which Pickett's Charge had been made, Skelly found Confederate soldiers as yet unburied. "They were lying on their backs," he wrote, "their faces toward the heavens, and burned as black as coal from exposure to the hot sun." The Federal army had supposedly won a great victory, townsfolk reminded themselves after the booming of the guns had stopped, but now Gettysburg, a town of 2,390, had become hell on earth.

As he walked across the ground south of Gettysburg, Skelly discovered what appeared to be hastily abandoned houses in between the scattered debris. They were farms familiar to him. South of town, he found the Abraham Trostle House "entirely deserted. In the kitchen the dinner table was still set with all the dishes from the meal, and fragments of food remained, indicating that the family had gotten up from their meal and made a hurried getaway." Northeast of this position, at the Lydia Leister House, Skelly inspected the small frame structure in which George Meade, the Federal commander, had made his headquarters. "In the front room . . . was a bed," he wrote, "the covers of it thrown back; and its condition indicated that a wounded soldier had occupied it." He later learned that Maj. Gen. Dan Butterfield, Meade's chief of staff, had lain in the bed after being struck by a shell fragment during the cannonade that preceded Pickett's Charge.

Skelly was one of the first to explore how war had touched Gettysburg and its environs with a deep stroke during the first days of July 1863. Indeed, the battle, and the war overall, was touching and transforming the lives of all Americans. What Skelly could not see, for example, was that his older brother Jack had been mortally wounded and lay dying in a hospital at Winchester, Virginia.

Only later would it become clear that the battle of Gettysburg was destined to be the largest and deadliest of the Civil War. Altogether, some 163,000 men approached and made war on one another in the hot Pennsylvania fields.

The battle produced 45,687 casualties. Of these, 7,058 were men killed on the field. Tactically, it reversed the rising confidence of Robert E. Lee's Army of Northern Virginia, which had swelled after a stunning victory at Chancellorsville. Strategically, it ruined Lee's ambitions to draw the war away from weary Virginia, take pressure off of besieged Vicksburg, forage extensively in the fertile Pennsylvania countryside, and with a victory perhaps even win recognition of the Confederacy from Britain or France. The high-water mark of the Confederacy, Gettysburg came to represent a point at which Lee's army would never again arrive. For the remaining two years of the bloody war, the great Southern army of the east would never again carry the war onto Northern soil on anything but a minute scale. Indeed, for many Americans, Gettysburg is the most revered battle in world history.

For Robert E. Lee, the gambles made during the Gettysburg campaign reflect a measure of the Confederate commander's desperation as much as his overconfidence in his army. Of the many Gettysburg controversies enthusiasts of the battle love to revel over, perhaps the greatest is "What could Lee have been thinking when he ordered Pickett's Charge?" Indeed, standing on the ground at the Lee Monument today and peering eastward toward the position of the Union center, marked by the Copse of Trees more than one and a quarter miles away, one must ponder Lee's judgment. On the battle's third day he ordered his ablest lieutenant, James Longstreet, to order the freshest units still available to march across that open ground under the direction of Maj. Gen. George E. Pickett to what became their doom. The charge, which most recently has been dubbed the Pickett-Pettigrew-Trimble Charge (for the three commanders who led it), was a titanic disaster, resulting in the loss, as either prisoners or casualties, of most of the more than 13,000 men who made it. It sealed the fate of the Gettysburg campaign. It reduced the momentum of the Confederate war effort to a point that would never again seriously threaten the sanctity of the Union. "It is all my fault," Lee told staff officers and private soldiers alike following the repulse of the charge.

Yet it was not as much Lee's fault as historians have often concluded. Lee had some reason to believe that the Yankee army had reinforced its northern and southern ends after they were attacked on the previous day (thus weakening the center), and the wily Federal artillery chief, Henry Hunt, had the cannoneers irregularly fire in a mock sputtering fashion during the cannonade that preceded the charge, as if they were running low on ammunition. It was a ruse that worked with deadly effectiveness; when the Confederates approached to within easy artillery range, Federal gunners opened up, with devastating results.

The battle of Gettysburg offers many similar stories. That the battle took place where it did, and how it did at all, was an accident. It was nearly the battle of Pipe Creek, and then later equally nearly the battle of Cashtown. Neither army intended to give general battle where and how they did, and each army was only vaguely aware of where the other lay in strength. The campaign began when Confederate cavalry under Maj. Gen. James E. B. Stuart, known affectionately as Jeb, moved out and screened the enemy along the Rappahannock River near Culpeper, Virginia. Yankee cavalry under Brig. Gen. Alfred Pleasonton, never considered the equals of the Southern horsemen, attacked at Brandy Station on June 9. The result was a great cavalry and infantry fight, with the Federals winning the day and gaining vast confidence in their abilities and those of their commanders. Stuart, a dashing cavalier who wore a yellow plume in his hat, was humiliated. His response to the humiliation would carry over into the actions that transpired three weeks later in Pennsylvania.

As the Gettysburg campaign accelerated, Stuart — given wide latitude in his orders by Lee — initiated a raid on June 25 in which he rode around the Federal army and captured supplies and wagons, harassing the lines of communication and confusing the Federal army in the process. Although the Federal commander of the Army of the Potomac, Maj. Gen. Joseph Hooker, did not need help in becoming confused — as he had demonstrated two months earlier at Chancellorsville — Stuart succeeded in thwarting the Yankees and capturing supplies and material. In his absence, however, Lee's Army of Northern Virginia lacked much of its cavalry and therefore had an even vaguer notion of where the Yankees were than it would have if Stuart had been present. Consequently, as the armies felt their way northward — Lee behind the screen of the South Mountain ridge and Hooker in slow pursuit, finally crossing the Potomac into Maryland on June 25 and June 28, respectively, they had little idea of where the opposing forces were.

The situations for battle now deepened with each passing day. Confederate forces under Lt. Gen. Richard S. Ewell spearheaded the movement through the fertile Cumberland Valley. Stuart's raiding column continued to slice through the countryside, now taking 125 captured Federal wagons with it. Rebel forces marched into Pennsylvania towns, including York and Carlisle, and skirmishes with scattered Federal troops and hastily assembled Pennsylvania militia erupted at Greencastle, McConnellsburg, and Sporting Hill. In the midst of imminent war in Pennsylvania, Hooker scuffled with the general-in-chief, Maj. Gen. Henry W. Halleck. It wasn't the first time, and Halleck and Lincoln had had enough. Maj. Gen. George G. Meade, a Pennsylvanian and veteran of the regular army, was assigned as the new commander of the Army of the Potomac. It was an uncomfortable time to change field commanders.

Meade pulled his seven scattered army corps northward, to surround Frederick and Middletown, in Maryland, and anticipated battle, ever cautious about the situation and the ground. After writing an influential circular to his corps commanders along Pipe Creek on June 30, in which he considered fortifying this line in northern Maryland, he pushed forward. Lee, meanwhile, disturbed by the continued absence of Stuart, began to appreciate the situation he found himself in. A spy employed by Lee's senior corps commander, Lt. Gen. James Longstreet, informed the Confederate high command that he had reconnoitered the Yankee positions and that they were much closer than Lee and Longstreet could have surmised. The spy, a mysterious individual named Harrison, planted the seed of what would become the Confederate tactical preparation for the battle. The Southern forces began to concentrate at Cashtown and Gettysburg, the former being a small crossroads, the latter a transportation artery of roads that arrayed outward like spokes from the center of a wheel.

And thus, as Meade's army floated northward in bits and pieces, Maj. Gen. Harry Heth's Confederate infantry clashed with troopers under Brig. Gen. John Buford, who had been reconnoitering west of Gettysburg, on the early morning of July 1. The battle was begun. Whether or not Heth's Confederates were hunting for shoes and other supplies is still a point of argument among Gettysburg buffs; almost certainly Lt. Marcellus E. Jones of the 8th Illinois Cavalry was the one who grabbed a carbine and fired off several shots at a distant Rebel officer on horseback, unleashing the general crackle of musketry along Willoughby's Run that followed.

Once it began on the morning of July 1, the battle accelerated by piecemeal additions to the fire on each side. It took on a life of its own, and neither side, though unprepared for major action, would break off and retreat. On the Federal side, Meade would not arrive on the field until the very early morning of July 2, after the whole first day's action had been fought. Instead, after it became clear that the battle had begun, Meade dispatched Maj. Gen. Winfield Scott Hancock to the field with orders to take control and devise a coherent tactical plan for the engagement. In the meantime, John Buford's cavalry had its hands full with a growing presence of gray-clad uniforms both west and north of Gettysburg. His brigade of horse soldiers, aided by a small investment of others, was having a hot time holding Lt. Gen. A. P. Hill's soldiers to the west, and it became clear that Lt. Gen. Richard Ewell's Confederates were bearing down on Buford from the direction of Carlisle.

A short time after the battle erupted along the Chambersburg Pike, through the Railroad (McPherson's) Woods and into the unfinished railroad cut, the first Yankee infantry — that of the 1st Corps, commanded by Maj. Gen. John F. Reynolds — arrived on the scene. The battle was now joined, but the slight recovery by the Union forces was stifled when a bullet from one of the Confederate volleys struck Reynolds in the head, killing him instantly. He was one of the highest-ranking officers killed during the Civil War.

The push to stave off the Confederate surge faltered, and as the afternoon wore on, Yankees scattered through the town and the residents of Gettysburg who had not fled witnessed war spilling directly through their streets. Hancock had arrived on Cemetery Hill, south of the town, and rallied his dazed Federal troops, regrouping them in front of a recently completed Cemetery Gatehouse. Night fell under a partly cloudy sky with an occasional light spray of rain but with a waning gibbous moon, nearly full, casting a dull light across the landscape, which rang occasionally with the shrieks and cries of the wounded.

As numbing as July 1 had been, it was a mere prelude to the real fighting that followed. Lee had hesitated early in the first day, preferring to wait to attack until Stuart's position was known and until Longstreet's corps had been brought up into position. When it became clear that the Confederates were pushing a weaker enemy back into Gettysburg, however, his dreams of strategic conquest lit anew, and he confidently ordered his commanders to press the attack. Lee established headquarters in a series of tents erected across the Chambersburg Pike from the Mary Thompson House, on ground fought across the previous morning. His solitary command style offered a stark contrast to that of the Yankees; whereas Meade and his commanders discussed their options at length, Lee thought alone and talked only briefly with a number of senior commanders before retiring. Meade, still in harried transit, finally found the Lydia Leister House on the Taneytown Road, south of town. Hancock assured Meade that he had arrayed the army in good order, an exercise that in fact continued throughout the night and resulted in a fishhook-shaped line of battle that in large part concentrated toward the high ground from which artillery could fire effectively.

The second day at Gettysburg, July 2, was the decisive day of battle. In terms of intensity of action and numbers of forces involved, it made the previous day appear to be a skirmish, and it gave many areas of the battlefield fame that would echo in the American psyche — Cemetery Hill, Culp's Hill, Little Round Top, Devil's Den, the Wheatfield, the Peach Orchard, Rose Woods, Spangler's Spring, the Trostle House, the Valley of Death, and the Slaughter Pen. The two armies faced each other as they established positions, reinforced, and prepared for action through the first half of the second day. With the Union army spread across Cemetery Hill and Cemetery Ridge south of the town, the Confederate army arrayed itself in a north-south line along Seminary Ridge, southwest of the town. Skirmishers lay flat on the ground in meadows and on the edges of fields of corn and shot randomly at enemy troops barely visible in the distance. Occasionally a Confederate skirmish line formed and surged toward the Federal lines with a Rebel yell and a crack of musketry fire.

For the Army of the Potomac, the notable event of the day thus far was that the irascible Maj. Gen. Daniel E. Sickles, a politician and sometime friend of James Buchanan's, had disobeyed orders and marched his 3d Corps well out into an exposed position toward the Confederate line. He spread troops past the Wheatfield, across the Abraham Trostle Farm, and into the Peach Orchard, where they created a salient that was vulnerable to Confederate artillery fire and direct attack. All the while, Confederates under Lt. Gen. James Longstreet were preparing to attack the ground over which Sickles's troops were thinly spread. They would push eastward through the Peach Orchard, the Wheatfield, and into the craggy rock pile known as the Devil's Den before contesting the rocky slope of Little Round Top. As the day wore on, Union scouts scurried up Big Round Top, the highest elevation in the area, finding it too heavily wooded for artillery. Just to the north, however, stood Little Round Top — 135 feet lower but recently cleared of timber and affording an outstanding artillery post that would command the southern part of the field. Suddenly, Meade's chief engineer, Gouverneur K. Warren, realized that Little Round Top held a tactical key to the battle and sent engineers and artillerists up the hill to occupy it.

By this time, Longstreet had launched his fearsome attack, which spread over the southern part of the field, led by Maj. Gen. John Bell Hood, a reckless fighter commanding mostly Georgia, Alabama, and Trans-Mississippi troops. Throughout late afternoon and early evening on July 2, a vicious firefight washed over the whole field. In the words of one participant, the Union battle line "exploded" all across its length, and ground such as the Wheatfield was fought over, taken, lost, recaptured, and lost again — at the expense of many hundreds of lives.

The story of Gettysburg follows, among others, the individuals who have become folk heroes in the Civil War community. Thus, at the end of the day on Little Round Top, the actions of Col. Joshua L. Chamberlain of the 20th Maine Infantry enabled his small force to anchor the left flank of the Union line, resisting Hood's attacking forces, which could have collapsed the Federal hold on this important position.

Later on the night of July 2, Confederate forces fought bitterly for Cemetery Hill and Culp's Hill, other spots of high ground to the north, which the Federals retained. Readers will see how Robert E. Lee, deep in the night between the second and third days of battle, was unable to move beyond the relatively simple notion of fighting at Gettysburg once the battle had erupted, and they will step inside the famous Union council of war, wherein each of Meade's corps commanders was polled over what to do on the battle's third day.

The battle culminated with the myriad actions on July 3, the battle's final day, including the renewed, bloody attack on Culp's Hill early in the morning and the cavalry fight east of the main battlefield. The most controversial Confederate command decision of the war, Lee's ordering of the Pickett-Pettigrew-Trimble Charge, also occurred. The story of the charge raises questions about Lee's judgment. How could he have ordered such an ill-fated attack? In a purely tactical frame, with hindsight, the question certainly leaves Gettysburg students in debate. But given Lee's strategic goals, his sense of desperation relating to the timing of foreign intervention, and the false belief that the Federal artillery was mostly depleted, his reasoning becomes slightly more understandable. Others played a pivotal role in the charge. They include Confederates Edward Porter Alexander, Lewis Armistead, Richard Garnett, and James Kemper, as well as, of course, George Pickett, J. Johnston Pettigrew, and Isaac R. Trimble. Key Federal participants who played a decisive role in the final story of the battle include Winfield Scott Hancock, Alexander Hays, John Gibbon, and the mortally wounded artillerist Alonzo H. Cushing.

And what of the meaning of Gettysburg? After examining the retreat of the Southern army, I suggest that — unlike has often been argued — Meade, too, was clearly far too depleted to fight further, having lost nearly a quarter of his men, and therefore he committed no blunder by "allowing Lee to escape." In the battle's wake, Gettysburg was transformed into a town full of casualties, hospitals, and the suffering and trauma brought on by wounds.

Lincoln's trip to the field four months after the battle to dedicate the new national cemetery cast a new meaning onto the town and into the war. Lincoln's brief remarks, intended almost as an afterthought to Edward Everett's two-hour address, still resonate over the field and formulate the basis for what draws Americans so strongly to the Civil War nearly a century and a half after the fact.

13

Jefferson F. Davis

The Confederate president, who may
have made a better field general than
an administrator, sanctioned the second
great invasion of the North, rather than
sending reinforcements to Bragg's
army to enable it to take the offensive
in Tennessee.

LEE'S ARMY MOVES NORTH

★ JUNE 9–JULY I, 1863 ★

Gen. Robert E. Lee

Lee, who had taken command of the Army of Northern Virginia on June I, 1862, after Gen. Joseph E. Johnston's wounding, forged it into an effective fighting machine. In Lee's mind, the risks inherent in a raid into Pennsylvania were more than offset by the potential benefits of winning a battle on Northern soil, threatening Northern cities, and drawing the fighting away from war-weary Virginia.

The year 1863 was a trying one for the American nation. The outcome of the American Civil War was still far off in a haze, not to be perceived by anyone on either side. It was starkly clear that the war would go on for unending months, and the nation's sons were dying or coming home wounded at an alarming rate. The Federal army and navy had a vast goal at hand: to militarily conquer and occupy the South, bringing the wayward states back under the control of the Union. Confederate forces on land and water could play a defensive game, hoping that either foreign intervention from Britain or France would decide the contest, or war-weary Northerners would sue for peace. As the year began, 918,191 Union troops were in the field, with 698,802 present for duty. In the Confederate armies, 465,584 soldiers were in the field.

On January 1, 1863, President Abraham Lincoln changed the psychological course of the war by issuing the Emancipation Proclamation. Now transformed into a holy war of freedom for slaves (even if many Northerners were themselves initially lukewarm about the prospects), the Civil War took on a new dimension beyond merely preserving the Federal Union. Now, although the participants couldn't know it at the time, it would be effectively impossible for Britain or France to intercede on behalf of the Confederacy in apparent support of slavery. The war had begun and would end as a purely American affair, the ultimate family dispute.

CHAPTER I : LEE'S ARMY MOVES NORTH

Maj. Gen. Andrew A. Humphreys

A veteran regular army man, Humphreys commanded a division in Sickles's 3d Corps at Gettysburg and thereafter served as Meade's chief of staff and 2d Corps commander.

Success in the contest thus far had visited both sides, with victories in Virginia for Confederate forces at First and Second Bull Run and monstrous triumphs at Fredericksburg and Chancellorsville, the latter taking place in early May 1863. In the west the story favored the Union, with victories at Forts Henry and Donelson, Pea Ridge, and Shiloh, and a combative major general named Ulysses S. Grant closing a noose around the Mississippi River bastion at Vicksburg, Mississippi. In the east, the Lincoln administration seemed unable to find the right commander for its principal force, the Army of the Potomac, which had seen three commanders, each unable to lead it to success. Maj. Gens. George B. McClellan and Ambrose E. Burnside failed during the Peninsular campaign and at Fredericksburg, and the third, Maj. Gen. Joseph Hooker, led the army to disastrous defeat at Chancellorsville, where he was knocked senseless by debris from a shell that exploded as he leaned against a column at his headquarters. Hooker's arrogance and rumored love for alcohol didn't help his cause, either. Age 48, Hooker was a Massachusetts native who had served during the Mexican War before becoming a California farmer prior to the Civil War. In early June 1863, he was on his heels and might have expected to lose his assignment.

17

Edwin M. Stanton

In Washington, Lincoln's gruff War Secretary Stanton fretted constantly over the protection of the capital during the Gettysburg campaign.

Maj. Gen. Henry W. Halleck

Coordinating communications between the field generals and politicians in Washington kept General-in-Chief Halleck, previously criticized as an inept field commander, in a useful role.

The principal Confederate army in the east, by contrast, was emboldened by victory. The Army of Northern Virginia was inherited on the Virginia Peninsula in 1862 by Gen. Robert E. Lee after his predecessor, Gen. Joseph E. Johnston, fell wounded at Seven Pines. Lee had led the army effectively and been the recipient of good fortune even when his command decisions were risky. He had thwarted McClellan on the Peninsula, defeated a combined force of armies at Second Bull Run, fought to a standoff before retreating at Antietam (on his first raid into the North), and won decisive strategic victories at Fredericksburg and Chancellorsville. At 56, Lee was the scion of a fallen branch from a famous family tree: great-grandson-in-law of George Washington, Lee had served spectacularly as an engineer during the Mexican War on the staff of Bvt. Lt. Gen. Winfield Scott and had a stint as superintendent of the U.S. Military Academy at West Point. His father, Lt. Col. Henry "Light-Horse Harry" Lee, had fought in the Revolution and served as governor of Virginia before falling from grace into alcoholism and debt and abandoning his family for the West Indies. Lee's loss of his father turned his heroic idolatry toward Washington, whom he had inherited as a relative by marriage (as well as his wife's inheritance of land and houses). Though his had been a distinguished career, Lee always felt he had something to prove, tainted as he was by past family blemishes.

After Chancellorsville, Hooker's 115,000 men and Lee's 75,000 reoccupied their old positions along the banks of the Rappahannock River. Lee's confidence and that of his army swelled to its highest level of the war. The Confederate army commander reorganized his army into three corps, commanded by Lt. Gens. James Longstreet, Richard S. Ewell, and Ambrose P. Hill. Ewell replaced Stonewall Jackson, who had been mortally wounded at Chancellorsville and died on May 10, eliminating the Confederacy's most celebrated field officer of the period. In Richmond, President Jefferson Davis shifted troops from the Carolinas into Lee's army and ordered its communications improved. Although Lee and his army felt highly charged, their confidence was only partly justified.

Many historians have concluded that the Civil War was won in the west; it certainly cast a long shadow over the eastern-theater operations and in the summer of

1863 dictated events. Confederate operations seemed stable in South Carolina, where Gen. G. T. Beauregard was holding up against the Union army and navy. The middle war in Tennessee was suspended after a bitter series of actions that culminated at Stones River sent the Confederate army of Gen. Braxton Bragg falling back behind the Duck River, as Federal Maj. Gen. William S. Rosecrans occupied Murfreesboro. In Arkansas and Louisiana, Confederate armies under Lt. Gen. Theophilus H. Holmes and Maj. Gen. Richard Taylor were carrying on scattered, small-scale actions. The pinch for the Confederacy came with Grant at Vicksburg, who had bottled up Lt. Gen. John C. Pemberton and the town's garrison and civilians. The only outcome at hand seemed to be starvation for the Southerners. Losing the stronghold would cut the Confederacy in two, leaving the Trans-Mississippi, the region west of the Mississippi River, isolated and worthless to the Confederate war effort.

The warm weather would certainly bring further action along the Virginia war front. Lee faced a critical decision in terms of his strategy, and he adopted the unlikely idea of again launching a raid onto Northern soil. Longstreet, his senior corps commander and most trusted lieutenant, proposed shifting troops westward to strike at Rosecrans in Tennessee, thereby lifting the pressure from Vicksburg by forcing Union troops east in support of Rosecrans. This would also draw the war away from Lee's treasured Virginia, which had been heavily burdened by the war and its destruction, and possibly would offer a decisive turning point in the conflict. But after serious contemplation, Lee refused. He was the commander of the Army of Northern Virginia and had gone to war primarily to protect his home state from the "foreign invaders." Lee had always shown a relative selfishness when it came to asking for vast quantities of men and supplies for his own army, and he wasn't about to unravel it all now to go and fight inside Tennessee. At this critical moment in the war, the conservatism and nineteenth-century localism that dominated Lee's thinking dictated his actions. Refusing to fight the contest as a whole, he looked inward to Virginia at the expense of Vicksburg, Tennessee, and everywhere else.

This decision launched what would become the Gettysburg campaign. Although he now lacked the recklessly bold Stonewall Jackson, Lee felt empowered by his army's victories, as well as a sense of urgency brought on by desperation. Lee decided that he could not attack Hooker directly because of the Federal army's strong position. A raid would not only draw the war away from Virginia but also resupply his men with provisions from the shops and fertile fields of Maryland and Pennsylvania. Moreover, by fighting and winning a battle on Northern soil, the army could prove its superiority, stunning the Federal civilians and perhaps igniting the burgeoning peace movement in the North. With a shocking enough victory, Lee reasoned, perhaps the waning ember of foreign intervention would even reignite. If he could win a victory and then threaten Harrisburg, Philadelphia, Baltimore, or even Washington, an end to the war might result. However he viewed it, Lee foresaw the potential for a negotiated peace. "We should neglect no honorable means of dividing and weakening our enemies that they may experience some of the difficulties experienced by ourselves," he wrote to Jefferson Davis on June 10. "It seems to me that the most effectual mode of accomplishing this object, now within our reach, is to give all the encouragement we can, consistently with truth, to the rising peace party of the North. Nor do I think we should in this connection make nice distinctions between those who declare for peace unconditionally and those who advocate it as a means of restoring the Union, however much we may prefer the former."

Early in June, Lee shifted his men to the west, hoping to move northward down the Shenandoah Valley, screened by the Blue Ridge and South Mountains. The Confederate commander cleverly kept A. P. Hill's corps along the Rappahannock trenches and moved it periodically to fool the Yankee scouts into believing the whole army was still present. Hooker's men deciphered the Southern movements, however, and on June 5 sent Maj. Gen. John Sedgwick's corps across the river to attack a portion of Hill's line. A reconnaissance in force resulted with action at Franklin's Crossing, also called Deep Run. The 26th New Jersey Infantry and 5th Vermont Infantry struck into the Confederates at Deep Run, who fired from well-constructed rifle pits, forcing the infantry to cross with great hazard on pontoon bridges before driving away a portion of the defenders, taking 35 prisoners and suffering 6 dead and 35 wounded. Sedgwick was convinced by the resistance that the whole Confederate army was still in position. Hooker then requested to move toward Richmond, but Lincoln refused, wishing Hooker to operate against the enemy army — not a city — and to protect Washington. (Lincoln, maturing as a battlefield strategist, would pen Hooker a note on June 14 asking, "If the head of Lee's army is at Martinsburg and the tail of it on the Plank Road between Fredericksburg and Chancellorsville, the animal must be very slim somewhere. Could you not break him?")

Hooker next sent his cavalry corps forward, led by Brig. Gen. Alfred Pleasonton, toward Culpeper Court House. Maj. Gen. James E. B. "Jeb" Stuart's Confederate horsemen occupied Brandy Station, northeast of Culpeper on the Orange & Alexandria Railroad. The first major action during the Gettysburg campaign occurred on June 9 as Pleasonton's troopers made their way into Brandy Station and struck into Stuart's horsemen, resulting in the largest cavalry battle of the war up until that time (the cavalry action at Trevilian Station would eclipse it the following year). The Brandy Station battle, also called Fleetwood, Beverly Ford, and Stevensburg, would redefine the perception of the Union cavalry.

Pleasonton organized his horsemen into two wings commanded by Brig. Gens. John Buford and David M. Gregg. Buford's right wing included the 1st Division and the reserve brigade, along with the infantry brigade of Brig. Gen. Adelbert Ames. Gregg's left wing comprised the 2d and 3d Divisions and Brig. Gen. David A. Russell's infantry brigade, so that the entire Federal force comprised about 8,000 cavalry supported by 3,000 infantry. The Confederate cavalry force consisted of the brigades of Brig. Gens. Fitzhugh Lee, Wade Hampton, William H. F. "Rooney" Lee (Gen. Lee's son; his brigade was commanded by Col. Thomas T. Munford), Albert G. Jenkins (who was not present at Brandy Station), Beverly H. Robertson, and William E. "Grumble" Jones, plus attached horse artillery.

The plan called for a Federal attack at dawn on June 9. To prepare, Pleasonton assembled Buford's cavalry brigade near Beverly Ford on the Rappahannock River. Pleasonton planned to cross his cavalry and strike southwestward into Grumble Jones's brigade while, six miles downstream at Kelly's Ford, Gregg and Col. Alfred N. Duffié struck into Robertson. Duffié would continue on to Stevensburg while the bulk of the force drew together at Brandy Station, where long Fleetwood Hill would provide an open ridge so the horsemen could operate unimpeded by thick woods. On June 8, as the Federal soldiers prepared for attack, Stuart was proudly displaying his cavalry division to Robert E. Lee in a grand review near Fleetwood Hill, a spectacle of 10,000 troopers with sabers gleaming and ready for admiration, if not battle.

Maj. Gen. George G. Meade and His Staff

The staff of an important general officer could be considerably large. Here Meade (center, seated) poses with his staff officers, aides, relatives, and assistants. Sometimes criticized as slow and bookish, Meade nevertheless had a biting temper. He would command the Army of the Potomac through the war's end.

Maj. Gen. George G. Meade

Following the disastrous performance of Joe Hooker at Chancellorsville, Meade was assigned command of the Army of the Potomac, the largest eastern army of the Union, only four days before the battle of Gettysburg commenced. Previously, Meade had been an effective brigade and division commander.

JUNE 9–JULY 1, 1863

Maj. Gen. Winfield Scott Hancock and His Staff

Of the seven Union corps commanders involved in the Gettysburg campaign, Hancock, leading the 2d Corps, played a stellar role. "Hancock the Superb," who always seemed to be in the thick of pivotal actions, here poses with his staff.

At 4 A.M. on June 9 the two columns of Union cavalry attacked, catching the Confederates unaware. Buford's men in blue fought savagely and forced Jones's men back to Brandy Station. Intense fighting flared over Fleetwood Hill, with many charges and countercharges producing frightening numbers of casualties on both sides. The battle was uncharacteristic of cavalry actions: horses were normally used for rapid transport, with the cavalrymen dismounting and fighting on foot once the battle commenced. But at Brandy Station the soldiers stayed on horseback and charged, fighting with pistols, carbines, and sabers drawn. This resulted from the sheer chaos and surprise of the battle's origin, the pride of Stuart's boys as horsemen, and Pleasonton's desire to see his cavalrymen gain respect relative to their Southern counterparts. The 1st New Jersey Cavalry made six charges throughout the 10 hours of fighting, and the action over the battlefield at Brandy Station raged for more than 12 hours. Gregg pushed Robertson back from Kelly's Ford and soon attacked from the south.

The action also raged nearby at Stevensburg, where Duffié struck into the 2d South Carolina Cavalry and 4th Virginia Cavalry, preventing his arrival at Brandy Station, but was thwarted by Hampton, and so the stunned Rebels retained the field. Stuart paid dearly for the battle, however, finding himself chastised by the Southern papers for being so roughly handled by the "inferior" Northern cavalrymen. The embarrassment Stuart experienced in the immediate wake of his boastful grand review would help to shape his actions over the remainder of the campaign. The Union casualties at Brandy Station were 69 killed, 352 wounded, and 486 missing (taken as prisoners); Confederate losses were 523 total. Among the casualties were Robert E. Lee's son Rooney, who was shot in the thigh. He was sent to Hickory Hill, near Hanover Court House, where he was captured on June 26.

In the wake of Brandy Station, Hooker sent portions of his army northwestward, occupying the old battleground at Manassas, and dispatched Pleasonton's cavalry to the west as a scouting force. As mid-June arrived Lee moved his army fully away from Fredericksburg, Hill's 3d Corps following the bulk of the army as a rear guard. The movements of the armies northward now commenced in earnest as Ewell's 2d Corps sped into the Shenandoah Valley. At Berryville, Virginia, on June 13, Maj. Gen. Robert E. Rodes's division moved to capture the Union garrison commanded by Col. Andrew T. McReynolds. Alerted, McReynolds quickly withdrew to Winchester, where his men occupied the town's Star Fort. Confederates captured a supply train and 75 prisoners nearby. This forced Union Maj. Gen. Robert H. Milroy to move from Winchester north to Harpers Ferry. As Rodes kept pushing northward, he struck the Union garrison at Martinsburg on June 14. Col. Benjamin F. Smith's Yankees broke after a short time and fled to Harpers Ferry, unpursued. Rodes's take included 700 prisoners and five field guns.

Winchester, meanwhile, a town that changed hands many times during the war, hosted a battle on June 14–15 that was also termed Stephenson's Depot. Ewell concocted a scheme to attack the town's western defenses, West Fort, Star Fort, and the Main (Flag) Fort, then defended by Milroy's force of 6,900. Supported by a heavy artillery bombardment, Maj. Gen. Jubal A. Early thrust forward, and captured West Fort, fighting briskly, commanded by Union Col. Joseph W. Keifer. As rounds from both sides scattered dirt high into the air, Brig. Gen. Harry T. Hays's Louisianans captured Fort West, forcing Milroy to fall back. That night, Milroy spiked his guns and burned his supply wagons to prevent their capture intact. By 1 A.M. he had begun his withdrawal, and a rare night action followed at 3:30 A.M. at Stephenson's Depot, four miles northwest of town. A Union debacle followed: Milroy was struck by the Confederate brigade of Col. Jesse M. Williams (Nicholls's brigade), which wrecked the Federal envelopment. Milroy's army suffered 95 killed, 348 wounded, and about 3,358 captured as prisoners; Confederate losses were 47 killed, 219 wounded, and 3 missing. Ewell also captured 23 field guns, 300 horses, and more than 300 wagons filled with supplies. The number of Union troops captured stunned the Lincoln administration, and Secretary of War Edwin M. Stanton called for additional militia to be "Federalized" into service.

23

Maj. Gen. John Sedgwick

Much beloved as "Uncle John" by the Union troops, Sedgwick led the 6th Corps at Gettysburg and played a limited role, being held in reserve for much of the battle. He would be killed the following spring at Spotsylvania.

Maj. Gen. Henry W. Slocum

Slocum's 12th Corps entered the battle late and fought principally on Culp's Hill, where the divisions of Alpheus Williams and John Geary fought stubbornly.

By the middle of June the campaign was maturing. The Confederates stretched nearly 100 miles in a huge line from Chester Gap, Virginia, to Hagerstown, Maryland; a few scattered cavalrymen had already crossed into Pennsylvania. A series of cavalry actions in Virginia next occurred. At Aldie, on June 17, Col. Thomas T. Munford's Southern horsemen (Fitz Lee's brigade) arrived to help screen Longstreet's right flank while Confederate Col. John R. Chambliss, Jr., (Rooney Lee's brigade) scouted toward Thoroughfare Gap, and Rebel Brig. Gen. Beverly H. Robertson moved to Rectortown. The brigade of Brig. Gen. H. Judson Kilpatrick, who was dubbed "Kill-Cavalry" for his recklessness, pushed back the Confederate scouts successfully at Aldie until Munford's 5th Virginia Cavalry mounted a charge with drawn sabers and stunted the Federal success. Munford's Confederates then established a line supported by horse artillery and resisted a series of Union attacks that lasted until darkness. Union losses were 305, Confederate casualties about 100.

Meanwhile, at Middleburg (seven miles west of Aldie), Duffié's 1st Rhode Island Cavalry was wrecked, losing 160 men as prisoners. Duffié initially had scattered Jeb Stuart and his staff but thereafter was surrounded and by hard riding escaped with only 31 of his men. Heavier fighting erupted at Middleburg on June 18 and 19. On the 18th, Pleasonton dispatched Col. John I. Gregg's brigade to Middleburg, but Gregg arrived too late to assist Duffié and withdrew to Aldie. The following day, Gregg's brigade again advanced on Middleburg and this time sent the 4th Pennsylvania Cavalry charging through the town, securing it for the Union. Brig. Gen. David M. Gregg's division next struck Stuart's troopers, driving them from the area; losses were about 99 Union and 40 Confederate. Minor skirmishing continued, the most significant clash coming at Upperville — six miles west-northwest of Middleburg and east of Ashby's Gap — on June 21. The Union cavalry was successfully driving Stuart back toward the main Confederate army, and here Stuart was attacked along Goose Creek. The Federal horsemen first drove Hampton and Robertson's horsemen into Upperville, and then Buford attempted to turn Stuart's left; this failed until the dashing Brig. Gen. Kilpatrick helped to push Robertson back through Upperville. The uneasy feeling of being whipped by Yankee horsemen continued in Stuart's mind. Stuart's mission of reconnoitering and supplying Lee with information had not worked, thanks to the Federal cavalry's harassment. The Southerners retreated to Ashby's Gap, with losses of 180; Union casualties were 209.

By late June it was becoming clear even to Hooker that Lee was in motion. He commenced marching the Army of the Potomac to Frederick, Maryland. Lee was less well informed of Hooker's whereabouts; not only had Stuart temporarily abandoned his role as the "eyes of the army," but Brig. Gen. John D. Imboden's cavalry raid down the Baltimore & Ohio Railroad had been fruitless. Pennsylvania civilians and militia found themselves in a growing panic, however: Gov. Andrew G. Curtin called for volunteers to turn away Confederates who were entering the state.

As the month of June faded, the two great armies were converging on each other in rural Pennsylvania. Southern soldiers marched in the cool mornings and hot afternoons, resupplying themselves from the countryside and relishing the opportunity to terrorize the Yankee civilians, who had not tasted war as those on the Southern homefront had. Confederate infantry crossed the Potomac River, passed farms, foraged in the fertile fields and woods, plundered stores, wrecked property, and encountered civilians, who demonstrated little support for the Southern cause.

Hooker found himself in a quandary. After suffering a blinding loss of confidence in himself, in the eyes of his soldiers, and from the Lincoln administration, he

Maj. Gen. Winfield Scott Hancock and Friends

Hancock, seated, posed with his close associates Francis C. Barlow (who commanded a division in the IIth Corps), John Gibbon (a division commander of Hancock's), and David B. Birney (a division commander in the 3d Corps). The photo was taken in 1864 near the time of the battle of Cold Harbor.

was ordered to simultaneously prevent Lee from operating freely in Pennsylvania and protect Washington. The hard-drinking commander planned an operation to attack Lee's lines of communications but then failed to initiate the movement; by June 27 he still had sent no orders. Hooker also played the game that McClellan had earlier, sending Lincoln a series of worrisome telegrams fretting over the perceived strength of the enemy force. When Hooker demanded that he pull the Federal troops away from Harpers Ferry and Secretary of War Stanton ordered them left in place, Hooker tersely asked to be relieved of command, probably expecting Stanton to reconsider. Instead, Lincoln immediately accepted Hooker's resignation and commenced plans to replace him. At 3 A.M. on June 28, Col. James A. Hardie, the powerful and feared assistant adjutant general attached to Secretary Stanton's office, arrived at Maj. Gen. George Gordon Meade's tent at Frederick and claimed he brought "trouble." Hardie handed Meade an order assigning him to the command of the army. Among the other candidates were John Sedgwick, Winfield Scott Hancock, Darius N. Couch, and John F. Reynolds. Reynolds, well liked by nearly everyone, had declined an outright offer of command reportedly because it didn't include a "free hand" to direct the army.

Lincoln didn't know it yet, but Meade would become the commander of the Army of the Potomac he had long searched for, leading it through to the war's end. Described by one of his soldiers as a "damned, goggle-eyed snapping turtle," the general's most famous attribute was his occasional fierce temper. Meade was also a bookish, careful thinker, and his knowledge of strategy and tactics would serve the army well. He was a Pennsylvanian, born in Cadiz, Spain, of American parents; he graduated relatively high in his West Point class of 1835 and, backed by his engineering training, had served gallantly in the Mexican War. His Civil War service had been impressive to date: he had been wounded at Glendale and at Antietam. "By direction of the President of the United States, I hereby assume command of the Army of the Potomac," Meade wrote on June 28. "Let each man determine to do his duty, leaving to all controlling providence the decision of the contest."

After Chancellorsville, the armies were reorganized. Meade's Army of the Potomac had about 85,000 men on the field. Lee's Army of Northern Virginia consisted of about 65,000. As Lee's army marched behind the screen of the Blue Ridge Mountains, the defense of Pennsylvania's capital was left to Maj. Gen. Darius N. Couch (Hooker's second in command at Chancellorsville). Primitive forts were constructed hastily along the Susquehanna River at Harrisburg and Wrightsville; many volunteers who would man the forts were clerks and shopkeepers from Harrisburg. Couch also sent troops to Chambersburg, believing the Confederate approach targeted that area. Soon after, the 8th and 71st New York Militia regiments took their places at Fort Washington, near Harrisburg. Delaying Ewell's oncoming Confederates at Chambersburg fell to Brig. Gen. Joseph F. Knipe, a Harrisburg resident, who established a line at the town with the two small New York militia regiments.

On June 22, the 71st New York Militia arrived in Chambersburg and prepared to block Jenkins's oncoming cavalry. On that day, local citizen Jacob Hoke reported, "a person supposed to be a woman came into camp. She was attired in mourning apparel, with her face almost concealed in a black bonnet of somewhat antiquated style. She went about the camp pretending to be silly, and inquired where a certain farmer lived who no one knew." The Federal soldiers in town soon learned that the person was a Confederate scout, and probably a male. Some of Jenkins's cavalry and Rodes's foot soldiers moved forward to Greencastle, between Chambersburg and Hagerstown, where a skirmish produced the first casualties north of the Mason-Dixon line during the Gettysburg campaign. Union Cpl. William F. Rihl of the 1st New York Cavalry was shot in the face, the bullet shattering his mouth and passing out the back of his head. He became the first soldier to die north of the Mason-Dixon line in the campaign; thousands more would meet the same fate in the ensuing days.

As Ewell's 25,000 men approached the Susquehanna River, Wrightsville and its Columbia Bridge became an obvious target, defended by sleepy camps of militia strung along the riverbanks. The bridge, spanning 5,620 feet, was allegedly the longest wooden span in the world at the time. On the river's western bank, the 27th Pennsylvania Militia protected it against a cavalry raid; other units included black laborers who took up rifles in defense of the bridge. The Yankees planned to withdraw across the bridge if attacked, exploding it with gunpowder charges they had placed. Brig. Gen. John B. Gordon, a brave Georgian who had been shot five times at Antietam's Sunken Road, led the Confederate approach on Wrightsville. Establishing a two-gun battery near the town, Gordon pelted the militiamen with shot and shell, forcing them to flee rapidly eastward, exploding the charges. The well-constructed bridge did not fall immediately, however: kerosene-soaked timbers caught fire,

Lee Crosses the Potomac River
June 25, 1863

Accompanying Lt. Gen. James Longstreet's Ist Army Corps, Gen. Robert E. Lee crossed the Potomac River from West Virginia into Maryland, initiating his second great raid of the North.

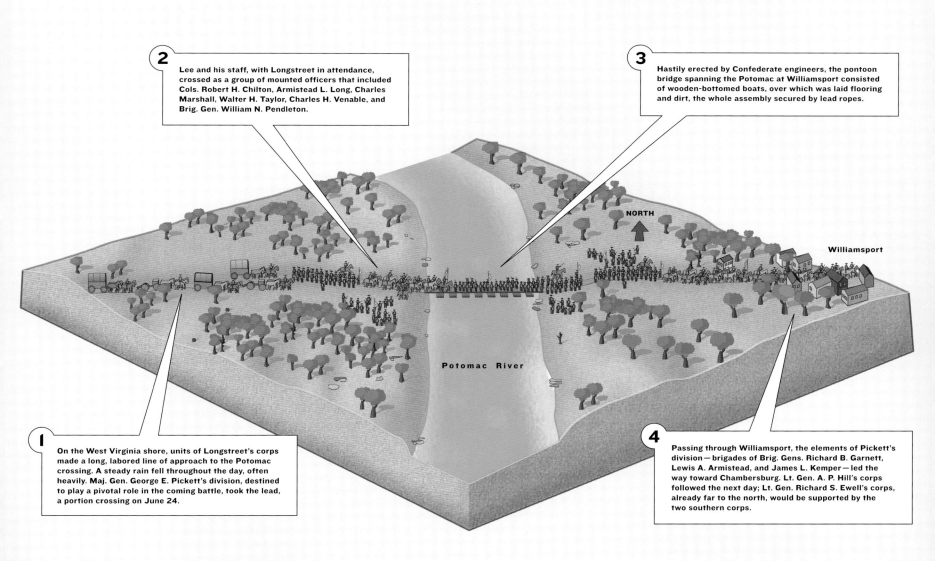

2 Lee and his staff, with Longstreet in attendance, crossed as a group of mounted officers that included Cols. Robert H. Chilton, Armistead L. Long, Charles Marshall, Walter H. Taylor, Charles H. Venable, and Brig. Gen. William N. Pendleton.

3 Hastily erected by Confederate engineers, the pontoon bridge spanning the Potomac at Williamsport consisted of wooden-bottomed boats, over which was laid flooring and dirt, the whole assembly secured by lead ropes.

NORTH

Williamsport

Potomac River

1 On the West Virginia shore, units of Longstreet's corps made a long, labored line of approach to the Potomac crossing. A steady rain fell throughout the day, often heavily. Maj. Gen. George E. Pickett's division, destined to play a pivotal role in the coming battle, took the lead, a portion crossing on June 24.

4 Passing through Williamsport, the elements of Pickett's division—brigades of Brig. Gens. Richard B. Garnett, Lewis A. Armistead, and James L. Kemper—led the way toward Chambersburg. Lt. Gen. A. P. Hill's corps followed the next day; Lt. Gen. Richard S. Ewell's corps, already far to the north, would be supported by the two southern corps.

Maj. Gens. Daniel E. Sickles and Samuel P. Heintzelman

Sickles, one of the most colorful characters of the war, led the Union 3d Corps into a precarious position at Gettysburg and received a cannonball to the right leg in return. Here, after his amputation, he poses with Heintzelman, who commanded the Department of Washington during the campaign.

creating a huge blaze visible as far away as Harrisburg. "Some of the arches remained stationary even when the timbers were all in flames," wrote a reporter for the *New York Gazette*, "seeming like a fiery skeleton bridge whose reflections was pictured [*sic*] in the water beneath. The moon was bright, and the blue clouds afforded the best contrast possible to the red glare of the conflagration." As it continued to burn, the bridge was destroyed.

The Confederate army had infiltrated the Pennsylvania countryside by June 28. Longstreet's corps, accompanied by Lee, occupied Chambersburg; A. P. Hill was spread to the east at Fayetteville and Greenwood; Ewell, with Rodes and Maj. Gen. Edward Johnson, was at Carlisle; Early was at York; Gordon was at Wrightsville, threatening Lancaster; and Jenkins's cavalry was along the Susquehanna River opposite Harrisburg. The Army of Northern Virginia foraged and gathered supplies liberally from the countryside and forced storekeepers to sell them materials, providing worthless Confederate currency in exchange. "I spent some time in Chambersburg, which is a pretty town of 5600 inhabitants," wrote Confederate soldier L. M. Blackford. "The stores were all closed when we entered the place, but many of them were opened by threats of violent entrance by armed force if it was not done quickly. . . . We bought what few things we could find that we wanted with C.S. money. . . . At some of the stores the soldiers got in, and not being restrained by a guard, took a good many things without pay. . . . Lee is making a bold stroke for peace. Pray that it may succeed." Others stole goods and money. At York, Early demanded from a committee of citizens $100,000 in U.S. currency as he threatened destruction; he let the town stand after receiving the sum of $28,600. Lee wanted Ewell chiefly to replenish his corps's supplies and remedy its hunger; he had permitted Ewell to strike at Harrisburg, but did not order it outright.

Indeed, Lee had been vague with his orders and his intentions for the campaign, wishing to see how things developed before committing to specifics. He was hindered by Stuart's absence and had poor information about the whereabouts of the Federal approach. But Stuart's absence was enabled by Lee's own order to him of June 22, which Stuart had received the next day. "If you find that [the enemy] is moving northward," penned Lee, "and that two brigades can guard the Blue Ridge and take care of your rear, you can move with the other three into Maryland, and take position on General Ewell's right, place yourself in communication with him, guard his flank, keep him informed of the enemy's movements, and collect all the supplies you can for the use of the army." In an accompanying letter from Longstreet, the corps commander wrote of Lee speaking of "leaving, via Hopewell Gap, and passing by the rear of the enemy. If you can get through by that route, I think that you will be less likely to indicate what our plans are than if you should cross by passing in our rear."

Lee often left orders open to too much interpretation. What if Stuart couldn't get through by the Hopewell Gap route? Armed with a vague set of suggestions and ample latitude for interpretation, Stuart took full advantage to avenge his embarrassment in the Southern press following Brandy Station. He set out to restore his name as the most dashing and heroic cavalry commander in the war by interposing himself between the Federal army and Washington, capturing as many supply wagons as he could, and raiding northward into Maryland via Rockville and toward Westminster before pushing toward Pennsylvania. The action was designed to restore Stuart's ego as much as it was to aid the current campaign. Stuart dispatched Beverly Robertson and Grumble Jones to guard the gaps along South Mountain and found that provisions for his horses were scarce along the trails ahead. The Southern horsemen found themselves skirting close to marching columns of Union infantry. Stuart crossed the Potomac on June 27–28 and moved on Hanover, east of Gettysburg, having proudly captured a 125-wagon supply train. (When Stuart finally reached Lee's army at Gettysburg on the afternoon of July 2, the perturbed Lee would tell Stuart the wagons were simply a "liability.") In his mind, Stuart had triumphed, and he arrived near Carlisle on July 1, looking for Ewell and as yet unaware of the developing battle to the south. Stuart ordered Carlisle to be cleared, but Smith retreated and readied his troops for action as Stuart shelled the town with his cannon.

Although Lee had generally planned a movement toward Harrisburg, on the evening of June 28 the situation changed with the arrival of a sometime scout of Longstreet's. The man, Henry Thomas Harrison, informed Longstreet and Lee that the Union corps were rapidly moving northward. This occurred near Chambersburg, and Harrison let Lee know on June 30 that the Union army was concentrated around Frederick and was now commanded by the cautious, bookish Meade. Without Stuart for confirmation, Lee hesitated briefly and then determined to trust Harrison, altering his plan and ordering his troops to converge on Gettysburg and Cashtown Gap, the former a hub of ten significant roads and the latter merely a crossroads with several structures seven miles northwest of Gettysburg on the other side of Marsh Run.

Meade, moving his huge army northward to feel Lee's position, found himself on the verge of a major battle only days after receiving his first army command. He ordered the seven Union corps to move northward from the Frederick area on June 29, at 4 A.M., not knowing where Stuart's cavalry was or the details of how the army communications worked, because of his predecessor's secrecy. Considering Meade's overt caution, he moved decisively, reflecting the gravity of the situation. Meade's orders received from the War Department had been as vague as those Lee dispensed: "Your army is free to act as you may deem proper under the circumstances as they arise," wrote Maj. Gen. Henry W. Halleck, the Union general-in-chief, on June 27. "You will, however, keep in view the important fact that the Army of the Potomac is the covering army of Washington as well as the army of operation against the invading forces of the rebels. You will, therefore, maneuver and fight in such a manner as to cover the capital and also Baltimore, as far as circumstances will admit." Because of the exigencies of the crisis, all Union forces in the area — including those commanded by the Middle Department in Baltimore (by Maj. Gen. Robert C. Schenck, who ranked Meade) — were placed under Meade's command. Additionally, he commanded Maj. Gens. Darius Couch (Department of Pennsylvania), Samuel P. Heintzelman (Department of Washington), and three of his own corps commanders, Maj. Gens. John F. Reynolds, Henry W. Slocum, and John Sedgwick, all of whom ranked him.

This town the armies would converge on was a sleepy little borough of 2,390 citizens. The only value it had was the convergence of roads. Indeed, because the Southern armies initially formed at nearby Cashtown, the resulting battle might easily have become the battle of Cashtown. At this stage it seems reasonable to believe that Lee was still developing a plan of operations, and with Stuart absent the formulation percolated more slowly than usual. Lee essentially ignored the cavalry forces that were north of the Mason-Dixon line, including those of Jenkins and Imboden, and he ordered only the cavalry brigades of Jones and Robertson forward from the Shenandoah Valley, as if by an afterthought, on June 29.

Meade, meanwhile, quickly began to show signs of stress and altered his plans from attacking Lee to establishing a defensive line. He concocted an order to establish a defensive line along Big Pipe Creek near Union Mills, Maryland, on June 30; thus, the coming battle also might easily have become the battle of Pipe Creek. Two of Meade's orders, issued a few hours apart, reveal a reversal on his part. In the afternoon of June 30, Meade penned that he would "push on tomorrow in the direction of Hanover Junction and Hanover"; in his celebrated "Pipe Creek circular," issued early on July 1, he wrote that the present objective of the army in advancing into Pennsylvania, to relieve Harrisburg and diffuse an invasion above the Susquehanna, had been achieved. He further stated that if the enemy attacked, he meant to withdraw his army "from its present position, and form [a] line of battle with the left

Maj. Gen. George Sykes

Known as "Tardy George" for his unspectacular battlefield movements, Sykes led the elite 5th Corps at Gettysburg, which included all the regular army infantry units and played a key role in securing the elevated hills south of the town on the battle's second day.

30

**Situation on the Evening of
June 28, 1863**

Gen. Robert E. Lee's Army of Northern
Virginia commenced its second great raid
into the North by swinging northward
behind the screen of the Blue Ridge
Mountains into Pennsylvania. Bookish
Maj. Gen. George G. Meade, newly
assigned commander of the Army of the
Potomac, followed cautiously.

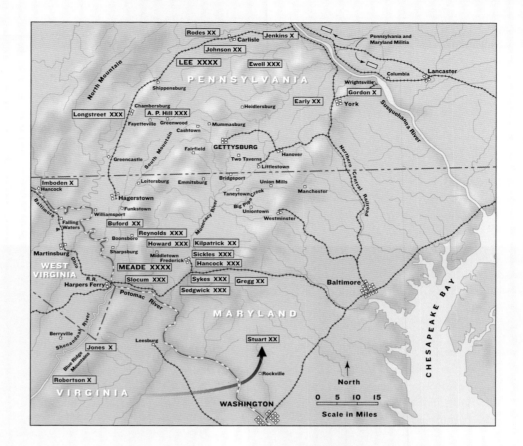

**Situation on the Evening of
June 30, 1863**

By the last day of June, both armies
were closely concentrated in southern
Pennsylvania. J. E. B. Stuart had commenced his ride around the Union army
through Maryland. Confederate units
had fought with militia and skirmished
with Union cavalry sporadically; a major
battle was shaping up, however, around
the town of Gettysburg, where many
roads converged.

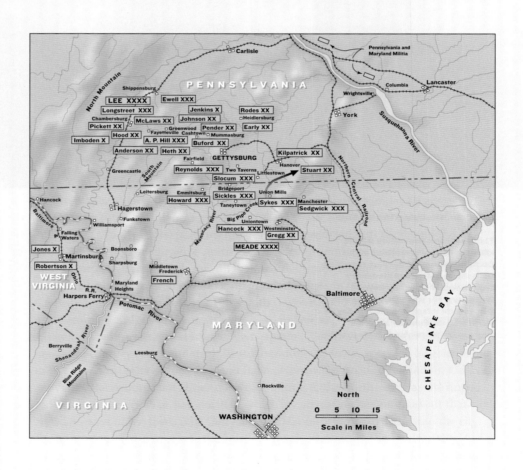

★ CHAPTER 2 ★

SHOTS CRACKLE ALONG WILLOUGHBY'S RUN

★ JULY 1, 1863 ★

McPherson's Woods
June 8, 1997

The battle of Gettysburg, the largest and costliest act of warfare ever played out in the Western Hemisphere, began essentially as an accident. Neither Union nor Confederate forces were ready for a battle. Early in the morning on July 1, about 5 A.M., Confederate Maj. Gen. Henry Heth ordered the brigades of Brig. Gens. James J. Archer and Joseph R. Davis eastward toward Gettysburg, sending them along the Chambersburg Pike. Some two hours later the situation for battle had developed: the Confederate infantry had reached a position about three miles west of Gettysburg, along Herr's Ridge, where it encountered the dismounted troopers of Brig. Gen. John Buford's division. The odds were in the favor of the South. Some 7,600 Confederate infantry marched toward the Union cavalry force of only 2,748 men. The Federal horsemen looked for cover, using trees, fence rails, or simply the ground as best they could. Although his men were outnumbered, Buford employed his breech-loading carbines effectively to buy time until more Federal units could arrive to relieve his brigade. He established a weak defensive line across the pike, east of Willoughby's Run, from McPherson's Woods on the south, across the unfinished rail line, and north toward Oak Hill. Col. William Gamble's brigade was spread along much of the line. Two regiments under Col. Thomas C. Devin anchored the Union right. By 7:30 A.M. the two forces had approached within distant sight of each other, and the first shot came not long after. Lt. Marcellus Jones of the 8th Illinois Cavalry fired his carbine, and the shot echoed along the swale containing Willoughby's Run.

CHAPTER 2 : SHOTS CRACKLE ALONG WILLOUGHBY'S RUN

**Willoughby's Run,
near McPherson's Woods
Charles and Isaac Tyson
ca. 1865**

**The initial clash at Gettysburg occurred
as an accidental encounter in the vicinity
of Willoughby's Run, depicted here some
two years after the battle.**

JULY 1, 1863

The Battle Opens on McPherson's Ridge
July l, 1863, about 9 A.M.

Essentially an accident, the battle
of Gettysburg commenced when the
eastward-marching troops of Maj. Gen.
Henry Heth clashed with the dismounted
Union cavalry of Brig. Gen. John Buford
on the morning of July l, 1863. Northwest
of Gettysburg, the battle escalated as
more units were pushed into the fight.

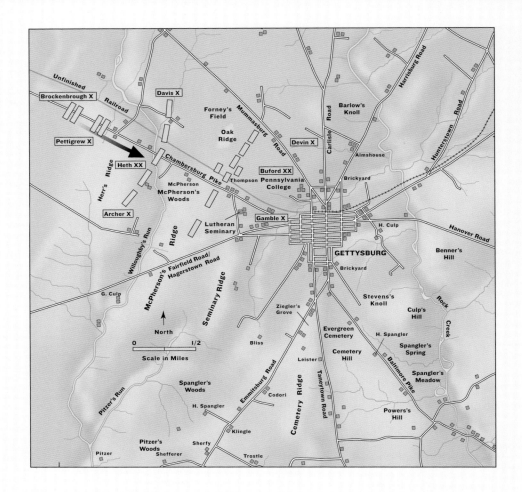

Within half an hour the Confederates had advanced and engaged the horsemen
in furious battle. The Union cavalrymen of Gamble and Devin, supported by six
guns from Capt. John C. Tidball's horse artillery, commanded by 2d Lt. John Calef,
held the Confederate infantry at bay. They hid behind a stone wall and fired blistering rounds with their breechloaders, producing three times as many shots as did the
Confederates with their conventional muskets. But Buford's troopers were hindered
by having to post many men idle, holding the horses, as most of the troopers fought.
Soon the numerical superiority of the Southern force began to turn the tide of battle.
By 9 A.M., the Federal horsemen had retreated to a line along McPherson's Ridge,
midway between Willoughby's Run and the Lutheran Seminary. This ridge held the
farm of U.S. deputy commissioner of internal revenue Edward McPherson, who
had earlier served as a volunteer aide on the staff of Maj. Gen. John F. Reynolds. By
9:30 A.M., Reynolds had arrived on the field, with the lead elements of the 1st Corps
in tow, much to the relief of Buford. The cavalry commander had received intelligence that he would need to contend not only with Heth's advance from the west,
but also with that of Ewell, who was reportedly advancing from Heidlersburg, to the
north. On the seminary grounds, Reynolds and Buford briefly discussed the situation
(although the authenticity of their alleged meeting at the cupola of what is now

CHAPTER 2 : SHOTS CRACKLE ALONG WILLOUGHBY'S RUN

First Shot Marker, Chambersburg Pike
June 5, 1997

About 7:30 A.M. on July I, Lt. Marcellus Jones of the 8th Illinois Cavalry discharged his carbine, and the largest-scale battle ever fought in the Western Hemisphere began. This marker, hidden in shrubbery on the Chambersburg Pike opposite Knoxlyn Road, marks the approximate position of the initial action.

Scene along the Chambersburg Pike

An early, possibly postwar view westward along the Chambersburg Pike depicts ground over which the first struggles at Gettysburg raged.

JULY I, 1863

Maj. Gen. Henry Heth

Heth, known to friends as "Harry," brought part of his infantry division toward Gettysburg on the morning of July 1, 1863, clashing with Buford's horsemen and starting the battle. Afterward, he attempted to rationalize going beyond his orders by spuriously claiming he was "searching for supplies, especially shoes."

Cashtown Inn, Cashtown, Pennsylvania
April 23, 1995

Heth's infantrymen, marching eastward toward Gettysburg, passed by the Cashtown Inn at a crossroads seven miles from Gettysburg, across Marsh Run. The structure was briefly used by A. P. Hill as his headquarters as the action nearby evolved.

Herr Tavern, Herr's Ridge
April 23, 1995

When gunshots rang out early on July 1, 1863, Frederick Herr's tavern, a brick eatery and boardinghouse constructed in 1815, stood prominently on Herr's Ridge, the point from which Heth launched his attack.

Schmucker Hall has been questioned). With crackles of musketry fire and booming cannon a short distance away, they briefly discussed tactics for the next phase of the fight. Reynolds moved to the rear and ordered fences torn down along the Emmitsburg Road, so that the advancing 1st Corps infantry could, on reaching the scene, cut across the fields to the action on McPherson's Ridge. Until about 10:45 A.M., the Union cavalry fought stubbornly, holding off the greater numbers of Rebels.

As Federal soldiers marched toward the battle, they did not know what they were getting into, although they could sense that a significant battle was under way. Whitish puffs of smoke were visible off in the distance, and the faint booming of cannon reverberated through the air. Brig. Gen. James S. Wadsworth's division advanced swiftly up the Emmitsburg Road, with Brig. Gen. Lysander Cutler's brigade in the lead. "We were being hurried at the utmost speed along the road on that hot July morning," wrote the chaplain of the 147th New York Infantry, "sweltering from every pore, as for me, my clothes could not have been wetter if I had fallen into a pond of water." Behind Cutler's brigade marched Brig. Gen. Solomon Meredith's unit, the so-called Iron Brigade, consisting of Wisconsin, Indiana, and Michigan troops who had fought stubbornly at Brawner's Farm and South Mountain, earning their sobriquet. A rumor swept through the line of march that George McClellan, still much adored by the boys, had retaken command of the army. It instilled new confidence in the soldiers, even if McClellan was actually in New Jersey doing absolutely nothing.

CHAPTER 2 : SHOTS CRACKLE ALONG WILLOUGHBY'S RUN

Brig. Gen. Joseph R. Davis

The Confederate president's nephew, Davis sent his brigade on the attack along with Archer's. Following a heavy fight with blasts of artillery and brisk small-arms fire, the Mississippians and North Carolinians retreated to Herr's Ridge.

Brig. Gen. John Buford

Buford's positioning of his small division on the first morning of action prevented a Union disaster, holding a relatively stable position until infantry arrived.

Brig. Gen. James J. Archer

In one of the first assaults of the morning, Archer was captured by soldiers of the Iron Brigade, becoming the first general officer taken at Gettysburg. Archer would not be released for more than a year, and soon thereafter he died from pneumonia, brought on by hard prison life.

Col. Thomas C. Devin

A hard-fighting New Yorker, Devin commanded the brigade of Buford's that anchored the initial Union right.

45

Brig. Gen. James S. Wadsworth

When the Union Ist Corps infantry arrived, it was led by the reliable Maj. Gen. John F. Reynolds. Reynolds's Ist Division fought under Wadsworth, one of the richest men who served in the Federal army. He would be killed less than a year later at the Wilderness.

Brig. Gen. Solomon Meredith

Wadsworth's Ist Brigade was the celebrated "Iron Brigade" of the west, comprising the 2d, 6th, and 7th Wisconsin, I9th Indiana, and 24th Michigan Infantries. It was led by the adopted Hoosier Meredith.

Col. Lucius Fairchild

The 2d Wisconsin of the Iron Brigade fought under Fairchild until he was wounded and captured, losing his left arm in the process. Having originally enlisted as a private soldier, Fairchild went on to the governorship of Wisconsin after the war.

Brig. Gen. Lysander Cutler

Cutler commanded Wadsworth's other brigade, which led the advance up the Emmitsburg Road toward the first sounds of battle. "We were . . . sweltering from every pore," one member wrote of the hot morning march. "My clothes could not have been wetter if I had fallen into a pond of water."

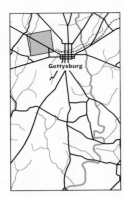

Clash along the Chambersburg Pike
July 1, 1863, Mid-Morning

Moving toward the town of Gettysburg, Confederate Maj. Gen. Henry Heth ordered Brig. Gens. James J. Archer and Joseph R. Davis forward early in the morning. About 7:30 A.M. the first shots were fired; some two hours later the battle had developed into a furious musketry duel between Rebel infantry and Union dismounted cavalry.

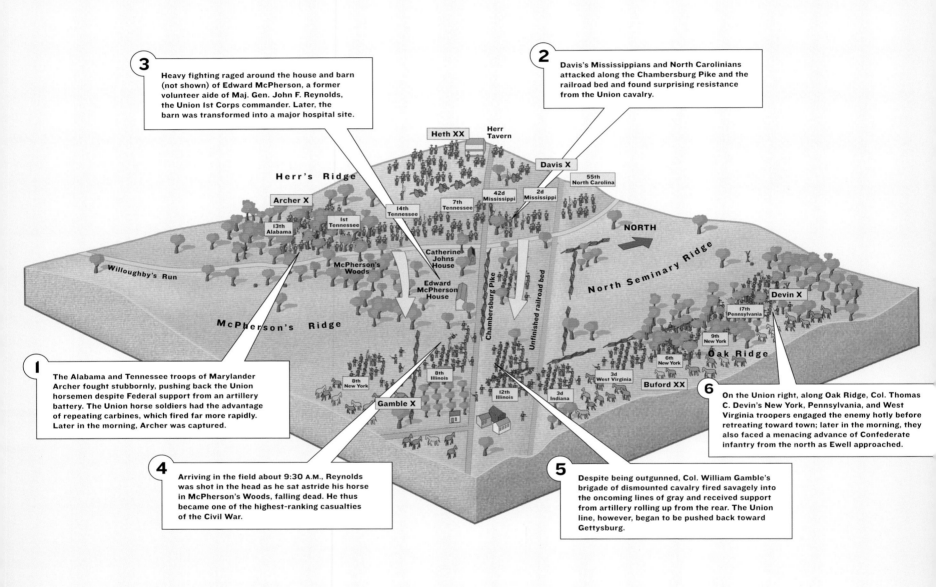

3 Heavy fighting raged around the house and barn (not shown) of Edward McPherson, a former volunteer aide of Maj. Gen. John F. Reynolds, the Union 1st Corps commander. Later, the barn was transformed into a major hospital site.

2 Davis's Mississippians and North Carolinians attacked along the Chambersburg Pike and the railroad bed and found surprising resistance from the Union cavalry.

1 The Alabama and Tennessee troops of Marylander Archer fought stubbornly, pushing back the Union horsemen despite Federal support from an artillery battery. The Union horse soldiers had the advantage of repeating carbines, which fired far more rapidly. Later in the morning, Archer was captured.

4 Arriving in the field about 9:30 A.M., Reynolds was shot in the head as he sat astride his horse in McPherson's Woods, falling dead. He thus became one of the highest-ranking casualties of the Civil War.

5 Despite being outgunned, Col. William Gamble's brigade of dismounted cavalry fired savagely into the oncoming lines of gray and received support from artillery rolling up from the rear. The Union line, however, began to be pushed back toward Gettysburg.

6 On the Union right, along Oak Ridge, Col. Thomas C. Devin's New York, Pennsylvania, and West Virginia troopers engaged the enemy hotly before retreating toward town; later in the morning, they also faced a menacing advance of Confederate infantry from the north as Ewell approached.

Scene along the Railroad Cut

Heavy fighting erupted around and in an unfinished railroad cut west of the town along the Chambersburg Pike. The 6th Wisconsin and 95th New York Infantries savagely attacked the 2d Mississippi in the cut, amassing a fearsome number of casualties and capturing many prisoners. This early view of the railroad cut is labeled "1863," but its date is unknown.

The Railroad Cut with Grave Marker
September 7, 1998

At the time of the battle, dead soldiers were originally buried close to where they had fallen; only later were they reinterred in the National Cemetery at Gettysburg or in cemeteries in other locales. Anywhere from several dozen to a few hundred casualties may remain buried on the field, however, having been missed by reinterment crews. In 1996 one such soldier was discovered in the railroad cut and reinterred in the National Cemetery. The soldier was a young white male; unit identification was not possible. Archaeologists found a .69 caliber musket ball, pieces of lead shot, and a glass button near the skeletonized remains, which had been hastily buried. A small marker stands in remembrance at his original grave site.

47

JULY 1, 1863

John Buford and John F. Reynolds Monuments, Chambersburg Pike April 23, 1995

Monuments honoring Buford and Reynolds (equestrian, background) adorn a portion of the initial ground fought over on July 1, 1863. The statues were erected in 1895 and 1899, respectively. Union memorialization vastly outweighs Confederate markers on the field, because of the lack of funds in the South with which to build monuments and the lack of desire to build memorials on a field of defeat.

Mathew B. Brady

New York photographer Mathew Brady brought three assistants to Gettysburg and arrived on the field about mid-July, 1863.

50

Buford's men were now hanging on perilously, though thousands of troops were approaching the field. Reynolds planned a counterattack. He had no intention of pulling back toward the Pipe Creek line. So he pushed the divisions of Wadsworth and Maj. Gen. Abner Doubleday into the fight, hurried Brig. Gen. John C. Robinson from the rear, and ordered Maj. Gen. Oliver O. Howard's 11th Corps forward as quickly as possible to stem the threat from Ewell. Cutler's brigade formed a line bisected by the railroad cut and, supported by artillery, faced Davis's Confederates to the north and the left flank of Archer's line in McPherson's Woods. To the south, the Iron Brigade, its soldiers characterized by distinctive black hats, pushed into Archer's line, flanking and crushing the 13th Alabama Infantry (Col. Birkett D. Fry), 1st Tennessee Infantry (Lt. Col. Newton D. George), and other regiments. Suddenly, Heth was convinced that heavy elements of the Army of the Potomac lay in front of him — this was no militia. In the attack of the Iron Brigade, the 2d Wisconsin Infantry (Col. Lucius Fairchild) captured about 75 Confederates. Among those taken was Archer himself. The Confederate high command in Richmond would never forgive Archer, nicknamed "Little Game Cock," for surrendering his sword so quickly on the morning's fight. He spent more than a year in Federal prison before being exchanged, and in October 1864 he died from the effects of pneumonia.

The Iron Brigade moved forward triumphantly. But tragedy would also strike the Union command. During the attack, Reynolds was killed by a gunshot wound to the head, making him one of the highest-ranking officers killed during the war. (Other high-ranking Union officers who fell were Maj. Gen. John Sedgwick at Spotsylvania Court House in the spring of 1864 and Maj. Gen. James B. McPherson at the Battle of Atlanta the following summer.) Struck by a stray bullet, Reynolds collapsed in his saddle; after he was lowered to the ground by aides, they discovered the wound. Reynolds gasped a single time, smiled slightly, and died from the ball that had entered behind his right ear. His body was taken into the town of Gettysburg, to the George George House, and readied for transport home to nearby Lancaster.

"He had taken his troops into a heavy growth of timber on the slope of a hill-side, and, under their regimental and brigade commanders, the men did their work well promptly," recalled Lt. Joseph G. Rosengarten, Reynolds's ordnance officer, years later. "Returning to join the expected divisions, he was struck by a Minié ball, fired by a sharpshooter hidden in the branches of a tree almost overhead, and killed at once; his horse bore him to the little clump of trees, where a cairn of stones and a rude mark on the bark, now almost overgrown, still tells the fatal spot." The Union command was momentarily stabilized when, following Reynolds's death, the unremarkable Doubleday assumed command of the Federal forces.

**Mathew Brady at a Small Pond,
McPherson's Woods**
Mathew B. Brady
View southwest
ca. July 15, 1863

Brady and his assistants, who may have
included David B. Woodbury and Anthony
Berger, set about documenting the most
dramatic scenes remaining after the
battle. Here Brady poses beside a small
pond at McPherson's Woods, close to
where the fighting erupted along the
Chambersburg Pike.

"Brady Pond"
April 23, 1995

Edward McPherson Farm
Mathew B. Brady
View northeast
ca. July 15, 1863

Brady's image of the McPherson Farm,
around which the first morning's battle
raged, was shot by an assistant and
includes Brady (standing) and perhaps
another assistant in the foreground.
Brady's interest in the farm buildings was
partly created by **Maj. Gen. John F.
Reynolds's** having been killed nearby.

McPherson Farm
August 21, 2000

52

Edward McPherson

McPherson, 33-year-old
owner of the celebrated
farm, was appointed
deputy commissioner
of internal revenue by
President Lincoln in
April 1863. Later in the
war he served as clerk
of the U.S. House of
Representatives; earlier
he had served as a vol-
unteer aide-de-camp
on the staffs of George
McCall and, ironically,
John F. Reynolds,
who died near
McPherson's Farm.

The Federals could stave off the inevitable for only so long. Most of Cutler's brigade was soon pushed into a retreat to Seminary Ridge, but for a time the 147th New York Infantry (Lt. Col. Francis C. Miller) held fast along the unfinished railroad bed. "The line of the [regiment] was lying in a [wheat]field at and below the ridge," wrote Capt. James Coey. "The fire of the enemy, the zipping of their bullets, cut the grain, completely covering the men, who would reach over the ridge, take deliberate aim, fire and then slide back under their canopy or covering of straw; reload and continue their firing. Those of the regiment wounded here were wounded in the head or upper part of the body, consequently more fatal." The New Yorkers then also were forced to withdraw to Seminary Ridge. This exposed the Union artillery and the right flank of the Iron Brigade.

By 11 A.M. a furious Union counterattack had commenced along the Chambersburg Pike, with the 84th New York Infantry (Col. Edward B. Fowler) driving across the pike northward toward the 42d Mississippi Infantry (Col. Hugh R. Miller), positioned along the railroad cut; to the east, the 95th New York Infantry (Maj. Edward Pye) similarly attacked, along with the 6th Wisconsin Infantry (Lt. Col. Rufus R. Dawes) of the Iron Brigade, which thrust into the 2d Mississippi Infantry (Col. John M. Stone) in a brutal fight.

The Confederates retreated back into the cut, which served as a natural rifle pit for a time, and the 6th Wisconsin, led by Dawes, fought hand to hand with the 2d Mississippi Infantry and the 55th North Carolina Infantry (Col. John H. K. Connally). A vicious melee now occurred: amid shouts of "Throw down your muskets!" the Wisconsin men fought stubbornly against the Mississippians, clubbing them with musket stocks, firing down into the cut, and lunging with Confederates in a desperate contest to see who might surrender. "My color guards were all killed and wounded in less than five minutes," wrote Cpl. W. B. Murphy of the 2d Mississippi, who carried the colors that morning. "My colors were shot more than one dozen times, and the flag staff was hit and splintered two or three times. . . . There were over a dozen shot down like sheep in their mad rush for the colors."

McPherson's Woods, Eastern Edge
Mathew B. Brady
View southeast
ca. July 15, 1863

Brady (in black coat) and an assistant
appear again in the foreground of a view
along the eastern edge of the woods in
which Union units fought stubbornly
while falling back toward the town during
the initial morning action. Visible in the
distance at left center is the cupola of
the Lutheran Theological Seminary,
used briefly as an observation post by
Federal officers.

53

McPherson's Woods
June 8, 1997

Mary Thompson House, Lee's Headquarters
Mathew B. Brady
View northeast
ca. July 15, 1863

On July 1, 1863, Lee established his headquarters on the Chambersburg Pike in a series of tents erected opposite the Thompson House. Lee used the house at brief intervals and ate several meals inside it. On the second and third days of battle, batteries of Southern artillery fired many rounds from the area. In this view Mrs. Thompson poses along with one of the Brady assistants.

Thompson House
August 21, 2000

General Headquarters Monument, Army of Northern Virginia, opposite Thompson House
April 25, 1995

Across the pike from Mary Thompson's house stood the complex of tents that operated as the nerve center of the Army of Northern Virginia during the battle. By Gettysburg battlefield custom, the position is now marked by an upturned cannon, denoting a corps or, in this case, army headquarters.

54

Thompson House
Mathew B. Brady
View northeast
ca. July 15, 1863

The house was built in the 1830s. This view, made a short time before or after the preceding view, prominently shows fence posts remaining along the pike.

Thompson House
August 21, 2000

Thompson House
Mathew B. Brady
View north
ca. July 15, 1863

Brady demonstrated great interest in the position of Lee's headquarters by making a number of variant images of the Thompson House.

55

Thompson House
View north
ca. 1865

A view made at war's end shows the rebuilt fence along the pike. In his only visit to the field at Gettysburg, Ulysses S. Grant visited the house in June 1867.

JULY 1, 1863

Maj. Gen. Abner Doubleday

Following Reynolds's death, the marginally capable Doubleday commanded the 1st Corps for the remainder of the day, worrying about his right to receive command and about how the battle was progressing. On July 2, 1863, Doubleday lost the assignment to Maj. Gen. John Newton.

Maj. Gen. John F. Reynolds

Reynolds was one of the highest-ranking officers killed during the war. He had been offered command of the Army of the Potomac prior to Meade but refused the assignment, sensing not enough independence of decision making from Washington authorities.

John F. Reynolds Death Monument
April 23, 1995

As the Iron Brigade surged ahead to attack the Rebel line early in the fight, tragedy struck the Union high command when 1st Corps commander Reynolds was hit in the head with a Minié bullet and killed instantly. He gasped a single time, smiled slightly, and died. The monument was erected in 1886.

James S. Wadsworth Monument, McPherson's Ridge
April 23, 1995

Wadsworth's division fought hard along the railroad cut and fields west of town before substantial pressure pushed them eastward. Wadsworth's monument was built in 1914.

Following the fight for the railroad cut, a temporary lull passed over the field. Stunned by the ferocity of the Union fight, Archer's and Davis's brigades retreated to Herr's Ridge, so named for its prominent stone Herr Tavern, to regroup. Heth asked for reinforcements from Maj. Gen. William Dorsey Pender's division to move up and take a position to support another attack, especially given the poor conditions of Archer's brigade. Around noon, Union Maj. Gen. Howard arrived on the field and assumed command from Doubleday; Howard immediately sent messages asking Maj. Gens. Henry W. Slocum and Daniel E. Sickles to move their corps into battle as fast as possible. He assigned Maj. Gen. Carl Schurz the command of his own 11th Corps. Howard positioned the division of Brig. Gen. Adolph von Steinwehr along Cemetery Hill, recognizing it as a naturally strong position. He also had great concern over the approach of Ewell's men in gray from the north. The leading division, that of Maj. Gen. Robert E. Rodes, was moving fast on Oak Ridge, and there Howard posted a line of defenders with Brig. Gen. John C. Robinson's division in the center. Doubleday spent part of the afternoon fretting about how he should have remained in command of some significant unit.

One of the great stories of the battle originated when a citizen of Gettysburg, John L. Burns, age 69, joined the Federal army. He took up arms alongside the 150th Pennsylvania Infantry (Col. Langhorne Wister), and later with the 7th Wisconsin Infantry (Col. William W. Robinson) during three hours of the afternoon fight on July 1. Several other civilian residents also fought in the action.

About 1:30 P.M. the great afternoon phase of the first day's battle erupted. Rodes's division, some 8,600 men strong and supported by 16 cannon, sent a deadly fire into the Union line along Oak Ridge, south of the Mummasburg Road and along

After Federal infantry arrived to reinforce the beleaguered cavalry, the battle raged north and west of town along the Chambersburg Pike, on Oak Ridge, and along the Carlisle Road. Confederate Lt. Gen. Richard S. Ewell launched a significant push southward early in the afternoon, with the heaviest fighting coming from Maj. Gen. Jubal A. Early's division.

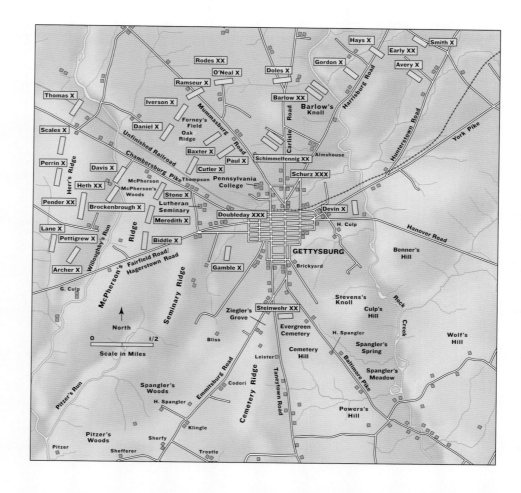

57

the southeastern edge of Forney's Field. Rodes planned to send the brigade of Col. Edward A. O'Neal obliquely into the right flank of the Federal line, rolling it up as it was attacked by his other brigade, that of Brig. Gen. Alfred Iverson. Robinson's force, consisting of only about 4,100 men, held the brigade of Brig. Gen. Henry Baxter, which occupied a position behind the stone fence alongside Forney's Field, and Cutler's brigade, to the south. The initial attack by Rodes failed, as Iverson did not participate and O'Neal's regiments encountered a stinging fire as they approached the Yankee line. At 2:30 P.M. Iverson's brigade finally did attack, again in uncoordinated fashion, with O'Neal to his left and the brigade of Brig. Gen. Junius Daniel on his right. To the later consternation of Confederate authorities, Iverson stayed behind the assault rather than joining it, raising allegations of cowardliness and even drunkenness. Iverson and his men simply failed to realize that such an opposing force awaited them behind the stone wall.

JULY 1, 1863

Lutheran Theological Seminary
ca. 1861–1865

An image of the seminary shot during or at the end of the war shows it under more normal conditions. The photographers may well have been Charles J. and Isaac G. Tyson of Gettysburg.

By midafternoon, despite the sloppy tactics on Oak Ridge, the driving Southern attacks were taking hold. Pettigrew's and Brockenbrough's brigades of Heth's division began assaults from the west anew, supported by well-placed Confederate cannon, with Pettigrew's fresh division now facing Meredith's Iron Brigade. Rodes threatened Oak Ridge, and Maj. Gen. Jubal A. Early arrived with his division, some 6,300 strong, from York, endangering the Union right flank. Shortly after 3 P.M. the veterans of the Iron Brigade were forced back from McPherson's Woods by Pettigrew's strong, coordinated sheets of musketry fire. On Seminary Ridge, Federal artillery blasted canister, small round balls packed with sawdust that acted as giant shotgun blasts, into Pettigrew's approaching ranks. After engaging along six lines of battle between late morning and late afternoon, the Iron Brigade was ordered to fall back to Cemetery Hill about 3:45 P.M. Gamble's Union cavalry attempted to cover the retreat, firing hotly into Pettigrew's men. Brig. Gen. Stephen Dodson Ramseur's brigade led an attack that speared into and scattered the Union regiments still on Oak Ridge. The resulting Union movement back through the town of Gettysburg, which still had plenty of civilians hiding in cellars and wondering which way the battle was moving, reflected a sense of panic. Pettigrew's attacked hotly at 4 P.M., driving the Union retreat into further chaos. He sent Col. Abner Perrin's brigade thrusting into the Union brigade of Col. Chapman Biddle west of the seminary, scattering it in retreat. Finally, believing that the Yankees were utterly routed, his men exhausted after six hours of fighting, Hill halted the attack.

Ewell's corps, moving southward toward the town, attacked headlong into the unfortunate, outnumbered Union 11th Corps, which had been so mauled at Chancellorsville by Jackson's flank attack. Schurz initially occupied a position just

574. Theological Seminary.

north of town, posting the divisions of Brig. Gen. Alexander Schimmelfennig along the Carlisle Road and Brig. Gen. Francis C. Barlow northeast of town. Barlow marched north past the Almshouse to occupy a slight rise on the ground known as Blocher's Knoll, subsequently as Barlow's Knoll. He dispatched the 900-man brigade of Col. Leopold von Gilsa to the knoll, which had an elevation of 519 feet. Von Gilsa deployed his men into a skirmish line to fire back and forth between the Confederates already spread across the area. By 3:15 P.M., Early launched an all-out push into the 11th Corps, sending the Confederate brigades of Brig. Gens. Harry T. Hays, John B. Gordon, George P. Doles, and Isaac E. Avery forward toward Gettysburg.

**Confederate Prisoners,
Lutheran Theological Seminary
Mathew B. Brady
View southeast
ca. July 15, 1863**

One of the celebrated images of
Gettysburg depicts three Confederates
along a fence line at the seminary after
being captured during the first day's fight.
A copy of the image at the Library of
Congress alleges that the men are members of the 8th Louisiana Infantry
of Harry Hays's brigade, the "Louisiana
Tigers," and that the men, left to right,
are an unidentified man, Pvt. Winborn
L. Chafin, and Pvt. W. H. Oliver.
Whether this is credible or spurious
is impossible to know.

**Site of the Prisoners, Lutheran
Theological Seminary
June 8, 1997**

The intensity of fire into Barlow's Knoll was overwhelming; Union casualties were severe. Gordon's men charged into Barlow's position, routing the Yankees and sending them scurrying. Many wounded soldiers covered the knoll after the desperate struggle, including the badly wounded Barlow, who had been shot in the left side. Age 29, Barlow was a well-liked New Yorker who had been a lawyer and newspaperman. As he lay alone, after the surviving Yankees had fled, Barlow was struck in the back by a second ball, which bruised him. Another bullet grazed a finger; a fourth struck his hat. Barlow was captured and taken to a house on the Blocher Farm, expecting to die. He survived, however, and was recaptured by Union troops when the Confederate army retreated from the field. Years later, Gordon, the Confederate general who attacked Barlow's position, spun a story about Barlow, in which he claimed the Union general officer had asked him to take possessions of his to pass along to Barlow's wife in case he should die; this appears to have been an invention of Gordon's for the sake of selling his 1903 autobiography.

After a vigorous stand against much larger numbers west of the town, the Union forces had crumbled on the afternoon of July 1. The battle of Gettysburg was shaping up to be a major Confederate victory — just what Gen. Lee believed he needed to pursue his strategic goals. Although the battle began by accident, now an all-out effort to strike the Federals on all fronts might collapse their lines and send them scurrying in retreat, sending chills of panic throughout the Yankee home front. It looked like it was going to be a memorable day for the South.

Peace Memorial, Oak Hill
April 23, 1995

In July 1938 more than 1,800 Civil War veterans converged (along with more than a quarter million spectators) for the 75th anniversary remembrance of the battle. President Franklin D. Roosevelt dedicated the Eternal Light Peace Memorial, which celebrates the reunification of the opposing sides. The eternal flame was extinguished in favor of sodium vapor light in 1978, but then was thankfully restored in the 1990s.

63

View along Seminary Ridge
June 8, 1997

CHAPTER 3

A DIZZYING RETREAT THROUGH TOWN

★ JULY 1, 1863 ★

The afternoon battle of July 1 at Gettysburg was now heavily favoring the South. Pushed by the southward attack of Early, Col. Wladimir Krzyzanowski's Union brigade collapsed and began a chaotic retreat toward the town. Early created a second line and continued to move his men forward, striking the Union battle lines with sharp volleys of musketry. Amid the Federal chaos, a pocket of resistance sprang up when Col. Charles R. Coster's brigade formed on the northern part of town along a brickyard operated by John Kuhn. As the divisions of Brig. Gens. Alexander Schimmelfennig and Adelbert Ames were falling back into the town, Coster made a last stand at the brickyard, deploying the 154th New York Infantry (Lt. Col. Daniel B. Allen) in the center, flanked by the 27th Pennsylvania Infantry (Lt. Col. Lorenz Cantador) on the left and 134th New York Infantry (Lt. Col. Allen H. Jackson) on the right. By 3:45 P.M. the brickyard fight had erupted in full fury as Coster's brigade came under attack by Brig. Gen. Robert F. Hoke's brigade (now commanded by Col. Isaac E. Avery) and the left wing of Harry Hays's brigade. A bloody hand-to-hand melee ensued, with stubborn fighting on both sides; the Union regiments were cut to pieces and numerous prisoners were taken. "I got up and went as fast as any of them," recalled Pvt. Janus Quilliam of the surrounded 154th New York, "but when we got to the road, it was full of Rebels and they were coming up behind us, so there we had to stay, and few got away."

Gettysburg Viewed from Seminary Ridge
Mathew B. Brady
View southeast
ca. July 15, 1863

A panorama looking toward the town shows the ground over which Union soldiers fled the scene of the first morning's fight, with the Chambersburg Pike cutting through the scene at right. The majority of the Ist Corps escaped eastward along the pike. The most prominent house on the pike is Carrie Sheads's Oak Hill Seminary; the house to its right, across the pike, is the James A. Grimes House. Above it in the background is Culp's Hill.

View along Seminary Ridge
June 8, 1997

Col. Ezra A. Carman

As Carman, colonel of the 13th New Jersey Infantry, approached the battle, he witnessed a crowd of citizens fleeing their homes for the countryside. "Our arrival in the town," he wrote, "was the cause of great rejoicing by the inhabitants, and from every house we received tokens of gratitude and delight in the shape of cooked provisions, biscuits, bread and butter, cakes, pies, and other luxuries which were keenly relished."

Maj. Gen. Jubal A. Early

Called "my bad old man" by Lee for his constant foul language, Early was a colorful character who struck hard into the Union IIth Corps, pressing it southward with a vicious attack on the first day.

Brig. Gen. Alfred Iverson

One of Rodes's brigade commanders was the Georgian Iverson, an incompetent field commander. When his brigade attacked on the afternoon of July I, he stayed behind and later faced allegations of cowardliness and drunkenness.

Maj. Gen. Robert E. Rodes

Virginian Rodes commanded a division in Ewell's corps; his initial attack on the first day was a failure. He would be mortally wounded at Winchester the following year.

Maj. Gen. William Dorsey Pender

After sloppy fighting on Oak and McPherson Ridges, Pender's division of Hill's Corps followed up the afternoon attacks of Heth's soldiers that had driven the Iron Brigade from McPherson's Woods and assailed the Federals. A rapid retreat ensued.

68

Maj. Gen. Carl Schurz

A Prussian revolutionary who emigrated to the United States in 1852, Schurz found his largely Germanic division in the IIth Corps outbattled by the southward attack of Ewell.

Brig. Gen. Adolph von Steinwehr

Also caught up in Ewell's attack and forced to retreat southward into the town of Steinwehr's division. Steinwehr had been born in Brunswick before coming to the United States in 1847.

Brig. Gen. Gabriel R. Paul

A well-liked regular army officer, Paul was hideously wounded on Oak Ridge when he was shot through both eyes and blinded.

Brig. Gen. John C. Robinson

Robinson's division fought skillfully on Oak Ridge despite the heavy attacks by Rodes.

With the areas of Union resistance crumbling, Confederates finally secured the town. Fleeing Union soldiers raced through the streets to the relative safety of Cemetery Hill. Casualties were strewn all over town; gunshots rang out through the streets; with the sight of Rebel soldiers in their town, civilians fled or hid. Many houses were quickly transformed into aid stations or hospitals, with casualties quickly laid out to be worked on. A chaplain, Horatio M. Howell (90th Pennsylvania Infantry), was killed on the steps of the Lutheran church. Danger to civilians in town lasted throughout the battle: On the morning of July 3, inside the McClellan House on Baltimore Street, Mary Virginia Wade, age 20, would be struck by a Minié bullet while baking bread and killed instantly. She would be the only civilian to die during the battle.

On July 1, fleeing soldiers also ran into danger. Schimmelfennig made the unfortunate decision to run down an alleyway that dead-ended at a barn in the yard of the Garlach family. There he hid between a barrel and a woodshed for three days before Union troops retook the town and liberated him. During this period the Garlachs brought the young general bread and water in a bucket supposed to be used for feeding pigs.

Meanwhile, Confederate tactical thinking was evolving. Lee, having observed the battle, appreciated the critical importance of Cemetery Hill, which rose to 615 feet, and Culp's Hill, at 620 feet. By 4:30 P.M. Lee had sent Ewell one of his famously ambiguous orders, asking Ewell to take the high ground of Cemetery and/or Culp's Hill "if practicable," a phrase that left open the widest possible range of interpretation. Approaching subordinates with such an attitude might have worked with the aggressive Stonewall Jackson, Ewell's predecessor, but Ewell was another type, characterized at this stage of the battle by caution. He believed that he could not position his artillery effectively to provide support for an infantry attack, felt that his troops were exhausted by fighting and marching, lacked one of his divisions (that of Maj. Gen. Edward Johnson), and had more than 4,000 Federal prisoners to contend with. He also felt that the troops he did have at his immediate disposal had been intermingled during the chaotic fighting through the narrow streets of the town as the Yankees had scattered southward. Moreover, early in the fight, Ewell had been knocked to the ground when his horse was killed by a shell fragment near Oak Ridge; that incident itself must have been alarming enough to caution him. In any event, at 5 P.M. Ewell arrived in the town square and saw masses of Confederate troops mingling with Union prisoners and virtually no citizens in sight. Johnson, meanwhile, finally reached Cashtown with his missing division and heard the sounds of battle. In the town, Ewell hesitated, riding forward with Maj. Gens. Robert E. Rodes and Jubal A. Early to examine Maj. Gen. Oliver O. Howard's Union line on Cemetery Hill. It was indeed clear that artillery could not be placed to advantage in the town; nonetheless, Ewell finally determined to make an attack on Cemetery Hill. A messenger from Lee, however, made it clear that no support would be available on the right, so Ewell decided not to attack, worrying more with each passing minute about the condition of Rodes's men. He then determined to move against Culp's Hill ("the wooded hill to my left") as soon as Johnson showed up.

69

Gettysburg from Seminary Ridge
Charles and Isaac Tyson
View east-northeast
August 1863

This view shows the town from a position along the Confederate battle line of the first day. The Fairfield Road (Hagerstown Road) cuts through the scene on the right; on the extreme left horizon are tents of Camp Letterman, the primary U.S. post-battle hospital. Prominent buildings in the scene, left to right, include the Sterner Iron Factory (long white structure at left edge); Christ Lutheran Church (steeple visible above tree near center of left-hand frame); St. James Lutheran Church (steeple to the right of Christ Church); Adams County Courthouse (boxlike building with tower on Baltimore Street); and St. Francis Xavier Catholic Church (center of right-hand frame).

70

View from Seminary Ridge
August 21, 2000

View along the Chambersburg Pike
Frederick Gutekunst
View northwest
ca. July 12, 1863

Gutekunst recorded one of his assistants standing on the Chambersburg Pike with the railroad cut along Oak Ridge clearly shown, as well as the private school for girls operated by Carrie Sheads and the C. Henry Dustman House just beyond it. The geography of the railroad cut makes it clear why soldiers fired out from it and were also caught within it by attackers.

Many officers of the Confederate army, accustomed to Jackson's brashness, were stunned by Ewell's apparent caution. In typical oversimplification, claims after the war hinged the life of the Confederacy on this moment. According to Lt. Col. H. C. Jones, "There was not an officer, not even a man, that did not expect that the war would be closed upon the hill that evening, for there was still two hours of daylight when the final charge was made, yet for reasons that have never been explained nor ever will be . . . someone made a blunder that lost the battle of Gettysburg, and humanly speaking, the Confederate cause." This was overreaching, but nonetheless, Ewell's hesitation was costly, even if tempered by real concerns. Attacking or seizing Culp's Hill and the adjoining portions of Cemetery Hill plainly would have yielded valuable ground for any fighting to come. Further, not only did he halt his plans, but Ewell, like Lee, also failed to use the available cavalry to scout the roads east of the town. So Ewell judged an attack on the high ground south of town "impracticable" and went about his business, much to the irritation of some of his subordinates, who favored aggressively attacking Culp's Hill, Cemetery Hill, or both.

**Anna B. Flint Grave,
Almshouse Burial
Ground, Barlow's Knoll
April 25, 1995**

North of the town, in
the path of Ewell's
southward attack, stood
the County Almshouse.
In the accompanying
cemetery for the poor,
simple gravestones
stood in the path of
battle, such as that of
Flint, who died in 1853.

**Francis C. Barlow
Monument,
Barlow's Knoll
June 5, 1997**

Near the Almshouse,
on a rise of ground
that came to be called
Barlow's Knoll, youthful
Barlow was badly
wounded, struck by
multiple balls while he
defended the position.

**Brig. Gen.
Francis C. Barlow**

Barlow survived his
wounding. The former
lawyer and journalist
commanded a division
in the Army of the
Potomac the following
spring and fought
valiantly at Spotsylvania.

**Brig. Gen.
John B. Gordon**

The much repeated
tale of Confederate
Gordon coming to
Barlow's aid and taking
his possessions to give
to the Union general's
wife appears to be a
fabrication for the sake
of selling Gordon's
turn-of-the-century
autobiography.

Though Union forces had been beaten back mercilessly through the town, they
were by late afternoon beginning to stabilize. From Taneytown, Meade had sent Maj.
Gen. Winfield Scott Hancock forward to Gettysburg, having issued orders for him to
assume command of the troops on the field. Hancock arrived about 4:30 P.M. and was
stunned to see the 1st and 11th Corps "retreating in disorder and confusion." Howard
and his subordinates had attempted to hold a line south of town but were struck by
repeated stinging volleys from sharpshooters taking cover behind buildings on the
southern edge of the town. Although Howard knew of Hancock's approach, it isn't
clear whether or not he realized Hancock had been given command of the army on
the field. After a hasty salute, Howard reminded Hancock that he was the senior officer in rank. Hancock replied that he was aware of that, but that he had been ordered
by Meade to assume command, and he would show Howard the document if neces-
sary. Howard allegedly replied that it wasn't, and after a brief, civil argument amid
the bullets whizzing by in the surrounding air, Howard and Hancock agreed that this
was a good place to fight the battle north of Pipe Creek, and that they would commence fighting the Rebels rather than each other.

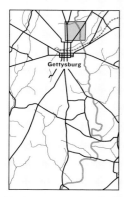

The Union IIth Corps Collapses
July I, 1863, Mid-Afternoon

Maj. Gen. Robert E. Rodes sent a thrust into the exhausted IIth Corps and collapsed the Union line of battle north of Gettysburg, sending it reeling through the town in retreat.

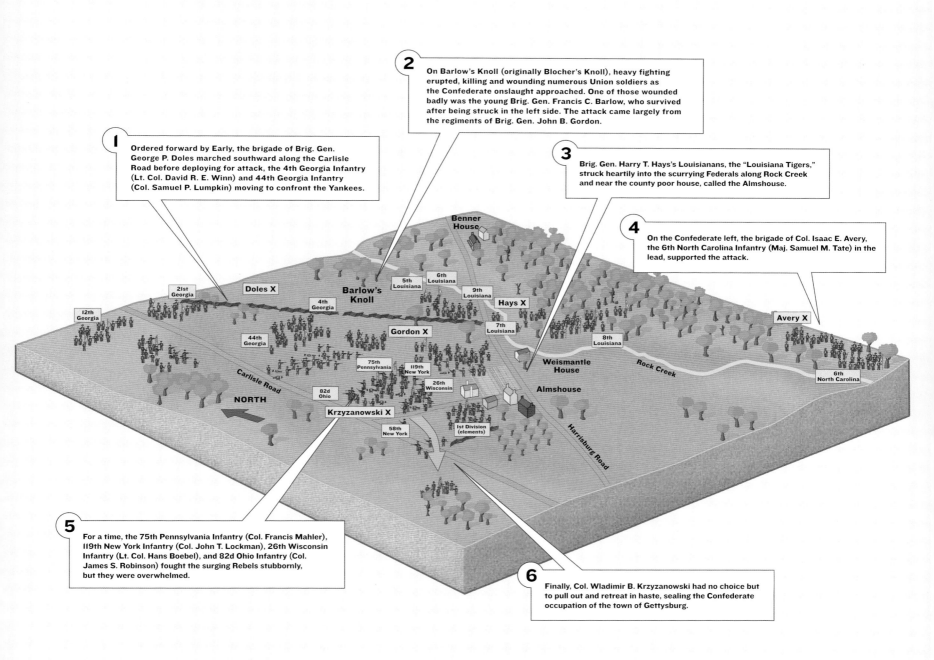

2 On Barlow's Knoll (originally Blocher's Knoll), heavy fighting erupted, killing and wounding numerous Union soldiers as the Confederate onslaught approached. One of those wounded badly was the young Brig. Gen. Francis C. Barlow, who survived after being struck in the left side. The attack came largely from the regiments of Brig. Gen. John B. Gordon.

1 Ordered forward by Early, the brigade of Brig. Gen. George P. Doles marched southward along the Carlisle Road before deploying for attack, the 4th Georgia Infantry (Lt. Col. David R. E. Winn) and 44th Georgia Infantry (Col. Samuel P. Lumpkin) moving to confront the Yankees.

3 Brig. Gen. Harry T. Hays's Louisianans, the "Louisiana Tigers," struck heartily into the scurrying Federals along Rock Creek and near the county poor house, called the Almshouse.

4 On the Confederate left, the brigade of Col. Isaac E. Avery, the 6th North Carolina Infantry (Maj. Samuel M. Tate) in the lead, supported the attack.

5 For a time, the 75th Pennsylvania Infantry (Col. Francis Mahler), 119th New York Infantry (Col. John T. Lockman), 26th Wisconsin Infantry (Lt. Col. Hans Boebel), and 82d Ohio Infantry (Col. James S. Robinson) fought the surging Rebels stubbornly, but they were overwhelmed.

6 Finally, Col. Wladimir B. Krzyzanowski had no choice but to pull out and retreat in haste, sealing the Confederate occupation of the town of Gettysburg.

Benner House

21st Georgia

Doles X

12th Georgia

4th Georgia

Barlow's Knoll

5th Louisiana

6th Louisiana

9th Louisiana

Hays X

7th Louisiana

Avery X

44th Georgia

Gordon X

8th Louisiana

6th North Carolina

75th Pennsylvania

119th New York

Weismantle House

Rock Creek

Carlisle Road

82d Ohio

26th Wisconsin

Almshouse

Krzyzanowski X

NORTH

1st Division (elements)

58th New York

Harrisburg Road

26th Pennsylvania Emergency Militia Infantry Monument, Chambersburg Street
April 25, 1995

Among the units raised to stem the tide of a Confederate invasion into Pennsylvania was the 26th Emergency Regiment, consisting of local militia who encountered Confederate cavalry and infantry near Gettysburg and skirmished on June 26. (Many of the roads are termed streets inside the town and turnpikes outside of it, as was the case with Chambersburg Street/Pike.)

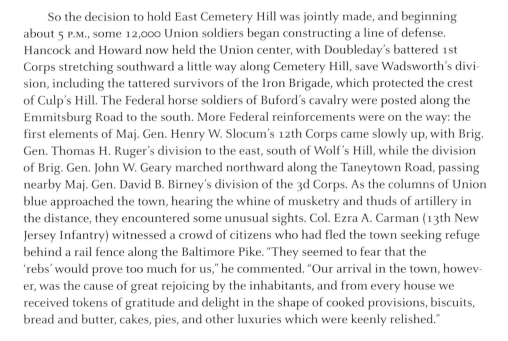

Pennsylvania College
Mathew B. Brady
View north
ca. July 15, 1863

Pennsylvania Hall (with cupola), the central structure of Gettysburg's Pennsylvania College, was built in 1837. (The college was later renamed Gettysburg College.) Classes initially were held on the first day of battle, but they were soon dismissed, and the students retreated. Maj. Gen. Oliver O. Howard's 11th Corps arrived on the scene to face Ewell's southward attack and fought over ground just north of the college before abandoning it and retreating southward.

Gettysburg College
August 21, 2000

So the decision to hold East Cemetery Hill was jointly made, and beginning about 5 P.M., some 12,000 Union soldiers began constructing a line of defense. Hancock and Howard now held the Union center, with Doubleday's battered 1st Corps stretching southward a little way along Cemetery Hill, save Wadsworth's division, including the tattered survivors of the Iron Brigade, which protected the crest of Culp's Hill. The Federal horse soldiers of Buford's cavalry were posted along the Emmitsburg Road to the south. More Federal reinforcements were on the way: the first elements of Maj. Gen. Henry W. Slocum's 12th Corps came slowly up, with Brig. Gen. Thomas H. Ruger's division to the east, south of Wolf's Hill, while the division of Brig. Gen. John W. Geary marched northward along the Taneytown Road, passing nearby Maj. Gen. David B. Birney's division of the 3d Corps. As the columns of Union blue approached the town, hearing the whine of musketry and thuds of artillery in the distance, they encountered some unusual sights. Col. Ezra A. Carman (13th New Jersey Infantry) witnessed a crowd of citizens who had fled the town seeking refuge behind a rail fence along the Baltimore Pike. "They seemed to fear that the 'rebs' would prove too much for us," he commented. "Our arrival in the town, however, was the cause of great rejoicing by the inhabitants, and from every house we received tokens of gratitude and delight in the shape of cooked provisions, biscuits, bread and butter, cakes, pies, and other luxuries which were keenly relished."

**Coster Avenue Mural and 154th
New York Infantry Monument
April 25, 1995**

As the Union retreat through the town
dissolved into chaos, Col. Charles R.
Coster's brigade made a stand at the
John Kuhn Brickyard on Gettysburg's
northern edge. The 154th New York
Infantry fought stubbornly before retreating in disarray. A mural now depicts these
moments of heated action.

John L. Burns Home,
Chambersburg Street
Frederick Gutekunst
View southeast
ca. July 15, 1863

Burns, age 69 and a local, was hailed
as "the hero of Gettysburg" following
the battle because he marched out to
the position of the armies and insisted
on shouldering a musket in defense
of his town. Burns poses with his wife
on the porch of their home.

John Burns Home
ca. 1863

Burns had been a veteran of the War of
1812; he fought on McPherson's Ridge
with the 150th Pennsylvania Infantry
and later with the 7th Wisconsin Infantry
during a three-hour stint. Here he again
poses on his porch; a photographer's
assistant stands below him.

Site of the
John Burns Home
June 8, 1997

John Burns Monument,
McPherson's Woods
April 23, 1995

In 1902 Burns received
the honor of a monu-
ment on the field, placed
near the spot where he
pleaded with Col.
Langhorne Wister to
join the men of the 150th
Pennsylvania Infantry
and soon thereafter
entered the fight.

John L. Burns

Wounded three times
during his service at
Gettysburg, in a leg
and an arm, Burns lived
eight more years in glory.

76

John Burns at Home, Variant
Mathew B. Brady
ca. July 15, 1863

A variant image of Burns with his crutches and flintlock was made shortly before or after the previous image.

John Burns at Home
Mathew B. Brady
ca. July 15, 1863

So impressive was the patriotism of Burns that when Lincoln visited Gettysburg he asked to meet Burns, and the two men attended services together at the town's Presbyterian church.

The Federal retreat through the town moved straight down the Chambersburg Pike into the town square, past these buildings. The corner building closest to the camera contained a savings bank and clothing store; Christ Lutheran Church stands several doors to the west. In the modern view, a tree mostly obscures the church's steeple.

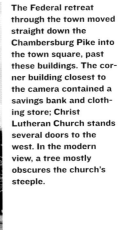

Chambersburg Street
Charles and Isaac Tyson
View west
August 1863

Chambersburg Street
June 8, 1997

This view depicts the tower of the Adams County Courthouse and the corner store of J. L. Schick, familiar sights to Yankee soldiers scurrying southward through the town's unfamiliar streets. The courthouse, constructed in 1859, served as a lookout for officers during the battle and a hospital following the action.

Baltimore Street
P. S. Weaver
View west
ca. October 1863

Baltimore Street
August 21, 2000

78

Samuel Fahnestock's Clothing Store was one of the largest brick structures in Gettysburg at the time of the battle. Maj. Gen. Oliver O. Howard observed the developing battle from its roof on July 1. Eight days later, when the photo was taken, the building had just been allocated to the Sanitary Commission, the civilian organization that looked after the soldiers' welfare.

U.S. Sanitary Commission Headquarters,
Baltimore Street
Alexander Gardner
View northwest
ca. July 9, 1863

Fahnestock Brothers Store,
Baltimore Street
June 8, 1997

**Henry Garlach House,
Baltimore Street**
May 8, 1996

During the Federal retreat through
town, Union Brig. Gen. Alexander
Schimmelfennig made the unfortunate
decision to run down a blind alley behind
Henry Garlach's house, at 323 Baltimore
Street. He hid behind the house for
three days, while the town was under
Confederate occupation, between
a barrel and a woodshed.

Sweeney House (Farnsworth House)
May 8, 1996

The wartime Sweeney House, now a
restaurant and bookshop called the
Farnsworth House, received significant
small-arms damage to its brick edifice
that is visible today.

On the evening of July 1, the battle of Gettysburg began to settle after a tumultuous first day. The action had thus far favored Lee's Army of Northern Virginia, but
mostly because it had fought an outnumbered enemy. Division and brigade commanders had escalated the fight into a major pitched battle, something that neither
side desired. Lee's army was scattered throughout southern Pennsylvania, his cavalry
mostly absent from the scene. Lee now faced continuing this escalating engagement
on ground that might greatly disadvantage his soldiers, with most of the Federal
army rapidly approaching. Maj. Gen. Edward "Alleghany" Johnson's tardy division
finally arrived around 7:30 P.M. and pulled into position north of Culp's Hill; Early
occupied the town itself, Rodes was positioned on the northwest edge of town, and
Pender stretched southward along Seminary Ridge. Maj. Gens. Henry Heth's and
Richard H. Anderson's divisions were still scattered west of town.

JULY 1, 1863

Carlisle Street
Sketch by Alfred R. Waud
View north
ca. July 4 or 5, 1863

Harper's Weekly artist Waud sketched a barricaded railroad track and the railroad station on the right side of Carlisle Street. This was one of several barricades erected across the town's streets as the fighting raged.

Carlisle Street
August 21, 2000

Gettysburg College
August 21, 2000

Pennsylvania College
Charles and Isaac Tyson
View north
ca. April 1862

The earliest known photograph of
Pennsylvania College is exceptionally rare
in that it depicts a view of Gettysburg
prior to the battle. A wagon and gas lamp
stand in the foreground. The Federal
retreat on the first day of battle washed
over this area, with many soldiers of the
1st and IIth Corps maneuvering south and
eastward into the town.

Finally, with darkness approaching, Ewell ordered Lts. Robert D. Early and
Thomas T. Turner to reconnoiter the summit of Culp's Hill. This peculiar reconnaissance would turn out to be a fateful event. Miraculously, they reached the summit
without detection by the nearby Union troops. Early and Turner reported the
enemy's line of battle to Ewell, who halfheartedly and finally asked Johnson to move
toward Culp's Hill and occupy it "if you find no enemy troops there." Incredulous,
Early urged that it be done because "if you do not go up there tonight, it will cost you
ten thousand men to get there tomorrow." Ewell was also repeatedly pushed by Maj.
Gen. Isaac R. Trimble, who claimed that "if we don't hold that hill, the enemy will certainly occupy it, as it is the key to the whole position about here." Ewell brusquely
responded that he didn't require advice from Trimble.

Johnson approached Culp's Hill by a peculiar route, forming east of the town,
fording Rock Creek, and moving toward Benner's Hill first. A small reconnaissance
party moved out ahead of the division, and as it approached the base of Culp's Hill
it encountered the pickets of the 7th Indiana Infantry (Col. Ira G. Grover), who
opened fire and caused the advancing Confederates to retreat in panic. Amazingly,
they also reported that an overwhelming force of Yankees lay ahead, causing Ewell to
nervously back off. At Ewell's headquarters a short time later, none other than Robert
E. Lee arrived to consult with the general. Also there were Rodes and Maj. Gen. Jubal
Early. After considering several options, Lee decided to leave Ewell's corps in position
for the night. Ewell later rode to Lee's headquarters, near the Mary Thompson House
along the Chambersburg Pike west of town, for further consultation. By 2 A.M. on
July 2, Ewell had ordered Johnson's division to regroup southeast of the town and
await further orders. The opportunity to attack Culp's Hill, which probably had
existed only around 6 P.M. the previous evening, was lost. During the late evening and
early morning hours, Federal troops on the hill had fortified the Union line and
moved fresh troops into position. In another of the multitudes of postwar specula-
tions, Early wrote, "Perhaps that victory might have been made decisive . . . by a
prompt advance of all the troops that had been engaged on our side against the hill
upon and behind which the enemy had taken refuge, but a common superior did not
happen to be present, and the opportunity was lost."

Baltimore Street and the Wagon Hotel
Alexander Gardner
View north
ca. July 1865

A northward view of the Wagon Hotel
shows the Rupp Tannery (left of center,
with smokestack), where the
Confederates stopped and fired during
the initial Union retreat.

View along Baltimore Street
August 21, 2000

Adams County Prison
June 8, 1997

Situated on High Street, the prison is celebrated
as the site of a council of war by Robert E. Lee
and his staff on July 2, which may have preceded
the attack on Cemetery Hill.

Aside from the movement on Culp's or Cemetery Hill, Lee's array of choices in the wee hours of July 2 was limited. As Longstreet's fresh corps marched toward the battlefield, Lee and Longstreet contemplated the best strategy for the morning. Cautious about the Federal battle line that was forming along the ridges extending southward from Gettysburg, Longstreet warned against attacking and instead suggested interposing the Confederate army between Meade's army and Washington. This would force Meade to take the initiative and move away from the formidable high ground. But Lee felt a desperate need for a victory on northern soil as soon as possible, and he had his blood up. He was anxious also not to disengage and possibly appear to be in retreat. Lee, therefore, formulated an offensive strategy after observing the Union line from Culp's Hill, Cemetery Hill, and Cemetery Ridge south to the Round Tops. With his 70,200 men and 262 field guns, Lee would attack on July 2 with a three-pronged movement, sending Longstreet around on the right flank to lead the assault, A. P. Hill in the center on Cemetery Ridge and southern Cemetery Hill, and Ewell into the Union right on Culp's Hill and eastern Cemetery Hill. Ewell's movement would be mostly a demonstration that would force the Union right to stay in position rather than shifting in support of the defense against Longstreet.

The Union high command also crystallized its plan late in the night. Arriving after his journey from Taneytown around 11:30 P.M. on July 1, Meade walked about the Federal line on Cemetery Hill. Near the brick gatehouse of Evergreen Cemetery, he spoke with generals Slocum, John Gibbon, Howard, Sickles, and Gouverneur Warren, formulating an opinion on the battlefield. One of the officers mentioned that they occupied "good ground," and Meade replied that it was just as well, as they could not now abandon the field. The Federal commander soon established his headquarters at the Lydia A. Leister House on the Taneytown Road and set to work formulating a tactical plan. The night remained hot and a bright moon hung overhead, which "presented a scene of weird, almost spectral impressiveness," recalled a veteran in the *National Tribune*. "The roads south and southeast of the town flowed with unceasing, unbroken rivers of armed men, marching swiftly, stolidly, silently. Their garments were covered with dust, and their gun barrels gleamed with a fierce brilliance in the bright moonlight. The striking silence of the march, the dust-gray figures, the witchery of the moonbeams, made it spectral and awesome. No drum beat, no trumpet blared, no harsh command broke the monotonous stillness of the steady surge forward."

82

The Wagon Hotel
View south
ca. 1861–1865

This hostelry at the intersection of Baltimore Pike and the Emmitsburg Road serviced teamsters; on July I it served as shelter for retreating Federal marksmen firing northward into a wall of Confederate snipers at the Rupp Tannery, down the street.

George George House
View west
ca. 1861–1865

After John Reynolds was fatally shot, his
body was carried to the George House, a
small stone structure on the Emmitsburg
Road, where it stayed ahead of the fighting only for a few hours. George later
claimed $100 in damages for his house's
use as a hospital.

George George House
May 8, 1996

The Wagon Hotel
Charles and Isaac Tyson
View north
ca. 1865

By war's end, normal activity had
returned to the streets of Gettysburg, and
in the first great push of Gettysburg
tourism, the Wagon Hotel soon changed
its name to the Battlefield Hotel.

Site of the Wagon Hotel
June 8, 1997

84

McClellan Home
May 8, 1996

John L. McClellan Home
Charles and Isaac Tyson
View southeast
ca. 1865

The lone civilian casualty of the battle
occurred in the McClellan Home on the
eastern side of the Baltimore Pike when
20-year-old Mary Virginia "Jennie" Wade,
busy baking bread, was struck by a stray
bullet on the morning of July 3. The
house, built about 1842, afforded apparently sturdy brick construction, but it did
not protect the young girl, who became
as celebrated in death as John Burns
did in life.

The slow, sullen march of Federal troops continued into the night. As more men
arrived, Meade deployed them into a form that began to resemble a fishhook with its
barb on Culp's Hill, curving through Cemetery Hill, and with a straight shank extending southward along Cemetery Ridge. This defensive line was established for four
reasons: such high ground offered a natural bastion from which to ward off expected
attacks from Lee; two subordinate officers, Slocum and Warren, strongly opposed
taking the offensive; his entire army was not yet present; and the troops on the field
were exhausted from the march. Few soldiers on either side slept for long on this
night, as neither side knew what exactly would transpire the next day.

JULY 1, 1863

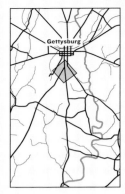

Union Troops Regroup on Cemetery Hill
July 1, 1863, Evening

After a day of heavy fighting in which they began by staving off a much larger Confederate force and then were shattered by Ewell's southward attack, the beleaguered Federal soldiers assembled south of town on Cemetery Hill.

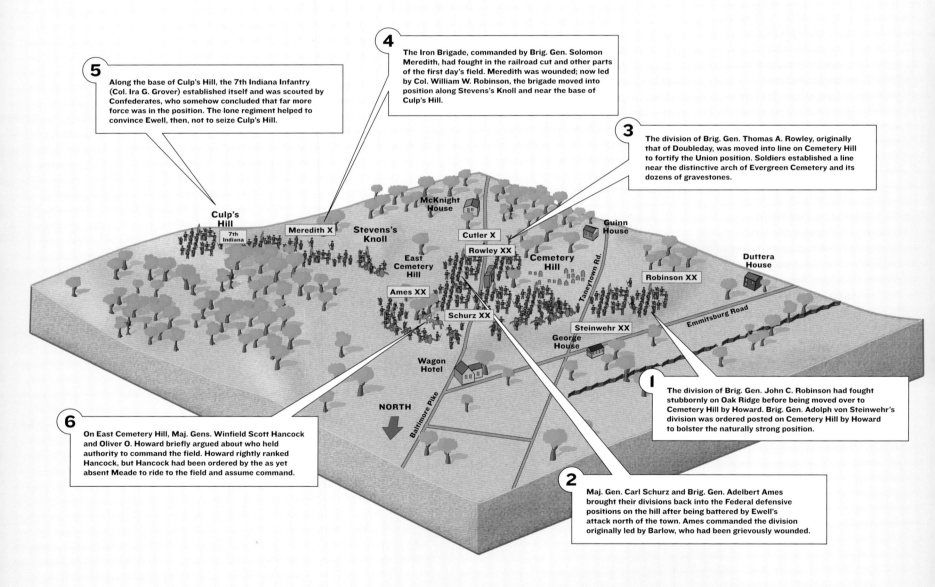

4 The Iron Brigade, commanded by Brig. Gen. Solomon Meredith, had fought in the railroad cut and other parts of the first day's field. Meredith was wounded; now led by Col. William W. Robinson, the brigade moved into position along Stevens's Knoll and near the base of Culp's Hill.

5 Along the base of Culp's Hill, the 7th Indiana Infantry (Col. Ira G. Grover) established itself and was scouted by Confederates, who somehow concluded that far more force was in the position. The lone regiment helped to convince Ewell, then, not to seize Culp's Hill.

3 The division of Brig. Gen. Thomas A. Rowley, originally that of Doubleday, was moved into line on Cemetery Hill to fortify the Union position. Soldiers established a line near the distinctive arch of Evergreen Cemetery and its dozens of gravestones.

1 The division of Brig. Gen. John C. Robinson had fought stubbornly on Oak Ridge before being moved over to Cemetery Hill by Howard. Brig. Gen. Adolph von Steinwehr's division was ordered posted on Cemetery Hill by Howard to bolster the naturally strong position.

6 On East Cemetery Hill, Maj. Gens. Winfield Scott Hancock and Oliver O. Howard briefly argued about who held authority to command the field. Howard rightly ranked Hancock, but Hancock had been ordered by the as yet absent Meade to ride to the field and assume command.

2 Maj. Gen. Carl Schurz and Brig. Gen. Adelbert Ames brought their divisions back into the Federal defensive positions on the hill after being battered by Ewell's attack north of the town. Ames commanded the division originally led by Barlow, who had been grievously wounded.

Culp's Hill

McKnight House

Meredith X

Stevens's Knoll

Cutler X

Rowley XX

Guinn House

Duttera House

7th Indiana

East Cemetery Hill

Cemetery Hill

Robinson XX

Ames XX

Taneytown Rd.

Schurz XX

Steinwehr XX

Emmitsburg Road

George House

Wagon Hotel

NORTH

Baltimore Pike

**Maj. Gen.
Winfield Scott Hancock**

Badly wounded on the
third day at Gettysburg,
Hancock recovered to
fight throughout the
Virginia campaigns
of 1864. He amassed
one of the most spectac-
ular records of a Union
major general.

**Winfield Scott Hancock Monument,
Cemetery Hill**
April 25, 1995

When Hancock was dispatched by
Meade to ride forward and assume
command of the field at Gettysburg
on July 1, he was not prepared to find
the 1st and 11th Corps "retreating in
disorder and confusion." Hancock's
equestrian monument dates
to 1896.

**Maj. Gen.
Oliver O. Howard**

A former teacher who
graduated high in his
West Point class,
Howard lost his right
arm at Fair Oaks in the
Peninsular campaign
of 1862. His reputation
was tarnished badly
when the 11th Corps
was mauled at
Chancellorsville, and
he fared poorly against
long odds on the first
day at Gettysburg.

**Oliver O. Howard Headquarters
Monument, Cemetery Hill**
April 25, 1995

As Federal forces scurried east and south
late on the first day, Maj. Gen. Oliver O.
Howard established the headquarters of
his 11th Corps on East Cemetery Hill. In
the wake of Reynolds's death, he
assumed that he would command the
field by seniority and was momentarily
offended by Hancock's assignment of
authority. But soon the two stopped argu-
ing and worked together to shore up a
Federal line. Howard's headquarters monument was erected in 1913.

A Visit to Cemetery Hill

by David Woodbury

Heading out Baltimore Street toward the high ground south of town, I can nearly imagine the scene on July 1, 1863, when thousands of Union troops scrambled through the streets of Gettysburg to rally on Cemetery Hill. At roughly 615 feet, it was, and remains, the most prominent elevation in the vicinity. It's little wonder that Maj. Gen. Oliver O. Howard chose this ground as the fallback position for hard-pressed Federals north and northwest of town, and as the cornerstone for the deployment of the hastily arriving components of the Army of the Potomac. "This seems to be a good position," Howard told his adjutant, Lt. Col. Theodore A. Meysenburg. The staff officer seconded the notion, rephrasing Howard's understatement: "It is the only position, general."

And so it was. The height afforded commanding views, and its relatively smooth, accessible crest was ideally suited for artillery placement. Cemetery Hill formed the natural apex of the Union line, bridging Culp's Hill and Cemetery Ridge, while anchoring the routes of supply and lines of retreat. The import of this eminence to Federal fortunes is sometimes underappreciated in the monolithic body of literature devoted to the three-day battle of Gettysburg. Or, it is lost in unrealistic presumptions about what Confederate Lt. Gen. Richard S. Ewell's predecessor could have accomplished on July 1, when possession of the high ground might still have been effectively contested. All things considered, Ewell's judgment appears to me as sound as Howard's was that day. Howard was attracted to the hill for the same reasons Ewell was wary of it.

Many more graves stand west of the pike today than did in the summer of 1863. The Soldiers' National Cemetery soon overshadowed the old Evergreen burial ground, and a subsequent expansion has added American dead from more recent wars. Mature trees obscure critical views offered by Cemetery Hill in the 1860s. I struggle to imagine the panorama to the west that surely must have transfixed Union artillerists as waves of Confederate infantrymen moved across the fields, finally slipping out of sight behind Ziegler's Grove, in the last day's climactic assault. In the same sketchy fashion, I try to conjure in my mind's eye images of Louisiana Tigers, late on July 2, rushing up the northeastern slope of Cemetery Hill (East Cemetery Hill, across the pike) to momentarily pierce the Union cordon atop the crest.

But unlike on other parts of the field, on Cemetery Hill I do not involuntarily become absorbed in the minutiae of the fighting; rather, my mind wanders beyond the immediate subject. Those of us with an abiding interest in days gone by — lovers of history and geography — cannot help but try to picture landscapes as they might have looked in antiquity, or at the moment history was unfolding, before the ravages of time irrevocably altered the transitory setting. Fortunately, at Gettysburg, the surviving work of numerous 19th-century photographers aids the imagination. Likewise, hours spent scrutinizing the work of William Frassanito and now Dave Eicher — whose juxtapositions of modern views with historic photos bridge the "now" and "then" in startling fashion — conditions the eye to look more closely. At Gettysburg I cannot look on a simple paved road without imagining the rutted paths of the past.

Gettysburg from Cemetery Hill
June 8, 1997

Gettysburg from Cemetery Hill
Timothy O'Sullivan
View north
July 7, 1863

O'Sullivan's unusual view, taken across the Baltimore Pike from the roof of the Evergreen Cemetery Gatehouse, shows the town of Gettysburg and Seminary Ridge (Oak Ridge to the north) on the horizon. The foreground tents belong to Federal militia who arrived and encamped on July 6.

Gettysburg from Cemetery Hill, Variant
Timothy O'Sullivan
View north
July 7, 1863

A variant of the previous exposure taken shortly before or after no longer depicts two civilians in the foreground but a person walking along the pike.

Evergreen Cemetery Gatehouse
Mathew B. Brady
View southwest
ca. July 15, 1863

The distinctive arched gatehouse to Evergreen Cemetery, near which Union troops rallied and formed a defensive line on the evening of July 1, became a popular subject for postbattle photographers. Visible in this scene taken two weeks after the battle are damaged windows in the 1855 structure. One of Brady's assistants poses at right while a militiaman stands behind the arch in Evergreen Cemetery.

Evergreen Cemetery Gatehouse
June 8, 1997

Evergreen Cemetery Gatehouse
Mathew B. Brady
View southwest
ca. July 15, 1863

Another Brady plate shows a similar scene.

Evergreen Cemetery Gatehouse
Mathew B. Brady
View southwest
ca. July 15, 1863

Still another Brady view was made from a slightly different angle.

92

Evergreen Cemetery Gatehouse
Charles and Isaac Tyson
View south
ca. 1864

The Tyson brothers' view, made a year later, provides a glimpse of the wartime appearance of East Cemetery Hill. The earthworks are now overgrown, and the gatehouse's windows and fences along the Baltimore Pike repaired.

Evergreen Cemetery Gatehouse
June 8, 1997

Evergreen Cemetery Gatehouse
Timothy O'Sullivan
View south
July 7, 1863

O'Sullivan's view was made about a week before Brady arrived on the field. Gettysburg photographic expert William Frassanito has approximated the time of this exposure to be 11 A.M., based on the shadows. This view was taken immediately after the withdrawal of the last units from the area and shows earthworks left from the 4th U.S. Artillery, Battery B, and a civilian wagon.

93

Evergreen Cemetery Gatehouse
June 8, 1997

**Position of Federal Lunettes,
Cemetery Hill**
June 8, 1997

**Federal Lunettes on Cemetery Hill and
Marie Tepe**
Frederick Gutekunst
View north-northwest
July 9–11, 1863

**Marie "French Mary" Tepe, vivandiere of
the 114th Pennsylvania Infantry, poses at
a fence post in this view of Union
lunettes made days after the action had
ceased. Such women were attached to a
regiment, which they followed, perform-
ing camp and nursing duties. This view
was taken from near the Evergreen
Gatehouse; an embalmer's tent stands
left of center. The ground here was
defended by Battery I (Wiedrich's) of
the 1st New York Artillery and attacked by
Louisiana infantry late on the second day.**

94

And so it is with Cemetery Hill. The trees remembered best in Gettysburg must
be the famous "copse" — the guiding point of the Pickett-Pettigrew-Trimble assault —
but at the time of the battle the most prominent tree for miles in every direction was
a 90-foot poplar crowning the mostly barren Cemetery Hill. (The tree was damaged
by lightning in 1876, and the last of the trunk was cut down 10 years later. See above,
a Frederick Gutekunst photo of the mighty poplar.) Now, heading out on Baltimore
Street on the high ground south of town, I project that tree onto the horizon.

I never gaze on the old Evergreen Cemetery Gatehouse without thinking of the
pregnant caretaker, Elizabeth Thorn, who made a midnight supper for Maj. Gens.
Howard, Slocum, and Sickles, and who, when she returned to her home on July 7,
saw the fresh graves of 17 men in her garden. And when I look at the old headstones
in Evergreen Cemetery, I cannot help but envision the strange and violent scene as
artillery shells and bits of shrapnel tore into graves and bowled over tombstones in the
horrific cannonade of July 3. These images and vignettes flit through my head while
I'm on the hill but seem oddly disconnected from the rote chronological narrative of
events I am otherwise mindful of in places like the railroad cut, or Little Round Top.

**Scene of the Charge of the
Louisiana Tigers, Cemetery Hill
View north-northeast
July 1863**

The swift attack of Early's division into
East Cemetery Hill late on the second
day sent the brigade of Brig. Gen. Harry
Hays, the "Louisiana Tigers," headlong
into the now defended Union position.
Struck heavily by Federal artillery fire,
the Louisiana troops charged up the
hill (approximately toward the camera),
and a vicious hand-to-hand struggle
ensued. The assault broke, however,
and Federal artillerists and infantrymen
retained the heights.

**Scene of the Charge of the
Louisiana Tigers
August 21, 2000**

Why this sense of discontinuity? It is the graves. In the presence of so many fallen soldiers my thoughts invariably drift beyond this particular field. Because of its burial grounds, Cemetery Hill, more than other parts of this hallowed landscape, transcends its time and place. Who can walk on this rise without pausing to consider Lincoln's few, appropriate remarks, and who can recall those remarks without contemplating the magnitude of the Civil War? Standing on Cemetery Hill, the tragedy, the horror, and the heroism of Gettysburg feel emblematic of the whole era and call forth images of somber sacrifice in all of our wars. Standing amid the headstones, where generations of Americans are now interred, it continually occurs to me that the last full measure of devotion was given all over this Pennsylvania battleground; it was given way out at Glorieta Pass and down on Roanoke Island. It was given at Manassas, too, and across the water in Normandy, and in valleys as disparate as the Shenandoah and the Ia Drang.

David Woodbury is author of The Library of Congress Civil War Desk Reference *(2001). Editor of and contributor to numerous Civil War books and periodicals, he is presently on staff at Stanford University Press and resides in Palo Alto, California.*

Position of the Confederate Attack on Cemetery Hill
View northwest
ca. July 1863

Taken toward the same ground shown in the previous image but far to the southeast, this view records ground fought over by Col. Isaac E. Avery's brigade of North Carolinians as they attacked Cemetery Hill late on July 2. In the bloody fighting that followed, marked by heavy cannonading and sheets of musket fire, Avery was killed. His body was found accompanied by a note: "Tell my father I died with my face to the enemy."

Position of the Confederate Attack on Cemetery Hill
August 21, 2000

The Peach Orchard the Postcards Missed

by Richard A. Sauers

Students of the battle of Gettysburg have all heard of farmer Joseph Sherfy's now famous Peach Orchard, on a knob of high ground traversed by the Emmitsburg Road a mile or more south of town. It was this elevation that so mesmerized Maj. Gen. Daniel E. Sickles on July 2, 1863, and caused him to disobey orders and advance his 3d Army Corps away from Cemetery Ridge, precipitating the fierce fighting on the southern end of the battlefield that James Longstreet later described as "the best three hours' fighting ever done by any troops on any battlefield."

But this orchard has largely disappeared from the present-day terrain. The thin, rocky soil in the area has meant that any replanting of the orchard, on whatever scale, will not last more than a couple of decades. Since the battle, numerous peach trees have attempted to thrive but always need to be replaced. The current orchard, south of the Wheatfield Road, ignores the half of the 1863 orchard planted north of the road. Late-twentieth-century visitors to the battlefield thus have to use their imagination to visualize the original extent of the peach trees and how they hindered visibility and hampered military movements through them.

I collect Gettysburg postcards. Of the thousands of different battlefield scenes printed since picture-postcards were introduced in the 1890s, I have only one view of the Peach Orchard. It was published by Gettysburg entrepreneur Leroy A. Smith sometime in the 1960s. The postcard industry thus has failed to popularize the orchard in this bastion of popular souvenirs.

I first saw the orchard in the early 1960s, when I toured the battlefield for the first time. Since then, I've come to know the battlefield quite well and have taken a particular interest in the Meade-Sickles controversy. I've walked the Peach Orchard area many times, and I continually wonder just what Dan Sickles thought that day. The orchard area indeed is on higher ground than the lower half of Cemetery Ridge, but Maj. Gen. George Meade was correct in maintaining that the slight orchard ridge was neutral ground, commanded by the guns of both armies. Neither army could hold it if the other wanted it. Thus, Sickles erred in thinking the Peach Orchard had to be controlled by his troops.

Today, visitors will see a dozen or so tablets and regimental monuments, plus some flank markers and a few cannon, standing silently, awaiting the Confederate attack. The freshly mowed grass and reconstructed period fences are a far cry from the confusion inherent in the fighting of July 2 as it ebbed and flowed around a Peach Orchard that Sickles thought was the key to his position on Cemetery Ridge.

Richard A. Sauers received his doctorate in history from Pennsylvania State University, where he studied under Warren W. Hassler, Jr. He is author of more than a dozen books, including A Caspian Sea of Ink: The Meade-Sickles Controversy *(1995),* Advance the Colors! Pennsylvania Civil War Battleflags *(1998), and* The Gettysburg Campaign: June 3–August 1, 1863 *(1982).*

James Longstreet Monument
September 7, 1998

Lee's right hand at Gettysburg,
Longstreet argued that the Confederate
army should move around the Union left,
interposing between it and Washington,
forcing action on ground more favorable
to the Southern troops. A statue of
Longstreet dedicated in 1998 appears
oddly stylized and diminutive compared
with the earlier equestrian monuments
on the field.

JAMES LONGSTREET
PREPARES
FOR ATTACK

★ JULY 2, 1863 ★

July 2, the second day at Gettysburg, would be one of the most heavily fought days of the war.
Arguably, it would also be the decisive day at Gettysburg, although another day of battle would follow. The second day was so filled with complex action that it would be difficult to reconstruct the exact nature of the waves of attacks and counterattacks that flowed across Gettysburg's many fields and hills. So many units were intermingled that determining the precise sequence of actions would be nearly impossible. But at least it's clear that from his headquarters near the Thompson House, Robert E. Lee envisioned his attack commencing sometime in the morning. Lee and Lt. Gen. James Longstreet both awakened early, perhaps as early as 3 A.M.

Though his headquarters tents were pitched north of the theological seminary, across the Chambersburg Pike from the Thompson House, Lee spent considerable time on a tree stump or fallen log north of the largest seminary building, talking with officers and writing out battlefield orders. Much has been made of Lee's poor health during the battle of Gettysburg, and he certainly was suffering to a degree from diarrhea and possibly a recurrence of his malaria, picked up while supervising work at Baltimore's Fort Carroll in 1849. But Lee was hardly incapacitated. He is known to have walked, vigorously discussed orders at length, ridden the battle lines, and although somewhat weakened, performed his duties adequately.

From the early morning hours up until about 11 A.M., Longstreet was in attendance at Lee's headquarters or near the general alongside the seminary. Also present for extensive consultation that morning were Maj. Gen. John Bell Hood, A. P. Hill, Maj. Gen. Lafayette McLaws, and other key officers. From their vantage point at the seminary, Lee may have viewed Federal artillery on Cemetery Hill one and a quarter miles away. Though he was still formulating his plans in the morning, Lee believed the right-flank route offered the greatest opportunity. He therefore sent scouting parties to explore that direction, led by staff officers Col. Armistead L. Long, his military secretary; artillery chief Brig. Gen. William N. Pendleton; and engineer Capt. Samuel R. Johnston. The three officers recorded unusual experiences. Pendleton moved down to Spangler's Woods, between the Emmitsburg Road and Pitzer's Run, and saw little except for the two stray Yankees he captured while they were drinking from a stream. Long explored potential artillery positions. Johnston set out at 4 A.M. and rode south along Willoughby's Run, turning eastward and climbing the slope of Seminary Ridge. Near the Peach Orchard, he explored the ground but reported seeing no Union troops, a very strange quirk, considering that many should have been visible from that position. Johnston's party moved to the Round Tops, exploring the base of Little Round Top, and, oddly, reported seeing no Federal soldiers in that area either. After three hours and a convoluted path that miraculously prevented them from spotting the enemy in force, they returned to Lee and reported their reconnaissance. Longstreet, then, was asked to move into position to ready for an attack on the Federal left.

Joseph Sherfy House
May 8, 1996

Sherfy's farm on the Emmitsburg Road stood near the exposed salient that Sickles had marched out toward the Confederate lines on July 2; the Rebel attack would swing past the structure on its way toward the Wheatfield, Devil's Den, and Round Tops.

The events that followed set into motion the Confederate attack formation. Lee rode ahead to assess the preparations for battle on the Confederate left. Leaving his headquarters about 9 A.M. and moving through the town, he could not find Ewell on his arrival at the 2d Corps headquarters on the east side, near Rock Creek, but he did find Maj. Gen. Isaac Trimble. Subsequently, Lee and Trimble climbed into the cupola at the Almshouse for a view of the surrounding terrain and reportedly lamented that they could not yet "pursue our advantage of yesterday." Lee next returned to his headquarters and supposedly remarked to Long, "What *can* detain Longstreet?" suggesting impatience with a tardy attack. The implication sparked a firestorm of controversy when former Confederates looked to assign blame for losing the battle, mostly after the war. Longstreet told Hood, some officers reported, "The General [Lee] is a little nervous this morning; he wishes me to attack; I do not wish to do so without Pickett. I never like to go into battle with one boot off." If true, this remark suggests that Lee had planned an early attack.

JULY 2, 1863

**Maj. Gen.
Daniel E. Sickles**

In direct contradiction to his orders, Sickles led his 3d Corps far in advance of the Union battle line on July 2, creating a vast salient that opened it to attack.

**Brig. Gen.
William N. Pendleton**

Pendleton, Lee's chief of artillery, also cast out on a reconnaissance that passed down to Spangler's Woods and accomplished little except for capturing two wandering Yankees drinking at a stream.

Col. Armistead L. Long

Lee sent Long, his military secretary, and several other officers on reconnaissances on the morning of July 2 that somehow missed spotting key concentrations of Federal troops.

Col. Hiram Berdan

One of the curious episodes of the early part of July 2 occurred when Berdan, commanding the 1st U.S. Sharpshooters, sent them out of the Peach Orchard westward into Pitzer's Woods, encountering Confederate skirmishers. After skirmishing for 20 minutes and observing heavy numbers of Confederates in the adjoining fields, Berdan's men withdrew.

**Maj. Gen.
John Bell Hood**

When the Confederate attack commenced on July 2, Hood spearheaded the right-flank of it with his division. Only minutes into the action, Hood was struck in the left arm, incapacitating it and removing him from the field. A Kentuckian who had moved to Texas, Hood had a curious career throughout the entirety of the war; he would lose a leg at Chickamauga and destroy his army in Tennessee near the war's end.

**Maj. Gen.
Lafayette McLaws**

McLaws's division of Longstreet's corps also attacked with ferocious force eastward, north of Hood. A Georgian and cousin-in-law of Jefferson Davis, McLaws later in the war found his career in jeopardy through poor planning and performance but was restored to command by Davis.

Many supporters of the Lee mythology later claimed he had ordered an attack by Longstreet at sunrise. This is clearly not the case. But it may be reasonable to believe that Lee wanted an attack as early as "practicable," when intelligence could be sorted out, troops positioned, and organizational details minded. Longstreet and others, however, claimed that Lee had issued no orders to attack until after he returned from his visit to Ewell's headquarters. Indeed, the written order from 11 A.M. instructs Longstreet to "move with the portion of [his] command that was up, around to gain the Emmitsburg Road, on the enemy's left." Therefore, actual preparations for the attack did not commence until between 11 A.M. and noon. Longstreet, already not a believer in attacking at Gettysburg, readied his corps for an assault on the Union left by late morning. Did the Confederate command structure fail? Did it break down by failing to initiate an attack sooner? How much of the blame should rest on Lee as army commander or Longstreet as a sullen subordinate? None of this really matters as much as some would like to believe. The attack happened the way it happened; in war, "might have beens" are meaningless.

The degree of Longstreet's uncooperative spirit might be debated, but he certainly was at least grumpy. He marched his corps over the unfamiliar Pennsylvania ground, with its rises and swales, stands of trees, and granite outcrops, following orders but perhaps without urgency. July 2 at Gettysburg was a hot, sunny day, and the wool uniforms and heavy equipment of the soldiers translated into exhausted, sweaty troops. Though Longstreet's corps started out together, the routes of the divisions of McLaws and Hood may have differed slightly. McLaws, in the lead, probably marched south from Herr's Ridge to a point south of the Black Horse Tavern (on the

Longstreet Forms for Attack
July 2, 1863, Noon–4 P.M.

On the late morning of July 2, Lee decided to attack the Union left flank on the southern portion of the field. He sent Lt. Gen. James Longstreet's corps southward to form for attack. After a confused, protracted march beginning west of town, Longstreet's divisions by mid-afternoon finally formed for attack west of and astride the Emmitsburg Road.

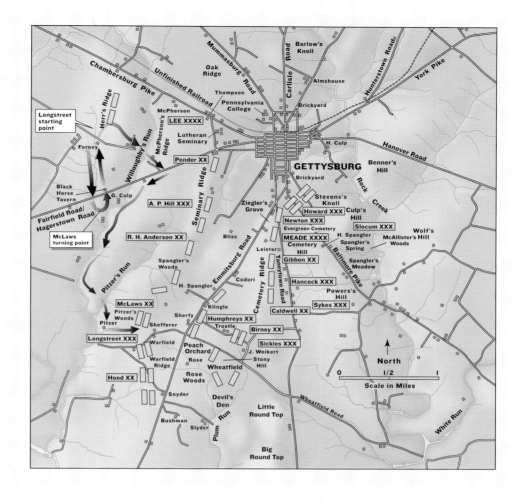

Fairfield Road), where the column turned around and marched northward, past the Forney House, turning eastward and eventually rejoining the Fairfield Road, then turning south and marching along Willoughby's Run, then turning southeast along the country road on which stood Pitzer's Schoolhouse. East of the schoolhouse, McLaws and Hood deployed into battle lines after this very long march. All the while, Longstreet's columns attempted to avoid being spotted by the Federal signal station on Little Round Top. At times the march was completely confused and inefficient. Maj. Gen. Richard Anderson's division, to the north, had been in position since noon, although A. P. Hill had been tardy in posting it. Longstreet's divisions of McLaws (center) and Hood (right) took much longer to deploy and organize than anyone had dreamed. Lee's plan thus unfolded with delays, missed communications, and wasted time. It was 4 P.M. before the wings of the army were in position along Seminary Ridge, ready for the day's action.

JULY 2, 1863

The Peach Orchard
April 25, 1995

When the battle of Gettysburg took place, Joseph Sherfy's Peach Orchard was covered with green peaches that would ripen later in the season. Heavy action occurred in and around the orchard on July 2.

James Warfield House, Warfield Ridge
September 7, 1998

One of the structures along the Confederate battle line arrayed on Seminary Ridge was the Warfield House, home of a free black, for which a portion of the ridgeline was named. Longstreet established his headquarters in this vicinity, though far away from the present headquarters marker; it was probably nearer to Pitzer's Schoolhouse, beside Willoughby's Run.

The Federal preparations for battle were also stricken with poor coordination and communication. Maj. Gen. Daniel E. Sickles, commanding the 3d Corps, had ordered his men to move out into a salient far in front of the rest of the Union army, to a position reasonably close to the Confederate lines. Longstreet's lead scouts, in fact, had been fired on by 3d Corps skirmishers as they approached on the march. Sickles advanced his corps to the Sherfy Peach Orchard along the Emmitsburg Road, with the divisions of Brig. Gen. Andrew A. Humphreys on the north and Maj. Gen. David B. Birney on the south, without any justification. Although the ground was somewhat higher along the Peach Orchard (591 feet) than that inside the southward line along Cemetery Ridge (perhaps 550 feet), which Meade understood Sickles would hold, Sickles believed the forward ground might offer a better artillery position and allow guarding of the Emmitsburg Road for the passage of artillery trains. For a short time Sickles's salient surprised and halted the Confederates who spotted it, but any positive effect it had for the Union was fleeting. Overall, Sickles had simply moved a portion of the Federal army into a vulnerable, exposed position.

Sickles had discussed this contemplated movement with Meade's chief of artillery, Brig. Gen. Henry J. Hunt, and asked for authority to make it, but Hunt had begged off and referred Sickles to Meade. After Hunt rode off to check on artillery, Sickles ordered Birney to make a reconnaissance on the woods in front of the Peach Orchard, and Birney dispatched four companies of the 1st United States Sharpshooters (Col. Hiram Berdan), with the 3d Maine Infantry (Col. Moses B.

Philip Snyder House, Warfield Ridge
May 8, 1996

The Snyder House stood near the
position where **McLaws's** right connected
with Hood's left as they formed for
Longstreet's attack of July 2. From near
this position, many **Confederate** soldiers
grouped to begin their journey toward the
high ground held by the Yankees.

Lakeman) in support. Berdan's men moved out of the Peach Orchard, crossed the
road, and moved into Pitzer's Woods, encountering Confederate skirmishers of Brig.
Gen. Cadmus M. Wilcox's brigade. Crackles of musketry echoed through the woods as
a sharp 20-minute action ensued. After Berdan's men spotted numerous
Confederates marching through the open fields beyond, the sharpshooters withdrew.

The Confederates continued on the advance. When McLaws's men moved out
from the woods about 3 P.M. and gazed over the countryside in their front, they were
stunned to see Sickles's men. Rather than discovering an open route to the Yankee
line posted in the distance, they stood in front of a formed line of battle supported by
artillery. "The enemy was massed in my front and extended to my right and left as far
as I could see," stated McLaws.

Now irritated that the attack had not commenced, Longstreet asked McLaws why
he did not press forward at once. Longstreet then discovered that the U.S. 3d Corps
blocked his path and ordered McLaws *not* to attack. While Hood's division deployed
to McLaws's right, Longstreet found that the Union line extended nearly all the way
to the Round Tops and that attacking up the Emmitsburg Road, as originally instructed by Lee, would expose the Confederate right. An adjustment needed to be made:
scouts reported no Union troops near Little Round Top, and so it dawned on
Longstreet that a movement around the Federal left might send troops behind the
Federal line, possibly collapsing it. But Lee's orders to Longstreet allowed no discre-
tion. Between 3:30 and 4 P.M., the artillery of Col. Edward Porter Alexander, commanding Longstreet's reserve guns, opened fire on the Federal position; shortly afterward, by 4:30 P.M., Hood's men had fired volleys and marched forward, and the attack
was under way.

JULY 2, 1863

Arkansas Monument, Seminary Ridge
April 25, 1995

Arkansas's state memorial consists of an impressive relief honoring the 3d Arkansas Infantry, which served in Robertson's Texas Brigade, the only unit from the state to fight at Gettysburg. The monument was dedicated in 1966.

Alabama Monument, Warfield Ridge
April 25, 1995

From the area where this monument stands, near the extreme right of the Army of Northern Virginia, Brig. Gen. Evander M. Law's brigade of Alabamians commenced its attack. The monument was dedicated in 1933.

South Carolina Monument, Seminary Ridge
April 25, 1995

Erected in 1963, South Carolina's memorial to its fallen sons was positioned approximately where Brig. Gen. Joseph B. Kershaw's brigade of South Carolinians formed for attack.

It was about 3 P.M. when Sickles had moved his corps into the exposed salient. At this time, with the final corps not yet in position, the Union 6th Corps of Maj. Gen. John Sedgwick was sighted approaching the battlefield along the Baltimore Pike. Meade hastily summoned his corps commanders to the Leister House for a meeting, and all showed up except for Sickles. Around this time the group suddenly heard cannon fire in the direction of the 3d Corps, and an aide of Brig. Gen. Gouverneur K. Warren, Meade's chief engineer, rode up and reported the situation was "not all straight" along Sickles's front. (Though often reported as a major general in July 1863, Warren was commissioned a major general only in 1864, and it was then backdated to the time of Gettysburg.) Alarmed and confused, Meade mounted his horse, Old Baldy, and rode with Warren toward Sickles's position, ordering Maj. Gen. George Sykes to move the 5th Corps over to the Federal left as quickly as possible. When they moved along the road, the generals found a gap where the 3d Corps was supposed to be. Behind the Peach Orchard, Meade finally caught up with Sickles and angrily asked for an explanation. Meade, with his fiery temper, bristled after Sickles explained, and the chagrined corps commander suggested he would withdraw to the assigned position. Meade, however, pointed out that the enemy would not allow it without attacking, and just about this time the Confederate line exploded with artillery fire. The agitated Meade quickly rode back to his headquarters to reorganize the situation.

In the so-called Meade-Sickles controversy that would erupt in the years following the battle (over whether Sickles had erred by moving his corps and whether or not he had directly disobeyed orders), the army commander was clearly right and Sickles wrong. The controversy provided some of the more entertaining sessions for the ill-fated but powerful Senate Committee on the Conduct of the War, which monitored a vast array of foolish battlefield decisions, and added yet another legendary event to the story of Gettysburg.

106

Sickles Creates a Salient
July 2, 1863, about 3 P.M.

By the second day of battle, Union tacticians had pulled the Yankee battle line into a "fishhook" along the ridges south of town. But the irascible Maj. Gen. Daniel E. Sickles, commanding the Federal 3d Corps, marched his troops westward, without orders, creating an exposed salient into the Sherfy Peach Orchard and inviting Confederate attack.

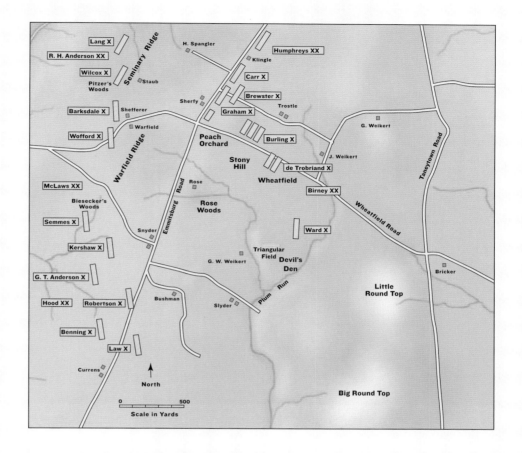

The Confederates' main attack of July 2 was, for better or worse, under way. From the southern terminus of Seminary Ridge and adjoining Warfield Ridge (named for the Warfield House, which stood atop it), the attack struck eastward with fury, soldiers screaming the Rebel yell and rushing into battle supported by vigorous blasts of artillery behind them. Southern soldiers of Hood's division fired as they headed toward the southern edge of the Rose Woods, toward the Devil's Den, and then toward Big Round Top. Withdrawing, Birney's division formed a battle line north of the Devil's Den, stretching up to the Wheatfield. Toward this position, half of Confederate Brig. Gen. Jerome B. Robertson's brigade, the 1st Texas Infantry (Lt. Col. Philip A. Work), and 3d Arkansas Infantry (Col. Van H. Manning) crossed the Emmitsburg Road and marched past the George W. Weikert Farm (also frequently called the Timbers Farm because of its inclusion as such in a postwar survey), advancing through the southern edge of the Rose Woods. They made tracks for

Mississippi Monument, Seminary Ridge
June 7, 1997

The bold statuary adorning Mississippi's monument was placed on the field in 1973 near where Brig. Gen. William Barksdale's brigade awaited the July 2 attack. Barksdale fell wounded and was captured as the attack gained momentum. He died not long after.

Soldiers and Sailors of the Confederacy Memorial, Warfield Ridge
June 7, 1997

The Civil War centennial brought about a desire to erect a monument at Gettysburg honoring all members of the Confederate forces. In 1965, some six years after the death of John D. Salling, probably the last verifiable veteran of the Confederate army, this monument was unveiled.

Louisiana Monument, Seminary Ridge
June 6, 1997

A figure of "the spirit of the Confederacy" hovers aloft in Louisiana's monument, dedicated in 1971.

CHAPTER 4 : JAMES LONGSTREET PREPARES FOR ATTACK

Capt. James E. Smith's 4th New York Artillery (posted north of the Devil's Den) and Brig. Gen. J. H. Hobart Ward's brigade. The 4th and 5th Texas Infantries (Cols. John C. G. Key and Robert M. Powell) marched just north of the George Bushman Farm, passed the John Slyder House ("Granite Farm"), and moved to the northern end of Big Round Top. On the assault's southern end, Brig. Gen. Evander M. Law's brigade moved straight eastward toward Big Round Top, with the exception of the 44th and 48th Alabama Infantries (Cols. William F. Perry and James L. Sheffield), which, on reaching the base of Big Round Top and Plum Run, headed northward toward the Devil's Den, shifting to Law's left. As the attack gained momentum, Brig. Gen. Henry L. Benning's brigade, in support, advanced toward the Devil's Den, and Anderson's brigade later moved into Rose Woods. Along the left of Ward's Union line north of the Devil's Den, the 4th Maine Infantry (Col. Elijah Walker) wheeled to the left to block a Confederate advance through Plum Run Valley. Already, events that would lead to the deaths of hundreds of young men were irrevocably unfolding.

Texas Monument, Warfield Ridge April 25, 1995	**Florida Monument, Seminary Ridge** June 6, 1997	**Georgia Monument, Seminary Ridge** April 25, 1995
Near the position where Brig. Gen. Jerome B. Robertson's Texas Brigade, the former brigade of Hood's, went into action, the Texas Monument commemorates Lone Star State members of the Army of Northern Virginia. The monument was erected in 1964.	Constructed in 1963, the Florida Monument remembers three regiments from the state that served in Col. David Lang's brigade (Perry's old brigade).	Georgia's tribute was erected in 1961 near the spot where Brig. Gen. Paul J. Semmes's brigade of Georgians formed for the July 2 attack. Semmes, cousin of Confederate naval captain Raphael Semmes, was mortally wounded in the assault.

UNION FORCES SEIZE THE HIGH GROUND

★ JULY 2, 1863 ★

A bronze statue of Maj. Gen. Gouverneur K. Warren, Meade's chief engineer, graces the summit of Little Round Top. Warren recognized the tactical importance of the hill and ordered troops to scramble up its slopes. April 25, 1995

The Confederate attack, once under way, dealt a sweeping blow to the disorganized Federal line of battle. Not only had Yankee soldiers hugged the ground during the fierce artillery duel that preceded the assault, but Minié bullets had whistled by the advancing and retreating ranks with equal zip. The Confederate attackers found themselves exposed to heavy volleys of musket fire from the front and from the artillery battle above them. Even Confederate division commanders were not immune to the battle's ferocity. Soon after the action commenced, a shell exploded over Maj. Gen. John Bell Hood's head, wounding him severely and causing him to lose the use of his left arm. "With this wound terminated my participation in this great battle," he later wrote. "As I was borne off on a litter to the rear, I could but experience deep distress of mind and heart at the thought of the inevitable fate of my brave fellow-soldiers . . . and I shall ever believe that had I been permitted to turn Round Top mountain, we would not only have gained their position, but have been able to finally rout the enemy." Hood may have been engaging in wishful thinking, but the action north of the Devil's Den was indeed heating up quickly. After scattered fighting, Brig. Gen. Evander M. Law's brigade and the 4th and 5th Texas regiments crossed Plum Run and found themselves moving around the northwestern slope of Big Round Top. Meanwhile, the 44th and 48th Alabama regiments began to shift northward along Plum Run into the Devil's Den. Views of the terrain were varied here, as the lay of the land changed from spot to spot. Big Round Top was heavily timbered and sloped steeply; to its north, Little Round Top's clear-cut western face and shallower slope made it much more inviting for artillery. Between the Round Tops was a shallow gorge; northwest of Big Round Top stood the collection of massive granite boulders that composed Devil's Den. Northwest of Devil's Den, along Houck's Ridge, was the Triangular Field, bordered by small, stacked granite rocks that created a makeshift fence. North of this area stood thick Rose Woods, and north of the woods was the exposed, relatively flat Wheatfield. Another rise, Stony Hill, was west of the Wheatfield. Plum Run ran through the whole scene, one branch (Rose Run), heading the Peach Orchard and the other fronting Seminary Ridge; the two joined and ran along the base of Big Round Top. The Rose Farm stood to the west.

Maj. Gen. Richard H. Anderson

North of Hood and McLaws in Longstreet's July 2 attack was the division of Dick Anderson of A. P. Hill's Corps, consisting of the brigades of Wilcox, Mahone, Wright, Posey, and Lang (Perry's brigade). Anderson attacked with three of his brigades into the Federals north of the Peach Orchard.

Brig. Gen. William Barksdale

A native Tennessean who moved to Mississippi and became a lawyer and journalist, Barksdale had also served as a member of the U.S. House of Representatives for nearly eight years before the war. He was struck in the thigh, left foot, and chest during the Confederate advance on July 2 and died in the Jacob Hummelbaugh House the following day.

Brig. Gen. Joseph B. Kershaw

South Carolinian Kershaw's brigade fought well into the Confederate attack of the second day, pressing into Rose Woods, against Stony Hill, and fighting in the Wheatfield.

Brig. Gen. Andrew A. Humphreys

Humphreys, a Philadelphian, would become Meade's chief of staff a few days after Gettysburg and continue in that role until late in 1864. He fought stubbornly along Emmitsburg Road and was then hammered by Barksdale's and Anderson's attacks and retreated to Cemetery Ridge.

The fighting through these areas was intense and only escalated in severity throughout the afternoon. The 1st Texas and 3d Arkansas regiments attacked savagely into Brig. Gen. J. H. Hobart Ward's brigade, firing on Capt. James E. Smith's battery of the 4th New York Artillery, to open the assault at the Devil's Den. A "fierce, charging yell" opened the first of two assaults on the line, with Smith's artillerists firing like devils in return and, to their chagrin, beginning to run low on ammunition. With their case shot expended, Smith shouted, "Give them shell! Give them solid shot! Damn them, give them anything!" Posted at a rock wall between the Wheatfield and Rose Woods, the 17th Maine Infantry (Lt. Col. Charles B. Merrill) opened a blistering fire on the attacking Confederates, and the 4th Maine blocked the advance of the Alabama regiments into Plum Run Valley (an area that came to be called the Valley of Death). Brig. Gen. Henry L. Benning's brigade of Georgians now attacked Ward's line; a counterattack by the 4th Maine and 99th Pennsylvania Infantries (Maj. John W. Moore) anchored Smith's position for a time, until Benning's and Brig. Gen. Jerome B. Robertson's brigades together struck the position that unhinged the Federal line. Covering the position along Plum Run, the 6th New Jersey Infantry (Lt. Col. Stephen R. Gilkyson) permitted the Federals to escape in reasonable order. The fighting at the Devil's Den had been severe, with "roaring cannon, crashing rifles, screeching shots, bursting shells, hissing bullets, cheers, shouts, shrieks, and groans," as described by Union Capt. William Silliman. At one point, when the Confederates had attacked strongly, Smith simply shouted, "For God's sake, men, don't let them take my guns away from me!" Among the dead during this phase was Col. Augustus van Horne Ellis, a New York fireman who had been struck in the head with a Minié bullet and was posthumously commissioned a brevet brigadier general for his valor.

113

Abraham Trostle House
Timothy O'Sullivan
View northeast
July 6, 1863

The Trostle House was a prominent
structure with a magnificent brick barn
that stood one and a half miles south of
town; it is also termed the Peter Trostle
House. During the fighting for the Union
left on July 2, Capt. John Bigelow's 9th
Battery of Massachusetts Artillery was
ordered to hold this position at all hazards. It was attacked by Barksdale's
Mississippians, and brutal hand-to-hand
fighting ensued around the house.

Trostle House
June 8, 1997

Abraham Trostle House and Barn
Timothy O'Sullivan
View northwest
July 6, 1863

During the fighting for the artillery posted at the Trostle House, four of Capt. John Bigelow's six field pieces were captured and more than 50 horses killed, some of which are shown in O'Sullivan's image. Artillery damage remains evident today on the barn's brickwork.

Trostle Barn
June 8, 1997

George Bushman Farm
May 7, 1996

Dating to the late 18th century, the George Bushman Farm, prominently placed east of the Emmitsburg Road, witnessed the sweep of the initial Confederate attack by Hood's division. (The house is also termed the Michael Bushman House and was leased at the time of the battle to David Essick; it is not to be confused with the George Bushman House far to the east along Rock Creek.) Not far from this house, Hood was wounded when a shell exploded over his head.

John Slyder House, "Granite Farm"
May 7, 1996

The Slyder House, known as the "Granite Farm," stood east of the Bushman Farm and in the path of the Confederate assault. A portion of the Slyder farmland between the house and Round Tops contains the "D-shaped field," where on July 3, Acting Brig. Gen. Elon J. Farnsworth's ill-fated cavalry charge was made against the Confederate right, resulting in total chaos and killing Farnsworth.

JULY 2, 1863

Dead Horse and Wrecked Artillery Limber
Alexander Gardner
July 6, 1863

Gardner's image, possibly taken near the Trostle House, shows one of the nearly 1,500 artillery horses killed during the second day's battle. Ammunition and artillery equipment are visible spilled from the limber.

Daniel E. Sickles Wounding Monument, Trostle Barn
April 25, 1995

Near the Trostle Barn, prior to the hand-to-hand struggle, Sickles transformed from a man in deep trouble for disobedience into a battlefield hero when his lower right leg was struck and shattered by a low-velocity case shot or cannonball. Ever the showman, Sickles coolly smoked a cigar and shouted orders as he was carried from the field on a litter. Erected in 1901, the monument marks the approximate position of Sickles's wounding.

As the fierce fighting witnessed the rattle of musketry and booming echoes of cannon fire throughout the southern end of the field, Brig. Gen. Gouverneur K. Warren, Meade's chief engineer, who had been investigating the Federal left, discovered the open nature of Little Round Top and that no one occupied it. Warren abruptly sent a note to Meade asking for a division to defend the tactically crucial hill. Meade initially assigned Maj. Gen. Andrew A. Humphreys to the task but quickly found that Maj. Gen. George Sykes's 5th Corps was coming up into position. Col. Strong Vincent, one of the 5th Corps brigade commanders (in Brig. Gen. James Barnes's 1st Division), on his own initiative moved his four regiments onto the military crest of Little Round Top, cleverly using an old logging path to avoid drawing artillery fire.

CHAPTER 5 : UNION FORCES SEIZE THE HIGH GROUND

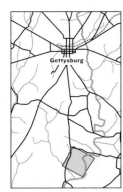

Longstreet's Men Attack
July 2, 1863, 4 P.M. and Later

Confederates strike out toward the Union left, hoping to smash it or possibly flank the line.

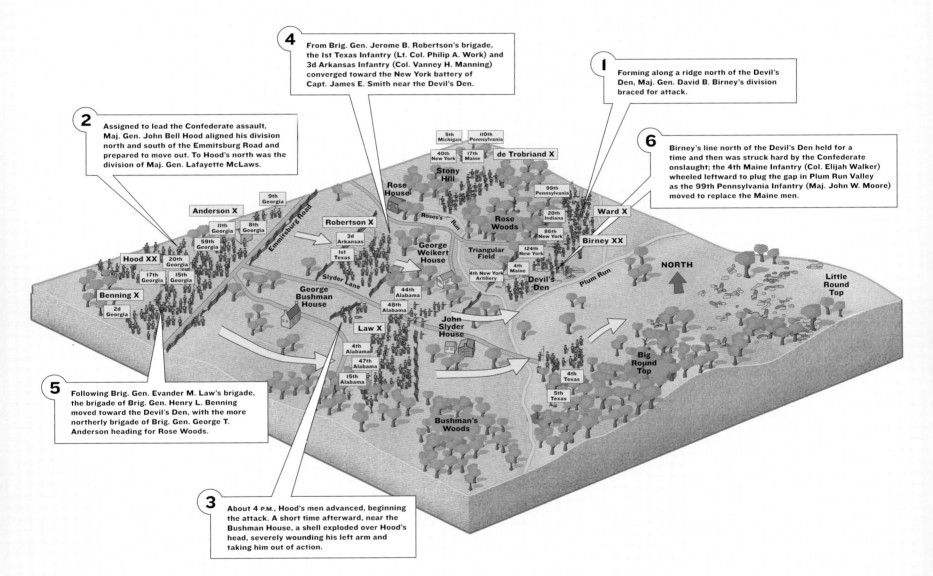

4 From Brig. Gen. Jerome B. Robertson's brigade, the 1st Texas Infantry (Lt. Col. Philip A. Work) and 3d Arkansas Infantry (Col. Vanney H. Manning) converged toward the New York battery of Capt. James E. Smith near the Devil's Den.

1 Forming along a ridge north of the Devil's Den, Maj. Gen. David B. Birney's division braced for attack.

2 Assigned to lead the Confederate assault, Maj. Gen. John Bell Hood aligned his division north and south of the Emmitsburg Road and prepared to move out. To Hood's north was the division of Maj. Gen. Lafayette McLaws.

6 Birney's line north of the Devil's Den held for a time and then was struck hard by the Confederate onslaught; the 4th Maine Infantry (Col. Elijah Walker) wheeled leftward to plug the gap in Plum Run Valley as the 99th Pennsylvania Infantry (Maj. John W. Moore) moved to replace the Maine men.

5 Following Brig. Gen. Evander M. Law's brigade, the brigade of Brig. Gen. Henry L. Benning moved toward the Devil's Den, with the more northerly brigade of Brig. Gen. George T. Anderson heading for Rose Woods.

3 About 4 P.M., Hood's men advanced, beginning the attack. A short time afterward, near the Bushman House, a shell exploded over Hood's head, severely wounding his left arm and taking him out of action.

**Brig. Gen.
Samuel K. Zook**

Zook died in a Federal field hospital on July 3. The former telegrapher had served competently as a New York militia officer before commanding a brigade in the Army of the Potomac.

**Col.
Philippe R. de Trobriand**

French-born de Trobriand, who gained the title Baron in 1840, was a lawyer, poet, and novelist who came to New York in 1841. He served as editor of a French-American newspaper prior to the war. De Trobriand's brigade fought savagely against Tige Anderson's Confederates in the opening Wheatfield action on the afternoon of July 2.

**Col.
Edward E. Cross**

As part of Caldwell's division, Cross's brigade formed in Trostle Woods and attacked waves of Confederates in the Wheatfield. Cross was struck by a Minié bullet in the abdomen during the attack and mortally wounded.

The Wheatfield
July 17, 1989

Some of the heaviest fighting of the Civil War occurred in the Wheatfield, known at the time as the "whirlpool." So ferocious and frequent were the attacks and counterattacks that a coherent record of the action may never be assembled. At least 14 Union and Confederate brigades fought savagely in the field during the evening of July 2.

Samuel K. Zook Death Monument, the Wheatfield
June 7, 1997

Among the numerous casualties in the Wheatfield was Pennsylvania Brig. Gen. Samuel K. Zook, who was struck in the abdomen near where his monument, erected in 1882, stands.

Irish Brigade Monument, near the Wheatfield
April 25, 1995

The so-called Irish Brigade, consisting of mostly ancestral Irish, was led by Col. Patrick Kelly into heavy fighting in the Wheatfield. The distinctive monument honoring the brigade, dedicated in 1888, consists of a decorated Celtic cross and features a bronze Irish wolfhound, symbolic of devotion to the cause.

William Corby Monument, Cemetery Ridge
April 25, 1995

Chaplain of the 88th New York Infantry, a regiment of the Irish Brigade, Corby provided absolution to the Irish Brigade soldiers before they entered the fight to reinforce the collapsing line of Sickles's salient. The monument to him was erected in 1910.

When Warren had discovered the openness of Little Round Top, all that stood on it was a Federal signal station. Now, south of the station on the hill's crest, the 16th Michigan Infantry (Lt. Col. Norval E. Welch), 44th New York Infantry (Col. James C. Rice), 83d Pennsylvania Infantry (Vincent's old regiment, Capt. Orpheus S. Woodward), and, on the extreme left of the Union line, the 20th Maine Infantry (Col. Joshua L. Chamberlain) were arrayed along the craggy ridge's military crest. The 20th Maine had the toughest assignment, as its position would surely be the one to be attacked most heavily should Confederate troops attempt to move around the Union left and collapse the line, assaulting it from the rear and forcing a withdrawal. To minimize this danger, Chamberlain, age 34 and a former professor of languages and religion at Bowdoin College, spread his 386 men along the spur of Little Round Top and detached 42 men under Capt. Walter G. Morrill eastward in a skirmish line. Morrill's Company B, reinforced by a scale of green-uniformed 2d U.S. Sharpshooters, then moved to a rock wall between and slightly east of the Round Tops, some 400 feet away from the regiment's left flank. This regiment was an unlikely choice to be holding such a critical position; it was inexperienced and had achieved only a modest record during the year of its existence. But war is chaos, and the chaos of the moment placed this unit, led by a casually experienced officer, at a critical spot.

George Weikert House, Cemetery Ridge
April 25, 1995

On Cemetery Ridge east of the Trostle House, George Weikert's residence stood in the path of the eastward Confederate advance of July 2.

Daniel Sheaffer House, Baltimore Pike
May 8, 1996

Sickles was taken to the Sheaffer House, built about 1780, far to the rear on the Baltimore Pike, where his leg was amputated, or it was amputated en route to the house, where he recovered. Sickles's leg was placed in a small coffin and sent to the Army Medical Museum in Washington; he visited his leg bones once a year, and they can still be seen at the museum.

120

John T. Weikert House, North of Little Round Top
April 25, 1995

Just north of the camera position of Brady's Little Round Top image stands the John T. Weikert House, another wartime structure of the many area Weikert houses that witnessed the heavy action on July 2. As did dozens of houses, Weikert's home served as a hospital and surgical station in the battle's wake, where amputations and other operations occurred.

The Confederate attack intensified in spurts over the field as the afternoon waned. By 5 P.M. the Alabama regiments had begun their attack on the left of Little Round Top. As the 4th Alabama Infantry and 4th and 5th Texas Infantries moved forward from the northwest face of Big Round Top against Vincent's battle line, the 15th Alabama Infantry (Col. William C. Oates) and 47th Alabama Infantry (Lt. Col. Michael J. Bulger) marched to the summit of Big Round Top and moved to assault the left flank of Vincent's line, the 20th Maine. The 4th Alabama opened a brisk volley into the right of Vincent's line from the base of Little Round Top; minutes later, the 47th Alabama and 15th Alabama regiments assaulted the 20th Maine in a confused hillside fight, with both sides covering behind trees and rocks where possible and exposing themselves only to deliver fire. "Soon we found the enemy flanking us," wrote Cpl. William T. Livermore of the 20th Maine, "and making fearful havoc in our ranks as every one who dared raise his head was sure of his man, but many lost their brains in the attempt." The Southern boys attacked savagely twice and were sent in retreat both times. Meanwhile, the 4th Maine Infantry continued to block access to Little Round Top by firing out into Plum Run Valley.

As both sides came to appreciate its tactical value, the action around Little Round Top heated up. Brisk musket fire between the 20th Maine and the 15th and 47th Alabama created large numbers of casualties as they shot through many rounds of ammunition. Finally, Benning's brigade dislodged the Union battle line ringing the base of Plum Run Valley and occupied the Devil's Den. Benning next posted two regiments between Devil's Den and the Triangular Field. The Yankees atop Little Round Top also held fast, with four regiments of Acting Brig. Gen. Stephen H. Weed's brigade added north of the 16th Michigan Infantry (Lt. Col. Augustus B. Farnham) — the 140th New York Infantry (Col. Patrick H. "Paddy" O'Rorke), 91st Pennsylvania Infantry (Lt. Col. Joseph H. Sinex), 146th New York Infantry (Col. Kenner Garrard), and 155th Pennsylvania Infantry (Lt. Col. John H. Cain). Heavy fighting commenced along the craggy ridge as both crackling rounds of musketry volleys and booming cannon fire raked the shelf of rocks atop the hill and the valley below. A third major wave of attack exploded against Vincent's line from the veterans in Law's and Robertson's brigades, threatening the Union hold on the hill. Regimental commanders such as Chamberlain had been told to preserve their positions at "all hazards." On the right wing of the 15th Alabama, Oates and his brother John led a savage thrust against the left of the 20th Maine, reaching the reverse slope from where they hoped to take in the rear the right wing of the Maine Regiment, who held the rest of the 15th and 47th Alabama under the heavy raking of musket fire. During brutal hand-to-hand fighting, some soldiers firing guns point-blank into the bodies of combatants falling into them, the 20th Maine rallied and retook the spur. In a decisive moment of the struggle, Oates turned and saw the enemy behind him. This was Capt. Morrill's Company B, which had risen from behind the rock wall between the Round Tops and delivered a volley into the backs of the Alabamians. Some of the Southern officers panicked, believing that "two regiments" might be closing in from behind. Oates was suddenly convinced that he was being surrounded.

The Round Tops
Mathew B. Brady
View southeast
ca. July 15, 1863

Brady's view was one of the earliest
taken of **Little Round Top** (and **Big Round
Top** on the right-hand edge), the position
that would prove tactically critical to the
battle. Engineers explored Big Round
Top but found it too heavily wooded to
afford an artillery position. The western
face of Little Round Top, by chance, had
recently been cleared of timber for hous-
ing materials. Federal commanders were
slow to grasp its significance, and when
Brig. Gen. Gouverneur K. Warren climbed
the hill as the Confederate attack began,
he found it unoccupied. Federal units
were rushed up the hill to secure it.
In this scene, two weeks after the battle,
Brady leans against a tree at left, near
the carriage.

The Round Tops
June 8, 1997

JULY 2, 1863

Big Round Top
View southeast
ca. 1860s

**An early view of Big Round Top from
the area of Stony Hill reveals much of
the Valley of Death.**

122

Chamberlain was also panic-stricken, his regiment running out of ammunition. "At this moment my anxiety was increased by the great roar of musketry from my rear," he penned, "on the farther or northerly slope of Little Round Top." The Maine commander believed the Union artillery on the hill might be overrun and turned against his men. Oates contemplated only retreat; Chamberlain considered a downhill attack as an option. "It was imperative to strike before we were struck by this overwhelming force in a hand-to-hand fight," recalled Chamberlain. "At that crisis I ordered the bayonet. The word was enough. It ran like fire along the line from man to man, and rose into a shout, with which they sprang forward upon the enemy, now not thirty yards away. The effect was surprising; many of the enemy's first line threw down their arms and surrendered. An officer fired his pistol at my head with one hand while he handed me his sword with the other." Aided by Lt. Holman Melcher's forward movement and Lt. Col. Ellis Spear's instinct to follow it, the 20th Maine swung downhill. "Suddenly, in the midst of the noise of musketry," wrote Spear, "I heard a shout on the center, of 'Forward,' & saw the line & colors begin to move. I had received no orders. . . . But there was no time to seek explanation. The center was going ahead, apparently charging the enemy, if any, then all of course, and we all joined in the shouts and movement, and went in a rush over the boulders and down the slope." Oates's men retreated in confusion. The 20th Maine and other regiments had held the high ground on Little Round Top as instructed. Although the ground here was important, the fate of the whole nation hardly rested on this one action, as some recent histories might suggest. Had Confederates made their way behind the left, Sedgwick's 6th Corps would have awaited them behind the hill.

Though the Union held the crest, Yankee forces paid a dear price. Col. Strong Vincent, age 26, a Pennsylvanian and a Harvard-educated lawyer, was mortally wounded by a Minié bullet during the fight. The bullet fractured his left thighbone and lodged in his right thigh. Five days later he died in a nearby farmhouse. (Occasionally, bad news came hastily in the chaos of the war. After the battle, an assistant adjutant general, Lt. Col. Fred T. Locke, wrote the War Department simply: "B. G. Strong Vincent died July 7th.") Vincent was posthumously commissioned a brigadier general of volunteers. Also in the fight, Acting Brig. Gen. Stephen H. Weed, a New Yorker, age 31 and a regular army man, was wounded in the spine and paralyzed below the shoulders. "I'm as dead a man as Julius Caesar," said the young soldier. Carried behind some boulders, Weed died within a few hours. Other youthful Unionists were killed in the action: artillerist 1st Lt. Charles E. Hazlett was struck in the head as he was speaking to his mortally wounded friend Weed. Paddy O'Rorke, age 27, an Irish-born engineer, was shot through the neck while shouting orders to his troops.

**96th Pennsylvania Infantry Monument,
Northern Base of Little Round Top**
June 7, 1997

A regiment of Brig. Gen. Joseph J.
Bartlett's brigade, Maj. William H.
Lessig's 96th Pennsylvania Infantry
moved into position just south of the
John Weikert House and held the
ground until battle's end. The monument
dates to 1888.

**93d Pennsylvania Infantry Monument,
Northern Base of Little Round Top, Detail**
May 7, 1996

Maj. John I. Nevin's 93d Pennsylvania
Infantry, part of Brig. Gen. Frank
Wheaton's brigade, held a portion of the
ground north of the crest of Little Round
Top. It assisted in the repulse of the
Confederate attack on the second day,
acquiring the pride reflected in its monument, which contains a distinctive blue-
tile inlay. It was built in 1888.

But the action late in the afternoon was hardly confined to Little Round Top.
By 5 P.M. activity also had commenced in the Wheatfield. Union Col. Philippe Régis
Dénis de Keredern de Trobriand, French-born, age 47, a skilled attorney, poet, novel-
ist, and publisher who had been titled Baron in 1840, led his brigade into the fight.
He faced Brig. Gen. George T. Anderson, nicknamed "Tige," a hard-fighting Georgian.
De Trobriand's brigade, along with the 115th Pennsylvania Infantry (Maj. John P.
Dunne) and 8th New Jersey Infantry (Col. John Ramsay), established a line along
a stone wall and held the area, as well as Stony Hill, which was occupied by the
brigades of Cols. William S. Tilton and Jacob B. Sweitzer. As the Confederate attacks
on Ward intensified to the south, near the Devil's Den, Tige Anderson's brigade
moved into Rose Woods and approached the right of Ward's line and de Trobriand's
brigade. Confused fighting erupted along the line, pushing back the 115th
Pennsylvania and 8th New Jersey. Anderson's initial attack on the Union troops ultimately failed, but he regrouped, and the second attack carried support from the
brigade of Brig. Gen. Joseph B. Kershaw. As it began along the edge of Biesecker's
Woods, this assault moved swiftly northward across the Rose Farm and onto Stony
Hill, causing the brigades of Tilton and Sweitzer to withdraw to the Trostle Woods,
north of the Wheatfield. Fighting a brief delaying action, de Trobriand's men fell
back to beyond the Wheatfield, and the Confederates advanced to Rose Woods and
Stony Hill and into the Devil's Den.

Boulder on Little Round Top
Mathew B. Brady
View north-northeast
ca. July 15, 1863

The boulder atop Little Round Top is
instantly recognizable to any visitor to
the hill. Important background features in
the scene include the George Weikert
House (just right of the boulder) and
patches of woods above center that
include Ziegler's Grove (above right edge
of boulder) and the southern end of
Evergreen Cemetery (to its right). This is
also the only wartime view of the famous
Copse of Trees, near the Angle (just
above and two-thirds of the way toward
the right edge of the boulder).

Boulder on Little Round Top
June 8, 1997

Gouverneur Kemble Warren Monument, Little Round Top
April 25, 1995

The Warren monument, one of the most celebrated at Gettysburg, honors Meade's chief engineer and his contribution of suddenly recognizing the tactical importance of Little Round Top. The bronze statue was dedicated in 1888.

Brig. Gen. Gouverneur K. Warren

A New Yorker, Warren graduated second in his West Point class and achieved a sterling reputation as an engineer prior to his Civil War service. He was wounded at Gaines's Mill in 1862 while leading a brigade in the 5th Corps; his staff service came about in the spring of 1863.

Samuel Wylie Crawford Monument, Valley of Death
April 25, 1995

Brig. Gen. Crawford's Pennsylvania Reserves fought stubbornly in what came to be known as the Valley of Death, west of the Round Tops. Crawford's monument, in the valley, unfortunately misspells his middle name.

Brig. Gen. Evander M. Law

A South Carolina native, Law attended The Citadel and became a professor of history before moving to Alabama and joining the state militia. Law's brigade of Alabamians attacked through the Devil's Den and up into Little Round Top, nearly achieving success.

View of Little Round Top
April 25, 1995

Little Round Top offers a majestic panoramic view of the Gettysburg battle-field, this view aimed northwest. The Warren statue stands on the hill's crest.

Union Breastworks on Little Round Top
Mathew B. Brady?
View south
ca. July 15, 1863

Probably taken by Brady's crew two weeks after the action, this view shows the breastworks of the 91st Pennsylvania in the foreground and Big Round Top looming in the background. Visible as debris on the ground are wooden ammunition boxes, rails or poles (possibly portions of a rail fence carried atop the hill by soldiers), and either photographer's assistants or unrelated civilians seated on a boulder.

Union Breastworks on Little Round Top
August 22, 2000

No areas of the second day's battle matched the intensity of the fight in the Wheatfield. Known as the "whirlpool," the Wheatfield (527 feet) and surrounding woods witnessed attacks and counterattacks by at least 14 Union and Confederate brigades during a two-hour period on the early evening of this day. Union Brig. Gen. John C. Caldwell's division (consisting of the brigades of Brig. Gen. Samuel K. Zook and Cols. Edward E. Cross, Patrick Kelly and his famed "Irish Brigade," and John R. Brooke) formed amid Trostle Woods and moved into the Wheatfield, striking the 1st Texas and 15th Alabama Infantries and the right side of Anderson's battle line. Prior to the attack, Cross, a veteran fighter who was not admired by his troops, had considered the attack with his corps commander, Maj. Gen. Winfield Scott Hancock. "Colonel Cross, this day will bring you a star," said Hancock. "No General," replied Cross, shaking his head, "this is my last battle." A short time later the aggressive colonel was struck by a ball in the abdomen and mortally wounded.

The Union assaults were all hit with heavy return fire from the Southern troops. "The Rebs had their slight protection," noted Lt. Charles A. Fuller, "but we were in the open without a thing better than wheat straw to catch a minnie bullet that weighed an ounce. Of course our men began to tumble." After the first assaults, Zook's brigade moved out from its attack point toward Kershaw's position on Stony Hill. Zook was a native Pennsylvanian who had moved to New York. Age 42, he had been a militia soldier and superintendent of the Washington and New York Telegraph Company before the war. "If you can't get out of the way, lie down and we'll march over you," Zook shouted at Brig. Gen. James Barnes's retreating men in blue as he commenced his forward movement. As Zook led his men toward the fight, he suddenly received a severe stinging sensation in his chest, and his head fell back and grew light. A Minié bullet had hit him in the left side of the stomach, perforated his sword belt, and lodged near his spine. He died in a field hospital the next day.

CHAPTER 5 : UNION FORCES SEIZE THE HIGH GROUND

Union Breastworks on Little Round Top
Alexander Gardner
View northeast
ca. July 7, 1863

Gardner's view, taken only about four days after the battle, shows the type of stone breastworks Federal soldiers hastily constructed on the night of July 2–3. The 91st Pennsylvania Infantry (Lt. Col. Joseph H. Sinex) built the works.

Union Breastworks on Little Round Top
August 22, 2000

129

Simultaneous with the attack of Zook, Kelly's Irish Brigade thrust toward the southern end of Stony Hill, causing Kershaw's men in the 3d and 7th South Carolina Infantries (Maj. Robert C. Maffett and Col. David W. Aiken) to retreat to the yard surrounding the Rose farmhouse. As the Union attack apparently gained momentum, Brooke's brigade battled Anderson's Confederates, driving them from Rose Woods. A Confederate counterattack loomed; Anderson and Kershaw regrouped, and supported by waves of gunfire from the brigade of Brig. Gen. Paul J. Semmes, they swung through the Wheatfield, scattering the Federals, including Sweitzer's brigade, which had been sent in to support Caldwell. Caldwell's attack, successful for a short time, was shattered. Dozens of dead and wounded soldiers were left littered across the Wheatfield, making it one of the most gruesome areas of the battlefield. Semmes, a Georgian, age 48 and cousin of Confederate naval captain Raphael Semmes, was wounded in the thigh with a Minié bullet and died a week later in West Virginia.

JULY 2, 1863

More savage battle would unfold in the deadly Wheatfield. The next Union
division to support Caldwell was that of Brig. Gen. Romeyn Beck Ayres. Born in New
York, age 37, Ayres was a well-trained regular army artillerist who had served with
distinction with most of the Army of the Potomac's campaigns. His brigade commanders were Cols. Hannibal Day, Sidney Burbank, and Kenner Garrard, who took
over for the mortally wounded Stephen H. Weed (the third brigade was up on Little
Round Top). Ayres's two brigades in the Wheatfield received heavy return fire. As
Burbank's brigade marched into the fight, about the same time Sweitzer's men were
being roughly handled, they moved into the Wheatfield hoping to maneuver into
Rose Woods. But Burbank's men were shot down with severe small-arms fire sent by
Anderson on the left and Kershaw and Wofford on the right, forcing Ayres's soldiers
to retreat swiftly eastward across Plum Run and assemble again north of Little
Round Top. Wofford pushed the Union division of Brig. Gen. James Barnes away
from Trostle Woods, clearing this sector of the field of Yankee soldiers.

Other areas of the field contributed to the ghastly casualties of Gettysburg's
second day. Heavy fighting broke out in the Peach Orchard, east of the Emmitsburg
Road, beginning about 5:30 P.M. McLaws's division struck hard into the Union divisions of Barnes, Humphreys, and Maj. Gen. David B. Birney. Not only was the fight
characterized by murderous sheets of musketry fire, but the area witnessed some of
the hottest artillery action of the war. Though Antietam is often described as "artillery
hell," the experienced Confederate artillerist Edward Porter Alexander described the
battle at Gettysburg's Peach Orchard by recalling, "I don't think there was ever in our
war a hotter, harder, sharper artillery afternoon than this."

The first Confederate attack on the Peach Orchard commenced after a blistering
barrage of cannon fire and saw Kershaw's brigade advance eastward, its right toward
Stony Hill and its left across the Emmitsburg Road and into the Peach Orchard.
Kershaw's men then turned left, moving against the Union artillery batteries posted
along the Wheatfield Road. After some delay, Brig. Gen. William Barksdale's brigade
also moved across the road and passed on either side of the Sherfy House on its way
to attacking Brig. Gen. Charles K. Graham's brigade.

The commanders now facing each other offered a considerable contrast.
Barksdale was an old-time Southerner, a 42-year-old Mississippi attorney and politician who in 1856 had assisted Preston Brooks in his Capitol-floor caning of
Massachusetts senator Charles Sumner, one of the ugly events that brought tensions
between the two political factions to a boil. Graham, age 39, was a New Yorker who'd
had a brief stint in the navy before becoming a lawyer and civil engineer. Barksdale's
men first attacked Graham's brigade between the Peach Orchard and the Sherfy Barn.
With a hot musketry battle testing the limits of both battle lines, the 73d New York
Infantry, the "Second Fire Zouaves" (Maj. Michael W. Burns), shifted left to support
the 114th Pennsylvania Infantry, "Collis's Zouaves" (Lt. Col. Frederick F. Cavada).
Beside the Wentz Farm, south of the Sherfy House on the Emmitsburg Road, the 21st
Mississippi Infantry (Col. Benjamin G. Humphreys) collapsed Graham's line and
routed the Yankees from the Peach Orchard. To help protect the Union retreat,
a battery commanded by Capt. John Bigelow was ordered to keep a heavy fire going
as long as they could. "I then saw Confederates swarming on our right flank," wrote
Bigelow, "some standing on the limber chests and firing at the gunners, who were still
serving their pieces; the horses were all down; overhead the air was alive with mis-
siles from the enemy." Supported by Kershaw's left, the 21st Mississippi then drove
the Union batteries out from their positions along the Wheatfield Road.

Union Breastworks on Little Round Top
James F. Gibson
View northeast
July 6, 1863

Stone works erected by the 44th New York Infantry (Col. James C. Rice, fore-ground) and 140th New York Infantry (Col. Patrick H. O'Rorke, background) on July 2 are visible on the southern edge of Little Round Top. The Confederate attack of Law's and Robertson's brigades struck this position during the afternoon of the second day.

Union Breastworks on Little Round Top
June 8, 1997

Union Breastworks on Little Round Top
Timothy O'Sullivan
View north
July 6, 1863

Another view of the works of the 140th New York depicts a pine tree that stood among the rocks until just a few years ago.

Union Breastworks on Little Round Top
August 22, 2000

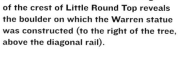
Union Breastworks on Little Round Top
Mathew B. Brady
View north
ca. July 15, 1863

The Brady view of Union works and scattered rocks on the western edge of the crest of Little Round Top reveals the boulder on which the Warren statue was constructed (to the right of the tree, above the diagonal rail).

Union Breastworks on Little Round Top
James F. Gibson
View north
July 6, 1863

The first of two images made only days and a few feet apart shows a portion of the Union breastworks only a short distance beneath the present-day monument to Gouverneur K. Warren. The Gibson view is much less sharp than the Brady view shown above.

Big Round Top from Little Round Top
Mathew B. Brady
View south
ca. July 15, 1863

Brady's assistant sits atop Little Round Top with Big Round Top looming in the background. The hastily erected works of stone protected many soldiers firing at the oncoming Rebels; the works were thrown up by the 91st Pennsylvania Infantry. Debris of battle still litters the ground.

Heavy Action at the Devil's Den
July 2, 1863, Late Afternoon

The Confederate attack of Longstreet's swept eastward through Rose Farm and Woods, up across the Triangular Field, and into the granite boulders of the Devil's Den.

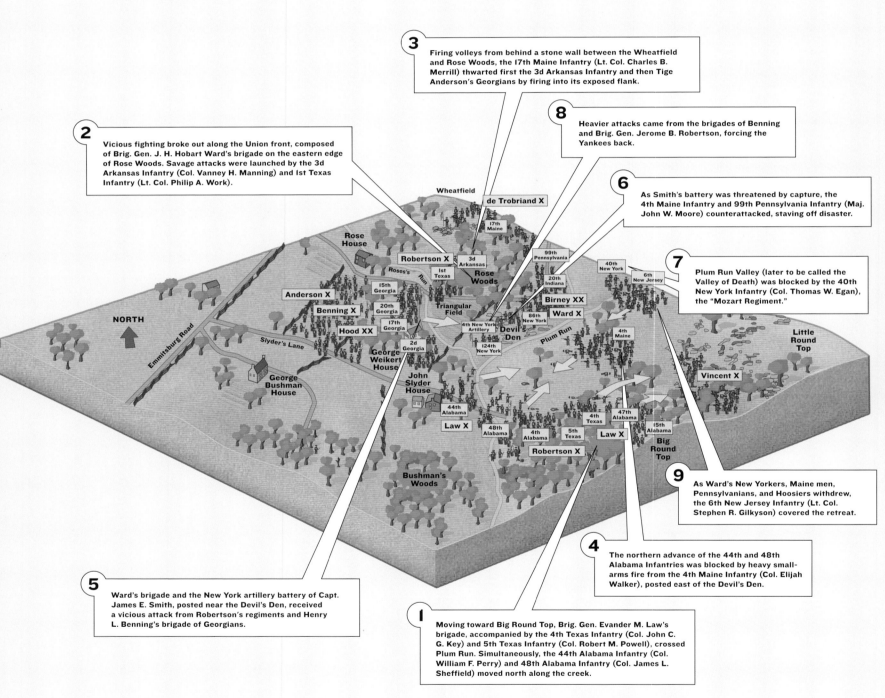

3 Firing volleys from behind a stone wall between the Wheatfield and Rose Woods, the 17th Maine Infantry (Lt. Col. Charles B. Merrill) thwarted first the 3d Arkansas Infantry and then Tige Anderson's Georgians by firing into its exposed flank.

8 Heavier attacks came from the brigades of Benning and Brig. Gen. Jerome B. Robertson, forcing the Yankees back.

2 Vicious fighting broke out along the Union front, composed of Brig. Gen. J. H. Hobart Ward's brigade on the eastern edge of Rose Woods. Savage attacks were launched by the 3d Arkansas Infantry (Col. Vanney H. Manning) and 1st Texas Infantry (Lt. Col. Philip A. Work).

6 As Smith's battery was threatened by capture, the 4th Maine Infantry and 99th Pennsylvania Infantry (Maj. John W. Moore) counterattacked, staving off disaster.

7 Plum Run Valley (later to be called the Valley of Death) was blocked by the 40th New York Infantry (Col. Thomas W. Egan), the "Mozart Regiment."

9 As Ward's New Yorkers, Maine men, Pennsylvanians, and Hoosiers withdrew, the 6th New Jersey Infantry (Lt. Col. Stephen R. Gilkyson) covered the retreat.

5 Ward's brigade and the New York artillery battery of Capt. James E. Smith, posted near the Devil's Den, received a vicious attack from Robertson's regiments and Henry L. Benning's brigade of Georgians.

4 The northern advance of the 44th and 48th Alabama Infantries was blocked by heavy small-arms fire from the 4th Maine Infantry (Col. Elijah Walker), posted east of the Devil's Den.

1 Moving toward Big Round Top, Brig. Gen. Evander M. Law's brigade, accompanied by the 4th Texas Infantry (Col. John C. G. Key) and 5th Texas Infantry (Col. Robert M. Powell), crossed Plum Run. Simultaneously, the 44th Alabama Infantry (Col. William F. Perry) and 48th Alabama Infantry (Col. James L. Sheffield) moved north along the creek.

**Acting Brig. Gen.
Stephen H. Weed**

Weed, a regular army
artillerist of high
capability, was struck
in the spine and para-
lyzed during the Little
Round Top fight. "I'm
as dead a man as Julius
Caesar," he proclaimed,
before expiring.

**Patrick H. O'Rorke
Death Monument,
Little Round Top**
June 7, 1997

The attack on the crest
of Little Round Top,
though ultimately a
Confederate failure,
proved costly in Federal
casualties. Several
important officers
fell dead or mortally
wounded, including the
beloved Col. "Paddy"
O'Rorke of the 140th
New York, who was
shot through the neck.
Rubbing Paddy's bronze
nose on his plaque on
the 140th's monument,
erected in 1889, is con-
sidered good luck.

**Strong Vincent Mortal
Wounding Monument,
Little Round Top**
June 7, 1997

Col. Strong Vincent,
commanding the brigade
posted on Little Round
Top's military crest, was
struck through the left
thigh and in the right
thigh; he died in a farm-
house five days later. In
1878, the marker was
placed at the approxi-
mate position of his
wounding.

**Rock Inscription,
"Strong Vincent Fell
Here," Little Round Top**
April 25, 1995

A rock near the 44th
New York Infantry
Monument bears an
inscription remembering
the Federal brigade
commander.

The swift, heavy fire characterizing Barksdale's attack now struck into Graham's
soldiers, positioned around the Sherfy buildings, sending them reeling in confusion.
The charge of the victorious Mississippians collapsed Sickles's salient, exposing
Humphreys's right and left flanks and forcing a Union withdrawal. Sickles witnessed
this collapse and, in the process, was struck and seriously wounded. Sitting in the
saddle near the Abraham Trostle House, north of Stony Hill, Sickles was hit at
the midpoint of the tibia by a low-speed round case shot or cannonball. The leg was
mangled, and Sickles was lifted onto a stretcher next to the Trostle Barn, where
despite loss of blood and the onset of shock, he continued talking with officers and
men, asked to have himself propped up so that his troops could see that he was alive,
and then requested and smoked a cigar. Transported behind the lines to a makeshift
field hospital at the Daniel Sheaffer House, Sickles had his lower right leg amputated,
wrapped, and placed inside a small coffin. Eventually it was sent to the Army Medical
Museum in Washington, where he visited it each year. In fact, the roguish Sickles
may have had the last laugh. Effectively taken out of the war at his most controversial
moment, he continued to aid the Lincoln administration in valuable ways and by
losing his leg made himself into a hero. In 1897, he received the Medal of Honor for
his heroics.

Sickles was a standout in a war full of standouts. After the war he served as
Minister to Spain and used his position to commence an affair with Queen Isabella,
former ruler of the country. This followed prewar notoriety from having shot and
killed his wife's paramour, Washington district attorney Philip Barton Key, the son of
the author of *The Star Spangled Banner*. In a sensational murder trial prosecuted by
Robert Ould (who would flee under a cloud of treason to become an assistant secretary of war for the Confederacy), Sickles was defended by Edwin M. Stanton (who
became Lincoln's secretary of war) and Thomas Francis Meagher, and was acquitted
by reason of temporary insanity — the first such successful defense in America. Even
more shocking to Victorian morals, he took his unfaithful wife back. Sickles outlived
his detractors. He survived until 1914 and presided over many Gettysburg reunions.
When he was asked why no monument had been erected to him, Sickles chortled,
"The whole damn battlefield is my monument."

135

JULY 2, 1863

Little Round Top from the Devil's Den
James F. Gibson
View east
July 6, 1863

Gibson's view of Little Round Top from the Devil's Den was made from one of the prominent boulders situated on the eastern face of the rocky outcrop. It suffers from atmospheric haze.

Little Round Top from the Devil's Den
June 8, 1997

Brig. Gen. Wright's brigade, north of Lang, moved forward toward the Codori homestead, pushing the 82d New York Infantry (Lt. Col. James Huston) and 15th Massachusetts Infantry (Col. George H. Ward) back in disarray and inflicting murderous casualties including Huston and Ward. The men in the ranks of the Union center continued to receive a heavy attack. Wright's men dashed forward to capture Lt. Gulian V. Weir's battery south of the Codori House and two guns of Lt. T. Fred Brown's battery between the Codori Farm and the Union line on Cemetery Ridge. On the ridge itself, Wright's attack struck Hancock's 2d Corps line as Southern boys charged into Col. Norman J. Hall's brigade; intense fighting along the line flared back and forth as Posey's men finally occupied the Bliss Farm and the 48th Mississippi Infantry (Col. Joseph M. Jayne) moved toward the Emmitsburg Road.

CHAPTER 5 : UNION FORCES SEIZE THE HIGH GROUND

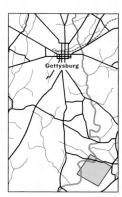

Little Round Top, Final Assault
July 2, 1863, Late Afternoon

Longstreet's attack charged eastward
toward the left flank of the Federal line.

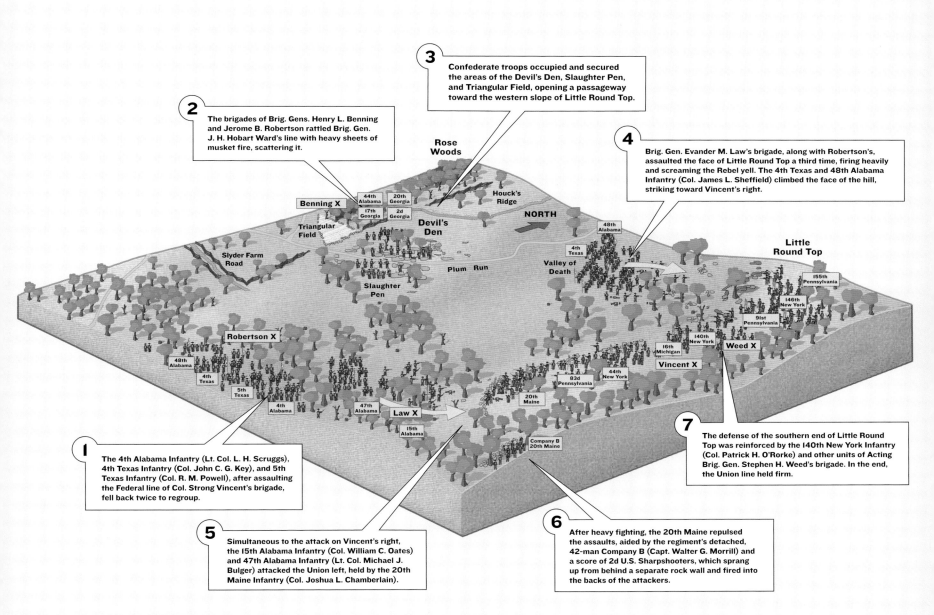

2 The brigades of Brig. Gens. Henry L. Benning
and Jerome B. Robertson rattled Brig. Gen.
J. H. Hobart Ward's line with heavy sheets of
musket fire, scattering it.

3 Confederate troops occupied and secured
the areas of the Devil's Den, Slaughter Pen,
and Triangular Field, opening a passageway
toward the western slope of Little Round Top.

4 Brig. Gen. Evander M. Law's brigade, along with Robertson's,
assaulted the face of Little Round Top a third time, firing heavily
and screaming the Rebel yell. The 4th Texas and 48th Alabama
Infantry (Col. James L. Sheffield) climbed the face of the hill,
striking toward Vincent's right.

1 The 4th Alabama Infantry (Lt. Col. L. H. Scruggs),
4th Texas Infantry (Col. John C. G. Key), and 5th
Texas Infantry (Col. R. M. Powell), after assaulting
the Federal line of Col. Strong Vincent's brigade,
fell back twice to regroup.

5 Simultaneous to the attack on Vincent's right,
the 15th Alabama Infantry (Col. William C. Oates)
and 47th Alabama Infantry (Lt. Col. Michael J.
Bulger) attacked the Union left, held by the 20th
Maine Infantry (Col. Joshua L. Chamberlain).

6 After heavy fighting, the 20th Maine repulsed
the assaults, aided by the regiment's detached,
42-man Company B (Capt. Walter G. Morrill) and
a score of 2d U.S. Sharpshooters, which sprang
up from behind a separate rock wall and fired into
the backs of the attackers.

7 The defense of the southern end of Little Round
Top was reinforced by the 140th New York Infantry
(Col. Patrick H. O'Rorke) and other units of Acting
Brig. Gen. Stephen H. Weed's brigade. In the end,
the Union line held firm.

Rose
Woods

Houck's
Ridge

NORTH

Devil's
Den

Triangular
Field

Benning X

44th
Alabama

20th
Georgia

17th
Georgia

2d
Georgia

48th
Alabama

4th
Texas

Little
Round Top

Slyder Farm
Road

Plum Run

Valley of
Death

155th
Pennsylvania

Slaughter
Pen

146th
New York

91st
Pennsylvania

Robertson X

140th
New York

16th
Michigan

Weed X

48th
Alabama

83d
Pennsylvania

44th
New York

Vincent X

4th
Texas

5th
Texas

20th
Maine

4th
Alabama

47th
Alabama

Law X

15th
Alabama

Company B
20th Maine

JULY 2, 1863

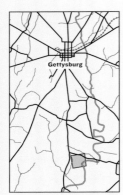

Bloody Attacks in the Wheatfield
July 2, 1863, Late Afternoon

The Confederate eastward attack surged forward into the area where at least 11 Union and Confederate brigades launched assaults and counterassaults.

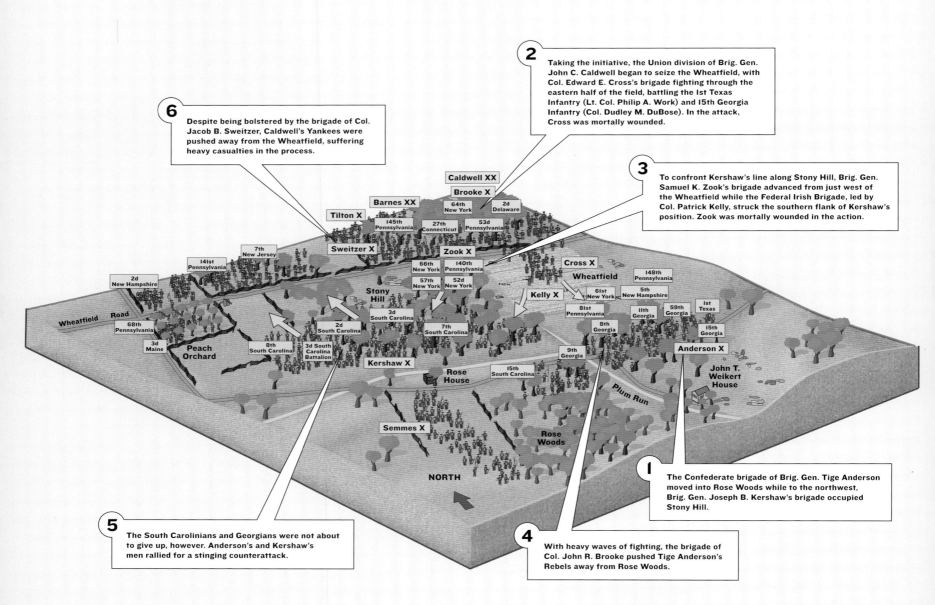

2 Taking the initiative, the Union division of Brig. Gen. John C. Caldwell began to seize the Wheatfield, with Col. Edward E. Cross's brigade fighting through the eastern half of the field, battling the 1st Texas Infantry (Lt. Col. Philip A. Work) and 15th Georgia Infantry (Col. Dudley M. DuBose). In the attack, Cross was mortally wounded.

6 Despite being bolstered by the brigade of Col. Jacob B. Sweitzer, Caldwell's Yankees were pushed away from the Wheatfield, suffering heavy casualties in the process.

3 To confront Kershaw's line along Stony Hill, Brig. Gen. Samuel K. Zook's brigade advanced from just west of the Wheatfield while the Federal Irish Brigade, led by Col. Patrick Kelly, struck the southern flank of Kershaw's position. Zook was mortally wounded in the action.

5 The South Carolinians and Georgians were not about to give up, however. Anderson's and Kershaw's men rallied for a stinging counterattack.

1 The Confederate brigade of Brig. Gen. Tige Anderson moved into Rose Woods while to the northwest, Brig. Gen. Joseph B. Kershaw's brigade occupied Stony Hill.

4 With heavy waves of fighting, the brigade of Col. John R. Brooke pushed Tige Anderson's Rebels away from Rose Woods.

Caldwell XX
Brooke X
Barnes XX
64th New York
2d Delaware
Tilton X
145th Pennsylvania
27th Connecticut
53d Pennsylvania
7th New Jersey
Sweitzer X
Zook X
Cross X
141st Pennsylvania
66th New York
140th Pennsylvania
Wheatfield
148th Pennsylvania
2d New Hampshire
57th New York
52d New York
Kelly X
61st New York
5th New Hampshire
Stony Hill
81st Pennsylvania
11th Georgia
59th Georgia
1st Texas
68th Pennsylvania
3d South Carolina
8th Georgia
15th Georgia
Wheatfield Road
2d South Carolina
7th South Carolina
9th Georgia
Anderson X
3d Maine
Peach Orchard
8th South Carolina
3d South Carolina Battalion
Kershaw X
John T. Weikert House
Rose House
15th South Carolina
Plum Run
Semmes X
Rose Woods
NORTH
Gettysburg

As darkness approached, the situation for the Union high command appeared to be discouraging. Fortune had struck with the salvation of Little Round Top by Vincent's and Weed's men, preserving tactically critical ground that would afford an artillery perch for later fighting. Confederates had made sweeping gains across the fields west of Little Round Top, however, forcing most of the Union line back into the original fishhook-shaped battle front along Cemetery Ridge. To the south, the Confederate brigades of Robertson and Benning occupied the Devil's Den and ground along the western base of Big Round Top; the brigades of Kershaw, Semmes, and Tige Anderson concentrated along Plum Run. Wofford's brigade settled along the northern side of the Wheatfield, west of the John Weikert House.

But the battle was still carried on in bursts. The blue-clad troops of Brig. Gen. Samuel Wylie Crawford's division, consisting of Pennsylvania Reserves, formed north of Little Round Top for a counterattack. Col. William McCandless's brigade, along with the 98th Pennsylvania Infantry (Maj. John B. Kohler), commenced an assault into the Wheatfield as soon as stunned and defeated Union troops on the retreat cleared the way. This charge of the Pennsylvania Reserves drove the Confederates back through the Wheatfield. To the north, Brig. Gen. Frank Wheaton's brigade similarly charged and pushed Wofford's men out of the area. Local citizen Tillie Alleman, age 15, described the thrill of seeing the charge of the reserves. "The Confederates faced toward them, fired, halted, and then began to retreat. I saw them falling as [they] were climbing over a stone wall and as they were shot in the open space. The fighting lasted but a short time, when the Confederates were driven back in the direction of Little Round Top." Largely held out until now, Sedgwick's 6th Corps began to enter the fight not only by supporting attacks but also by securing this ground with fresh troops. A portion of Sykes's 5th Corps, the brigades of Vincent (now commanded by Col. James C. Rice) and Col. Joseph W. Fisher, the surviving veterans of the Little Round Top struggle among them, now moved to scale and secure Big Round Top, occupying the summit in darkness.

East of the main battlefield, meanwhile, action erupted near Brinkerhoff's Ridge. The 9th Massachusetts Infantry (Col. Patrick R. Guiney), on picket duty near the Deardorf House, had skirmished with elements of the Stonewall Brigade (Brig. Gen. James A. Walker) throughout the afternoon. The Massachusetts men were then relieved by the 10th New York Cavalry (Maj. Matthew H. Avery), which spread itself along the Hanover Road and joined the fight against the Virginians. Frustrated with the continuing fire, the 2d Virginia Infantry (Col. John Q. A. Nadenbousch) moved north of the road and pushed forward into the Federal cavalrymen. By 7 P.M. the 10th New York Cavalry was relieved by elements of the 3d Pennsylvania Cavalry (Lt. Col. Edward S. Jones), 1st New Jersey Cavalry (Maj. Myron Beaumont), and Purnell's Legion (Capt. Robert E. Duvall), which sustained heavy fire. Following fighting between the 2d Virginia Infantry and the 3d Pennsylvania Cavalry along a heavily contested fence line, the Pennsylvania troops occupied the area and held it; the fight died out at dusk.

Another major action was shaping up in the waning twilight. Lt. Gen. Richard S. Ewell finally planned and launched an attack on the Union right, taking aim at the high ground on Culp's Hill. The Yankee line in the area had been established throughout the first night and reinforced during the afternoon of the second day. The task of attacking it would be monumental: the hill's topography afforded a naturally strong position, and Union engineers incorporated granite outcrops into the works as best they could. They also employed felled trees as makeshift defenses. Union positions

Brig. Gen. Samuel W. Crawford

Crawford's Pennsylvania Reserves staged a vicious counterattack into the Wheatfield late on July 2, after the action on Little Round Top began to wane. Crawford had been a participant from the war's first days, serving as a surgeon at Fort Sumter during the Confederate bombardment.

141

Little Round Top from the Devil's Den
Timothy O'Sullivan
View east
July 6, 1863

The only two-frame panorama made by one of the earliest photographers to record images of Gettysburg, this O'Sullivan pair may have been made toward the end of his Gettysburg series, when he became less concerned over his supply of plates.

Little Round Top from the Devil's Den
June 8, 1997

142

were concentrated between the Baltimore Pike and Rock Creek, along the high ground, and were manned by Brig. Gen. James S. Wadsworth's and Brig. Gen. John W. Geary's divisions along Culp's Hill and Brig. Gen. Thomas H. Ruger's division to the south. Maj. Gen. Henry W. Slocum's 12th Corps, latecomers to the battle, contributed many units to the area. In Geary's division, which manned the main portions of the line, the brigade of Brig. Gen. George S. Greene occupied a principal stretch along the southern slope of the hill. Held in reserve to the rear were the brigades of Col. Charles Candy and Brig. Gen. Thomas L. Kane. Ruger's men covered the far southern slope of the hill, extending into the area around Spangler's Spring and McAllister's Woods.

Ewell, meanwhile, had been busy moving guns. To support his long-awaited attack on Culp's Hill, he positioned artillery on Benner's Hill and also on Seminary Ridge north of Fairfield Road. A. P. Hill's corps also deployed cannon, mostly along Seminary Ridge south of Fairfield Road. These Confederate batteries totaled 73 guns prior to the attack. To counter this threat, the Union guns of the 11th Corps numbered 43 pieces inside or near Evergreen Cemetery, 33 oriented toward Seminary Ridge, and 10 facing Benner's Hill. Twenty-five pieces of the 1st Corps artillery pointed toward Benner's Hill.

Ewell sent Maj. Gen. Edward Johnson driving toward Culp's Hill about 7 P.M. Units of the Union 12th Corps shifted their lines, and Greene's Union brigade moved to the right to cover the area between the summit of Culp's Hill and the lower hill, to

Union Breastworks on Little Round Top
Alexander Gardner
View south
July 6, 1863

This remarkable view depicts a position
on the southern slope of Little Round Top
that constituted a gun pit. The image was
made just a short distance from the
breastwork photo that contained a prominent pine tree (see page 132). Debris of
battle and a series of sticks or pieces of
tree branch litter the foreground, the
Federal side of the rocks.

Union Breastworks on Little Round Top
June 7, 1997

Union Breastworks on Little Round Top
Alexander Gardner
View south
July 6, 1863

A view of the same "gun pit" made from a
slightly different angle records different
scenes of the same debris.

the south. As dusk approached, a well-planned Confederate assault sent the brigades of Brig. Gen. John M. Jones, Col. Jesse M. Williams (Nicholls's brigade), and Brig. Gen. George H. "Maryland" Steuart attacking the left, center, and right of Greene's position. Heavy sheets of musketry fire rang out in the dusk air; the furious assault stunned the Union soldiers waiting in line for action. The woods along this portion of the hill were thick, and the visibility was poor with the waning daylight. "Moments passed which were years of agony," recorded one Federal soldier. "The pale faces, starting eye-balls, and nervous hands grasping loaded muskets, told how terrible were those moments of suspense." Soon the smoke filled the woods so thickly that soldiers could not see what they were firing at but merely had to fire in the direction of sounds. On the lower elevation of the hill, Col. Archibald L. McDougall's Union brigade abandoned a line of works that was soon taken over by advancing Confederates from Steuart's brigade. Steuart's men viciously attacked Greene's right and threatened the entire Union position, but after a short time the Yankees reinforced the line, despite the abandonment of their position by the 137th New York Infantry (Col. David Ireland). As darkness deepened, the fighting died away and the brigades of Candy and Kane moved back to their former positions.

Ewell's attack intensified around 7:30 P.M., when Maj. Gen. Jubal A. Early's division attacked headlong into the Union-held stone walls and batteries atop East Cemetery Hill. The movement was spearheaded by the brigades of Brig. Gen. Harry T. Hays and Col. Isaac E. Avery (Brig. Gen. Robert F. Hoke's old brigade). Complicating the Federal defense of the area was that Union Brig. Gen. Adelbert Ames, concerned about the movement by Johnson to the east, shifted two regiments eastward into Culp's Meadow and moved the 17th Connecticut Infantry (Maj. Allen G. Brady) to the right, which created a gap near the Federal left. As the soldiers of Hays's brigade moved quickly across a brickyard site east of Baltimore Street on the southern edge of town and fanned out to attack uphill into the Union line, small-arms fire rang out from both battle lines and the advanced Union infantry fell back to a concentrated line atop the hill. Strengthening their position around the core of New York regiments posted in Col. Leopold von Gilsa's line, the Yankees readied for a major assault.

143

The Peach Orchard
July 2, 1863, 5:30–7:30 P.M.

As the Confederate attack continued,
Maj. Gen. Lafayette McLaws struck into
the Peach Orchard, his men firing sheets
of musket volleys as the divisions of
Maj. Gen. David B. Birney and Brig. Gens.
James Barnes and John C. Caldwell
responded, supported by a murderous
artillery barrage. As Brig. Gen. William
Barksdale's Mississippians charged,
this politician-turned-soldier was
mortally wounded.

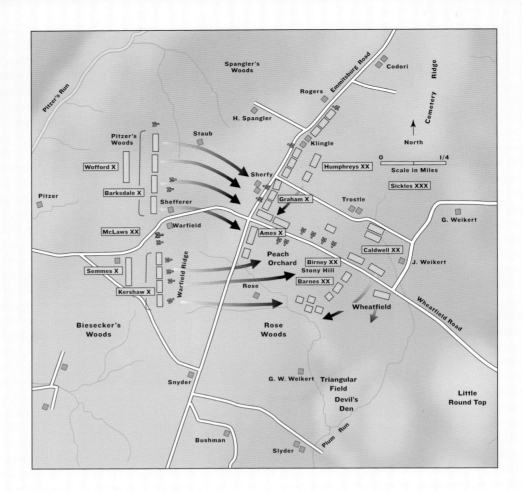

Cemetery Ridge
July 2, 1863, 7–8 P.M.

As dusk fell on the second day's field of
battle, the Confederate division of Maj.
Gen. Richard H. Anderson led a spirited
attack against the Union center along
Cemetery Ridge that briefly jeopardized
the Federal position. Heavy skirmishing
transpired between Brig. Gen. Carnot
Posey's brigade and Union troops around
the Bliss Farm. Fierce fighting commenced from Brig. Gen. Ambrose R.
Wright's men, who stormed across the
Emmitsburg Road, capturing five cannon
and approached the Copse of Trees
before being hurled back by contacting
Hays's Federals.

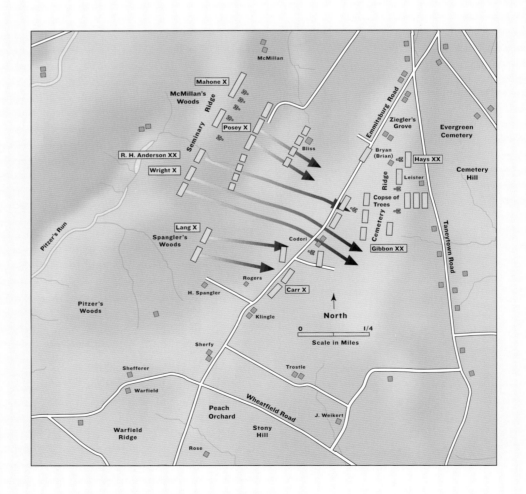

Union Breastworks on Little Round Top
ca. 1863

A detail image of debris amid breastworks was taken by an unknown photographer at an unknown position on the hill.

Union Breastworks on Little Round Top
ca. 1863

Another unidentified image of breastworks on Little Round Top was made
by an unknown photographer.

145

Hays's Louisianans "moved forward as steadily, amid this hail of shot and minnie
ball, as though they were on parade far removed from danger," recorded Col. Andrew
L. Harris, who held the Union left flank on the hill. Hays's Louisiana Tigers initially
struck into Harris's Ohioans, scattering them in bloody fighting and pushing up the
hill toward the battery of Capt. Michael Wiedrich, which fired canister rounds and,
when the canister was depleted, "rotten shot," spherical case shot loaded without
fuses, which would explode just outside the muzzle and send balls screaming forward
like a poor man's canister. Together, in the confused, chaotic darkness, Hays's Tigers
and Avery's Tarheels scrambled up East Cemetery Hill piecemeal, fighting at close
range and scattering the center of Gilsa's line. Despite the Confederate success,
however, four Union regiments — the 75th Ohio Infantry (Harris), 17th Connecticut
Infantry, 41st New York Infantry (Lt. Col. Detleo von Einsiedel), and 33d Massachusetts Infantry (Col. Adin B. Underwood) — held their positions at the foot of East
Cemetery Hill, in the Brickyard Lane.

One of the casualties of the attack was Col. Avery, who was struck in the neck by
a ball and knocked from his horse. Alone and unrecognized in the darkness, as battle
raged around him, the North Carolinian pulled a pencil and scrap of paper from his
pocket and, in a scrawl, wrote, "Tell my father I died with my face to the enemy. I. E.
Avery." The bloodstained paper was found with his dead body.

Ewell's bloody attack on Cemetery Hill developed further as Maj. Gen. Robert E.
Rodes's division entered the fray. Though the Confederate thrust of Hays and Avery

**Col.
Joshua L. Chamberlain**

Chamberlain, lionized
by the recent motion
picture *Gettysburg*, was
a 34-year-old former
professor of languages,
rhetoric, and religion
at Bowdoin College.
His rapid rise in the army
reflected a complex
personality: he had "the
soul of the lion but the
heart of the woman," as
Bvt. Brig. Gen. Horatio
G. Sickel phrased it.
Chamberlain rose to the
grade of Bvt. Maj.
Gen. and after the war
became governor
of Maine and later presi-
dent of Bowdoin College.

Capt. Walter G. Morrill

A former laborer from
the slate quarries of
Brownville, Maine,
Morrill led his 42-man
detachment against the
attacking Confederates
at a critical time in the
battle, helping the 20th
Maine to wheel down
Little Round Top and
push the I5th Alabama
Infantry back.

had succeeded in part by pushing many of the Union soldiers away from the main
line on East Cemetery Hill capturing seven cannon and endangering the Union batteries posted near the Cemetery Gatehouse, many of the scattered Union men rallied
near the guns and regrouped after a short time. The Union batteries were seriously
jeopardized, how-ever; one oft-repeated story mentions a Confederate in the charge
of the Louisiana troops placing his torso across the muzzle of a Federal cannon and
declaring, "I take command of the gun." The cannoneer, still holding the lanyard,
replied, "Du sollst sie haben!" ("You should have it!") and pulled away, blasting the
Rebel to pieces.

The 11th Corps regiments west of the Baltimore Pike moved in to support the
crumbling Union line, and from Cemetery Ridge, Col. Samuel S. Carroll's brigade
marched in reinforcements. After savage fighting atop the hill, Hays's and Avery's
Southerners were driven back. They regrouped in the darkness along Winebrenner's
Run, considerably north of Brickyard Lane and near Brig. Gen. John B. Gordon's
brigade. Following the failed attack by Early, Rodes swung his division southward
into position for an attack from the west, with the brigades of Brig. Gen. George P.
Doles, Brig. Gen. Alfred Iverson, and Brig. Gen. Stephen Dodson Ramseur in front.
But this tardy movement accomplished nothing, as Rodes halted his men along
Long Lane.

As darkness deepened, the fighting continued along the Union center. North
of the Round Tops, the Confederate attack was repulsed. East of the Trostle Farm,
Lt. Col. Freeman McGilvery established a line of cannon to harass the Confederates
approaching via that route. Through sharp, often hand-to-hand fighting, Confederates of the 21st Mississippi Infantry captured Lt. Malbone Watson's battery, which
was then retaken by the 39th New York Infantry. Two Union brigades, those of Brig.
Gen. Henry H. Lockwood and Col. George L. Willard, recaptured some of the valuable
ground lost earlier in the day: Lockwood retook the area surrounding the Trostle
Farm and four guns of Bigelow's battery that had been lost to the Confederates;
Willard's men pushed Barksdale's advance back to the Emmitsburg Road and retook
some Federal artillery, although Willard was killed in the process.

Meanwhile, desperate for troops with which to counter the Confederate surge,
Hancock had tracked down the 1st Minnesota Infantry (Col. William Colvill, Jr.). He
pointed toward Wilcox's Confederate line and shouted at Colvill, "Advance, Colonel,
and take those colors!" Of the 262 soldiers of the 1st Minnesota who attacked, 215 lay
dead or wounded after they charged, compiling one of the highest casualty rates of
any unit during the war. The attack worked, however, stalling Wilcox's Confederates
and pushing them westward to the other side of the Emmitsburg Road. Perry's
Florida brigade, meanwhile, south of the Codori Farm with Lang in command,
received substantial fire from units along the Federal center, and when the officers
learned of Wilcox's withdrawal, Lang pulled his men back too. In the deepest
Confederate penetration of the day, Brig. Gen. Ambrose Wright's right wing fought
its way onto the crest of Cemetery Ridge and fought stubbornly with the Union
brigades of Hall and Brig. Gen. Alexander S. Webb, which repulsed the assault in
a whirlwind of bullets and cannon fire, assisted by the dogged fighting of the 13th
Vermont Infantry. Rallying behind their sudden counterattack, Union regiments
of the 2d and 3d Corps, chiefly those of Brig. Gens. John Gibbon's and Andrew
Humphreys's divisions, advanced to the Emmitsburg Road and reclaimed most
of the cannon lost that afternoon.

**Early's Division Attacks
East Cemetery Hill**
July 2, 1863, about 7:30 P.M.

Late on the second day Maj. Gen.
Jubal A. Early struck headlong into
the elevated Union line of Maj. Gen.
Oliver O. Howard along the fortified
ridge of East Cemetery Hill. Fearsome
casualties resulted.

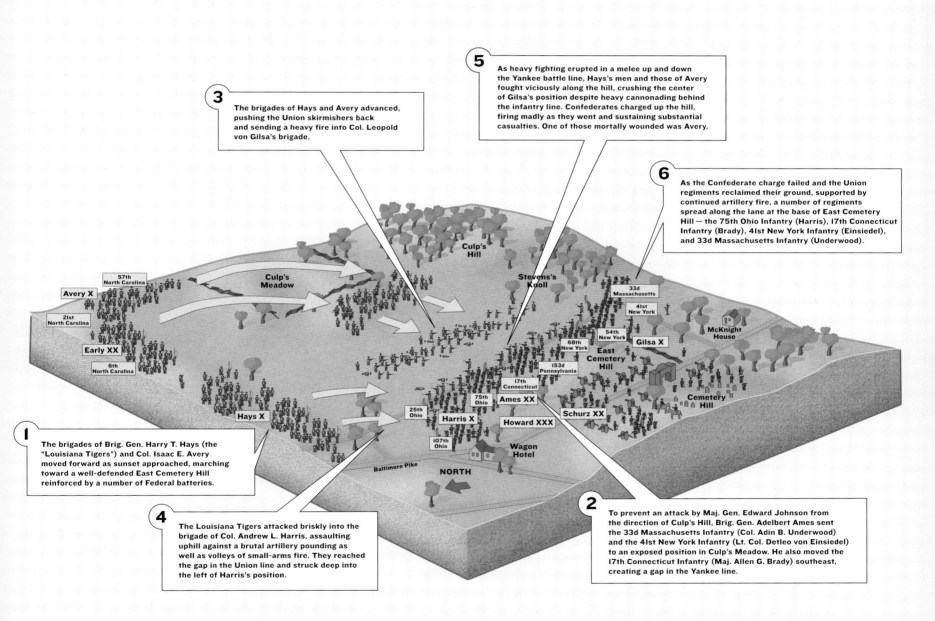

3 The brigades of Hays and Avery advanced,
pushing the Union skirmishers back
and sending a heavy fire into Col. Leopold
von Gilsa's brigade.

5 As heavy fighting erupted in a melee up and down
the Yankee battle line, Hays's men and those of Avery
fought viciously along the hill, crushing the center
of Gilsa's position despite heavy cannonading behind
the infantry line. Confederates charged up the hill,
firing madly as they went and sustaining substantial
casualties. One of those mortally wounded was Avery.

6 As the Confederate charge failed and the Union
regiments reclaimed their ground, supported by
continued artillery fire, a number of regiments
spread along the lane at the base of East Cemetery
Hill — the 75th Ohio Infantry (Harris), 17th Connecticut
Infantry (Brady), 41st New York Infantry (Einsiedel),
and 33d Massachusetts Infantry (Underwood).

1 The brigades of Brig. Gen. Harry T. Hays (the
"Louisiana Tigers") and Col. Isaac E. Avery
moved forward as sunset approached, marching
toward a well-defended East Cemetery Hill
reinforced by a number of Federal batteries.

4 The Louisiana Tigers attacked briskly into the
brigade of Col. Andrew L. Harris, assaulting
uphill against a brutal artillery pounding as
well as volleys of small-arms fire. They reached
the gap in the Union line and struck deep into
the left of Harris's position.

2 To prevent an attack by Maj. Gen. Edward Johnson from
the direction of Culp's Hill, Brig. Gen. Adelbert Ames sent
the 33d Massachusetts Infantry (Col. Adin B. Underwood)
and the 41st New York Infantry (Lt. Col. Detleo von Einsiedel)
to an exposed position in Culp's Meadow. He also moved the
17th Connecticut Infantry (Maj. Allen G. Brady) southeast,
creating a gap in the Yankee line.

Maj. Gen. Daniel Butterfield

Butterfield, a lawyer, superintendent of the American Express Company, and volunteer soldier, was Meade's chief of staff at Gettysburg. Often erroneously credited with composing the bugle call "Taps," Butterfield nevertheless was a capable soldier who faithfully recorded the commanding general's council of war held late on July 2.

Maj. Gen. Alfred Pleasonton

A career soldier and Washington native, Pleasonton rose to command the Army of the Potomac's Cavalry Corps just five weeks before the battle of Gettysburg. He successfully harassed J. E. B. Stuart at Brandy Station on the first day of the Pennsylvania campaign and battled the Southern horsemen on the final day at Gettysburg.

Brig. Gen. John Newton

A native Virginian who remained loyal to the Union, Newton graduated high in his West Point class and excelled as an engineer. He succeeded Abner Doubleday as commander of the 1st Corps after Reynolds's death and advised solidifying the Union position but not attacking on July 3.

Darkness ended the day's desperate struggles, with only the chaos of battlefield reorganization and the cries and moans of the wounded to interrupt the stillness. When an officer mentioned to Meade that the situation for much of July 2 seemed to be tenuous, the goggle-eyed general replied simply, "Yes, but it is all right now; it is all right now." About 9 P.M., Meade gathered and met with his wing commanders (Hancock and Slocum), chief engineer Warren, and corps commanders inside the tiny Leister House on the Taneytown Road, wanting to poll them on a course of action for the next day. Meade's chief of staff, Maj. Gen. Dan Butterfield, created a memoir of the event that was found in the general's papers in 1881. Its questions and answers read:

1. Under existing circumstances, is it advisable for this army to remain in its present position, or to retire in another, nearer its base of supplies?
2. It being determined to remain in present position, shall the army attack or await the attack of the enemy?
3. If we await attack, how long?

The replies followed.

Gibbon: 1. Correct the position of army, but would not retreat. 2. In no condition to attack, in his opinion. 3. Until he moves.
Williams: 1. Stay. 2. Await attack. 3. One day.
Birney, same as Williams.
Sykes, same as Williams.
Newton: 1. Correct position of army, but would not retreat. 2. By all means not to attack. 3. If we wait, it will give them a chance to cut our line.
Howard: 1. Remain. 2. Await attack until 4 P.M. tomorrow. 3. If they don't attack, attack them.
Hancock: 1. Rectify position without moving so as not to give up field. 2. Not attack unless our communications are cut. 3. Can't wait long, can't be idle.
Sedgwick: 1. Remain. 2. Await attack. 3. At least one day.
Slocum: Stay and fight.

Newton thinks it a bad position, Hancock puzzled about practicability of retiring, thinks by holding on [illegible] to mass forces and attack. Howard in favor of not retiring. Birney don't know. 3rd Corps used up and not in good condition to fight. Sedgwick [illegible]. Effective strength about 9,000, 12,500, 9,000, 6,000, 8,500, 6,000, 7,000. Total, 58,000.

Supported by the prevailing opinions of his subordinates, Meade decided to stay and fight for a third day at Gettysburg. Slocum repositioned his 12th Corps throughout the night, attempting to coordinate an attack that would recapture all the positions he formerly held on and around Culp's Hill. Though one more grisly day of battle lay ahead at Gettysburg, July 2 would prove the decisive day of the campaign.

Rock Wall of the 20th Maine Infantry, Little Round Top
September 7, 1998

Following the fighting of July 2, the 20th Maine Infantry erected a stone wall of breastworks along the military crest of Little Round Top. This view approximates their vantage point as the Confederates approached.

Company B, 20th Maine Infantry Monument, Little Round Top
September 7, 1998

Chamberlain detached one company of his regiment, Company B, under Capt. Walter G. Morrill, sending 42 men down the slope to hook up with skirmishers from the 2d U.S. Sharpshooters. The marker of Company B's position was erected in 1889.

20th Maine Infantry Monument, Little Round Top
September 7, 1998

Holding the left flank of the Federal line on Little Round Top, Col. Joshua L. Chamberlain's 20th Maine Infantry performed well and executed an unlikely downhill maneuver amid fleeing Rebels of the 15th Alabama Infantry (Col. William C. Oates). The regiment's monument was built in 1886.

JULY 2, 1863

Confederate "Sharpshooter Position"
at the Devil's Den
Timothy O'Sullivan
View southeast
July 6-7, 1863

This celebrated image was shown to be a hoax by Gettysburg image expert William Frassanito. Working for Gardner, O'Sullivan created a scene of the "sharp-shooter" amid what was certainly used as a shelter in the Devil's Den, but first pho-tographed the same body some 72 yards to the west near a prominent rectangular rock situated between the Devil's Den and Triangular Field. To maximize the effect of the photo at the "sharpshooter's position," he dragged the body and placed it along with the rifle used as a prop.

Confederate "Sharpshooter Position"
at the Devil's Den
June 13, 1997

150

**Dead Confederate Soldier
near the Triangular Field
Timothy O'Sullivan
View east**
July 6-7, 1863

The same soldier posed in the infamous
"sharpshooter's position" on the western
edge of the Devil's Den was first photographed near a large boulder 72 yards
to the west, between Devil's Den and the
Triangular Field, as analyzed by William
Frassanito. The .58 caliber U.S. rifle is
apparently the same gun seen in both
places and was picked up in Rose Woods,
Frassanito surmises, and carried by
O'Sullivan to serve as a prop in the
other locations.

Position of Dead Confederate Soldier
June 5, 1997

**Dead Confederate Soldier
near the Triangular Field
Timothy O'Sullivan
View south**
July 6–7, 1863

Another angle on the unfortunate
Confederate soldier (see page 151) shows
the prominent rectangular slab of rock
beside his presumed original position.

Position of Dead Confederate Soldier
June 8, 1997

In addition to the modern companion
view, a tertiary image shows how
Gettysburg students have outlined
the approximate position of the
body in stones gathered from the
Triangular Field.

**Confederate "Sharpshooter
Position" at the Devil's Den**
Timothy O'Sullivan
View southeast
July 6–7, 1863

This variant of the photo shown
on page 150 was shot from a
slightly different angle. O'Sullivan
photographed the same young
Confederate six times altogether,
perhaps because it was not bloated
by the release of gases, as happens
several days after death. This soldier,
who displays evidence of rigor
mortis, was probably buried near the
Devil's Den photography site; when
Gardner returned in November for
the Gettysburg Address ceremonies,
he claimed to have seen the partially
unburied skeleton of the same
man. He may have been a soldier
of the 1st Texas Infantry (Lt. Col.
Philip A. Work) or 17th Georgia
Infantry (Col. Wesley C. Hodges).

Dead Confederate Soldier
near the Triangular Field
Timothy O'Sullivan
View east
July 6–7, 1863

A variant image of the same dead soldier
reveals crisper details, including the rifle,
the soldier's hat, his frock coat, the strap
caught around his neck, and other debris
scattered near his head and body.

Dead Confederate Soldier
near the Triangular Field
Timothy O'Sullivan
View east
July 6–7, 1863

Another view taken from behind
the soldier's head lacks the clarity
of the previous two.

Position of Dead Confederate Soldier
June 8, 1997

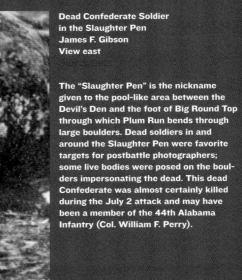

**Dead Confederate Soldier
in the Slaughter Pen**
James F. Gibson
View east
July 2, 1863

The "Slaughter Pen" is the nickname
given to the pool-like area between the
Devil's Den and the foot of Big Round Top
through which Plum Run bends through
large boulders. Dead soldiers in and
around the Slaughter Pen were favorite
targets for postbattle photographers;
some live bodies were posed on the boulders impersonating the dead. This dead
Confederate was almost certainly killed
during the July 2 attack and may have
been a member of the 44th Alabama
Infantry (Col. William F. Perry).

**Position of Dead Confederate Soldier
in the Slaughter Pen**

154

Dead Soldiers in the Slaughter Pen
Timothy O'Sullivan
View southeast
July 6–7, 1863

One of the most reproduced images of the Gettysburg field, this overall view of the Slaughter Pen shows many dead Confederate soldiers lying where they were posted as sharpshooters or skirmishers, near the wood line running along the base of Big Round Top. The identification of the area, from Gardner's celebrated *Photographic Sketch Book*, was somewhat vague until William Frassanito identified a prominent "table-like" split boulder in the scene and also on the field today. The boulder stands a short distance west of a line between the "pond" area of the Slaughter Pen and the modern Park Service comfort station in the woods.

The Slaughter Pen
June 6, 1997

Frassanito's Split "Tablelike Boulder"
June 6, 1997

Dead Soldiers in the Slaughter Pen
Timothy O'Sullivan
View southeast
July 6–7, 1863

A variant image of the Slaughter Pen
scene shows the dead from a slightly
different angle and the tablelike boulder
partly obscured by a short tree.

View in the Slaughter Pen
ca. July 6–7, 1863

Another image of the Slaughter Pen dead
survived with less impressive details.

Dead Confederates in the Slaughter Pen
Alexander Gardner
View northeast
July 6, 1863

These dead Rebel soldiers in the
Slaughter Pen were undoubtedly slain in
the same vicious attacks that cut through
the area on the battle's second day.

**Position of Dead Confederates in the
Slaughter Pen**
June 8, 1997

CHAPTER 5 : UNION FORCES SEIZE THE HIGH GROUND

Dead Confederate Soldier
in the Slaughter Pen
Alexander Gardner
View east
July 6, 1863

In 1987, a 16-year-old high school student, Gene Walker, discovered the position where this famous image of a dead Confederate was made in the Slaughter Pen. Heavily overgrown with brush for years, the area is now relatively clear. The unfortunate soldier may well have been a member of the 44th Alabama Infantry, 48th Alabama Infantry (Col. James L. Sheffield), or 2d Georgia Infantry (Lt. Col. William T. Harris). Gardner originally titled this view "All over now — Confederate Sharp-shooter at foot of Round Top, Gettysburg."

Position of the Dead Confederate Soldier
August 22, 2000

157

JULY 2, 1863

Confederate Dead at the Foot of Big Round Top
James F. Gibson
View north
July 6–7, 1863

This group of six slain Confederates was photographed three times by Gardner and his assistant Gibson. The elusive position of these images, which lies relatively close to the walking trail that now winds along the base of Big Round Top (marking an abandoned trolley line that had been constructed in 1893) past the modern comfort station and east of the Slaughter Pen, was identified by William Frassanito in 1989.

Position of Confederate Dead at the Foot of Big Round Top
August 22, 2000

158

Confederate Dead at the Foot of Big Round Top
Alexander Gardner
View southeast
July 6, 1863

Another view of the six dead Rebels along the base of Big Round Top shows the decayed nature of the foreground body perhaps four to five days after death. These soldiers were likely members of the 44th or 48th Alabama Infantry and killed on July 2.

Position of Confederate Dead at the Foot of Big Round Top
August 21, 1995

159

Confederate Dead at the Base of Big Round Top
James F. Gibson
July 6, 1863

A final shot of the six dead Confederates reveals the bloated nature of the bodies and apparently dark clothing that suggests some of the soldiers were wearing a dark butternut or brown uniform, not an uncommon practice.

160

**Soldiers Posing as "Dead"
in the Devil's Den**
P. S. Weaver
View east
November 11, 1863

Weaver, a Gettysburg photographer, created a series of images on November 11,
1863, a week prior to the Gettysburg
Address festivities, using live people as
posed "dead" among the rocks of the
Devil's Den. Rifles were propped in
many of the photos to lend authenticity.
The date of the images was identified
by Timothy R. Brookes and William
Frassanito in a diary entry of musician
Jacob Shenkel of the 62d Pennsylvania
Infantry (Lt. Col. James C. Hull). In this
view, Shenkel appears with left arm
extended, just right of the man at center
with the broad-brimmed hat.

Position of Dead Confederate Soldier
June 8, 1997

161

JULY 2, 1863

**Alfred R. Waud at the
Base of the Devil's Den**
Timothy O'Sullivan
View west
July 6–7, 1863

"Alfred R. Waud Rock," Devil's Den
June 8, 1997

Harper's Weekly artist Waud traveled
extensively to cover the war, producing
numerous drawings used for one of the
leading journals of the day. O'Sullivan's
recording of Waud among the boulders
of Devil's Den suggests that if the two
encountered each other by accident,
O'Sullivan felt enough association
with the artist to expend a plate on
their friendship.

The Slaughter Pen
Sketch by Alfred R. Waud
View northeast
July 6, 1863

Waud's sketch of the Slaughter Pen was
meticulously drawn three days after the
battle, perhaps in part from the very rock
on which he posed for O'Sullivan. It's
likely that either of these two men coined
the name "Slaughter Pen."

**Soldiers Posing as "Dead"
in the Slaughter Pen
P. S. Weaver
View east
November 11, 1863**

Another Weaver scene of posed "dead" soldiers was created with four soldiers and two doctors. Using scenes recorded at Camp Letterman, William Frassanito deduced the two doctors to be a Dr. Chamberlain and a Dr. Lyford, who operated an embalming firm.

**Position of Posed Soldiers, Devil's Den
June 8, 1997**

**Soldiers Posing as "Dead"
in the Devil's Den
P. S. Weaver
View east
November 11, 1863**

163

Another view of some of the same men posing as dead soldiers was made shortly before or after the image on page 160.

Posed Scene of "Dead" at the Devil's Den
P. S. Weaver
View north
November 11, 1863

Weaver posed "dead" on the primary
rocks of the Devil's Den on the same day
he photographed soldiers and doctors to
create his close-up views. These are
among the earliest views made of the
large boulders of the Devil's Den. This
rare copy, the only known, bears a photographer's stamp "White's Studio,
Hanover, Pa." at the bottom right. Ivan
White, in fact, took over one of Weaver's
galleries and acquired the negative sometime in the early 20th century.

Position of Posed Dead at the Devil's Den
August 22, 2000

CHAPTER 5 : UNION FORCES SEIZE THE HIGH GROUND

Posed Scene at the Devil's Den
P. S. Weaver
View west
November 11, 1863

Another rare, early Weaver view of four soldiers atop the large boulders of Devil's Den was made on the same day. According to William Frassanito, Dr. Lyford is the man standing in the left foreground. The southern end of the Seminary Ridge woods, on the Bushman property, is visible in the left background.

Position of Posed Scene at the Devil's Den
August 22, 2000

Jacob Weikert House, Southeast of Little Round Top
May 6, 1996

On the western side of the Taneytown Road, the house was employed as a hospital for five days during and following the battle. On its porch, after the terrible action of July 2, lay the bodies of three victims of Little Round Top: Acting Brig. Gen. Stephen H. Weed, Col. Paddy O'Rorke, and 1st Lt. Charles E. Hazlett.

Early Visitors to the Devil's Den
View west
ca. 1860s

Because of its huge granite boulders, the scenes of dead scattered around it, and the stories of intense fighting that washed through it, the Devil's Den became a postbattle focus of curiosity and tourism. A civilian group sits atop the rocks in this early postbattle or postwar shot.

JULY 2, 1863

Little Round Top from the Devil's Den
James F. Gibson
View east
July 6–7, 1863

This spectacular stereo view presents
a grand image of the Valley of Death as
seen from the Devil's Den. Two civilians
are visible in the right foreground;
William Frassanito points out the possibility that the men are O'Sullivan (left)
and Gardner. A dead Confederate soldier
lies near the rock visible close to
Gardner's head.

967

167

Little Round Top from the Devil's Den
August 22, 2000

JULY 2, 1863

The Triangular Field

The Triangular Field
June 7, 1997

The Triangular Field today stands full of brush but with its perimeter marked, as always, by the granite rocks collected long ago from the Devil's Den and surrounding fields.

The Triangular Field, fenced by stones placed along its three sides, was in 1863 a part of the George W. Weikert Farm. This image of a fallen Confederate soldier depicts a scene along the western edge of the Triangular Field, at a position easily found though overgrown with brush today. The attack against Houck's Ridge that swept through the field on July 2 involved the 1st Texas Infantry and several Georgia regiments of Brig. Gen. Henry L. Benning's brigade. The prominent logs propped along the rock enclosure may have helped to seal what was used as a shelter or may simply have been firewood stacked and waiting its turn.

**Dead Confederate Soldier
in the Triangular Field**
James F. Gibson
View west
July 5–7, 1863

Position of the Dead Confederate Soldier
August 22, 2000

168

**Union Dead on the
Southern Part of the Field
Timothy O'Sullivan**
July 5–6, 1863

O'Sullivan's view of the same group of
soldiers, taken from nearly the opposite
angle, was a much published image
shortly after the war, with the title
"A Harvest of Death."

**Union Dead on the
Southern Part of the Field
James F. Gibson**
July 5–6, 1863

Though the location of this image has not
been identified, it was probably made on
the southern part of the field and possibly
on or near Rose Farm. This photograph
and the two adjacent constitute the only
views known to show dead Union soldiers
at Gettysburg.

JULY 2, 1863.

169

**Union Dead on the
Southern Part of the Field
James F. Gibson?**
July 5–6, 1863

A variant made from a slightly different
angle and a short time before or after the
previous exposure reveals details of the
uniforms, which confirm Union identities
for these fallen soldiers.

Rose Woods

One of the most gruesome images of a dead soldier taken during the war, this scene — originally titled "Effects of a Shell at the Battle of Gettysburg" — brings home the human cost of warfare like few others. The rifle laid across the soldier's legs, and the perforated canteen, are effective props, but the damage to the poor boy's frame — the tremendous damage to his midsection, and the severed hand — is appalling. Whether or not the soldier was struck by artillery or simply killed by small-arms fire and subsequently scavenged by animals after death is a matter of conjecture.

Confederate Dead in Rose Woods
Alexander Gardner
View southeast
July 5–6, 1863

Just two or three days after the battle, Gardner shot 12 images of Confederate dead on the southwestern edge of Rose Woods, which as William Frassanito has pointed out constitutes the largest photographic study of a group of dead soldiers made during the Civil War. Altogether, 44 bodies of Confederates appear in the series. They were likely Georgians or South Carolinians, members of the brigades of Brig. Gens. Paul J. Semmes or Joseph B. Kershaw. It appears likely that many of the casualties may be the result of the encounter on July 2 between Semmes and Col. John R. Brooke's Federal brigade.

Position of Confederate Dead in Rose Woods
August 22, 2000

Position of Dead Confederate Soldier in Rose Woods
August 22, 2000

170

George Rose House
April 25, 1995

The Rose Farm, fought over during the battle, transformed into a Confederate aid station on July 2 and 3, and the adjoining 236 acres of land contained as many as 1,500 graves shortly after the war. A detailed itinerary of 1866 showed 80 identified graves, all Confederate, attesting to the fierce Confederate losses on the property.

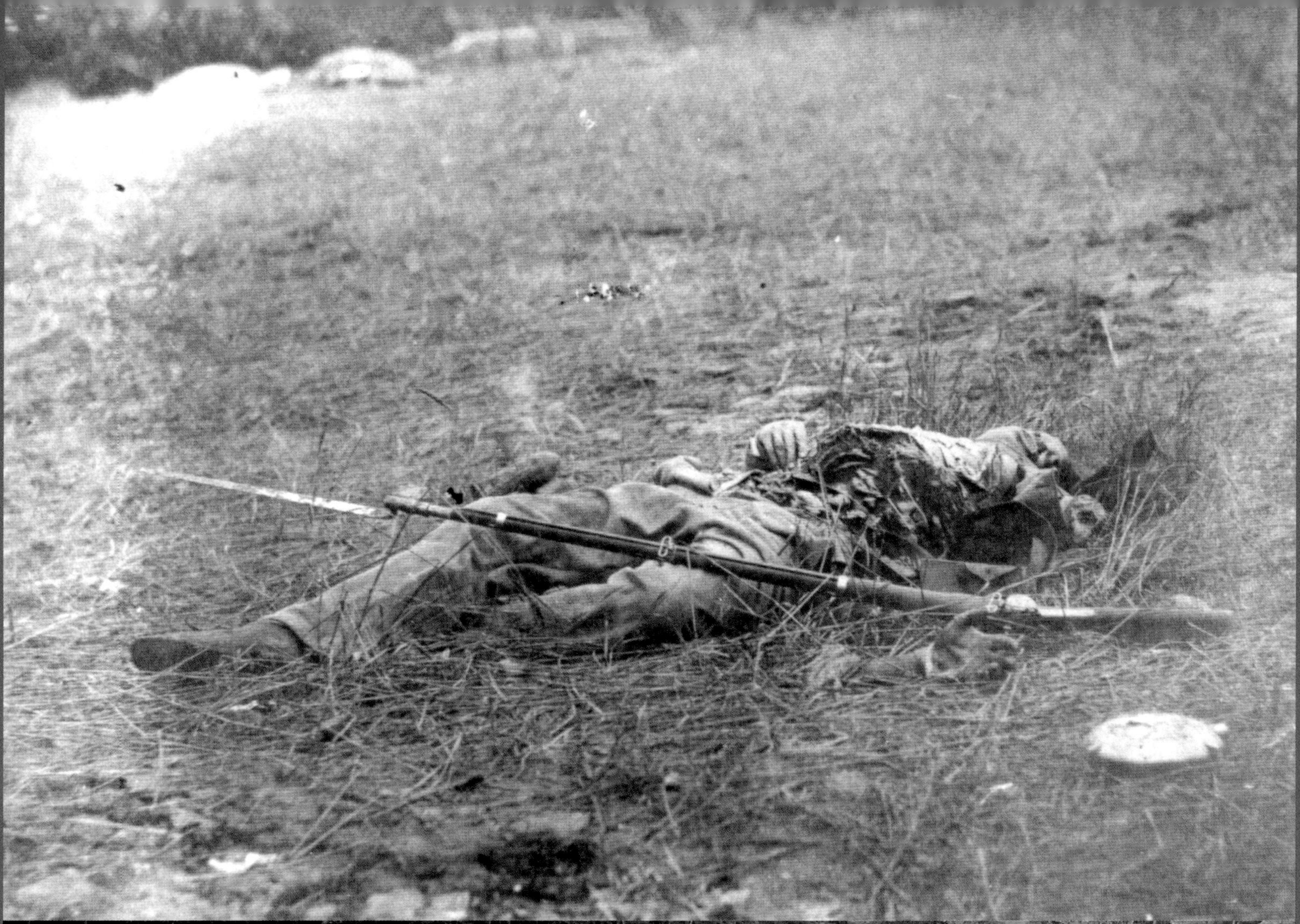
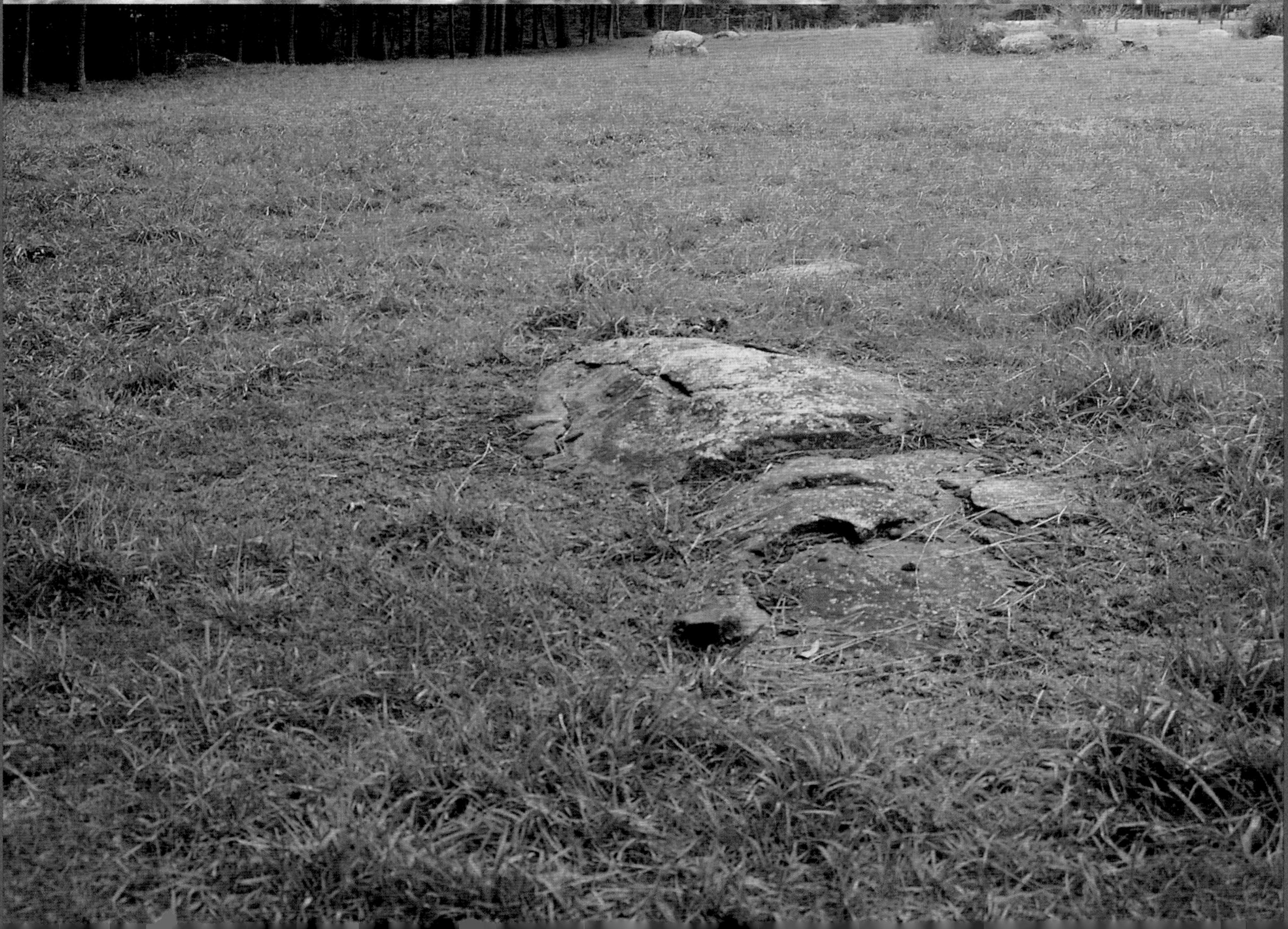

Dead Confederate Soldier in Rose Woods
Alexander Gardner
View south
July 5–6, 1863

Though taken from the same position,
Gardner's stereo version captured
a slightly different angle because of
the shorter focal length of the lens. The
canteen has been repositioned to make
a tighter grouping of personal effects.

**Position of Confederate Dead
in Rose Woods**
August 22, 2000

172

Confederate Dead in Rose Woods
Alexander Gardner
View southeast
July 5–6, 1863

Dead Confederates along the southwestern fence line of Rose Woods. The
prominent split boulder at right is a key
to identifying the position of this group.

Confederate Dead in Rose Woods
Timothy O'Sullivan
July 5–6, 1863

Another view of dead Confederates in Rose Woods reveals gaping wounds that may have been caused by battle or by mammalian scavengers after the mens' deaths, most notably in the body nearest the tree.

Confederate Dead in Rose Woods
Alexander Gardner
View southwest
July 5–6, 1863

The southern line of Seminary Ridge, also called Warfield Ridge, is visible in the background of this image of fallen Confederates on the Rose Farm. In this area the great Confederate attack of July 2 commenced, the soldiers marching and fighting toward the camera position, where some of the Georgians or South Carolinians in this view perished.

Position of Confederate Dead in Rose Woods
August 22, 2000

173

JULY 2, 1863

Confederate Dead in Rose Woods
Alexander Gardner
View southwest
July 5–6, 1863

This view was taken a few feet from the previous image. In this view a soldier lies against the prominent rock; he was either placed there or moved away, depending on the time sequence. It's likely this view was taken first and the previous one afterward, during which time a burial crew began working on the area.

Position of Confederate Dead in Rose Woods
August 22, 2000

174

Confederate Dead in Rose Woods
Alexander Gardner
View northwest
July 5–6, 1863

These dead have been gathered and lined up in rows for burial, forming a prominent V-shape in several of the following images. The view points toward the Sherfy Peach Orchard, where murderous casualties occurred. Gardner's darkroom wagon stands in the background. The dead soldiers here may have been members of Semmes's 51st Georgia Infantry (Col. Edward Ball) or 53d Georgia Infantry (Col. James P. Simms), or Kershaw's 15th South Carolina Infantry (Col. William D. de Saussure).

Position of Confederate Dead in Rose Woods
August 22, 2000

Confederate Dead in Rose Woods
Alexander Gardner
View north
July 5–6, 1863

As William Frassanito has pointed out, another view of the same group of dead with the darkroom wagon shows that the horses were unhitched from the wagon, and therefore Gardner believed he would be spending significant time photographing what was the largest group of bodies he had yet encountered on a battlefield.

**Position of Confederate Dead
in Rose Woods**
August 22, 2000

Confederate Dead in Rose Woods
Alexander Gardner
View northwest
July 5–6, 1863

Another view of the Rose Woods group
reveals limbs tied together with rope
prior to burial.

CHAPTER 5 : UNION FORCES SEIZE THE HIGH GROUND

177

**Position of Confederate Dead
in Rose Woods**
August 22, 2000

JULY 2, 1863

Confederate Dead in Rose Woods
Alexander Gardner
View north
July 5–6, 1863

Another view of the V-shaped group
of bodies laid out prior to burial.
The darkroom wagon again appears
in the background.

**Position of Confederate Dead
in Rose Woods**
August 22, 2000

Confederate Dead in Rose Woods
Alexander Gardner
View southeast
July 5–6, 1863

This view of the V-shaped group of dead comprises a portion of the southwestern edge of Rose Woods and the split-rail fence bordering it.

Position of Confederate Dead in Rose Woods
August 22, 2000

179

JULY 2, 1863

A Boy in Devil's Den

by Brian C. Pohanka

My first visit to the battlefield of Gettysburg was on a hot summer afternoon in 1964 during a family outing from our home near Rockville, Maryland. I was a rather chubby nine-year-old and with my buzz-cut hairstyle bore more than a passing resemblance to the ubiquitous kid in the "Far Side" cartoons. In those days no one seemed to see anything sinister or perverse in boys my age "playing war," and my friends and I had quite a substantial arsenal of toy guns, which we used to good effect in our skirmishes through the backyards of suburbia. These battles were for the most part loosely based on various World War II movies that we'd seen — but over the last year or so I had become increasingly and rather inexplicably obsessed with the American Civil War. This interest did not derive from family heritage, or through the influence of a historically minded mentor. It may have been due, in part, to media coverage of the Civil War Centennial commemorations, or to Walt Disney's TV film *Johnny Shiloh,* which I thoroughly enjoyed. But more than anything else I think it was a Christmas gift of Bruce Catton's heavily illustrated two-volume *American Heritage History of the Civil War* that transformed me into an embryonic enthusiast.

The battle maps in those American Heritage books fascinated me. The terrain was compressed and the scale all wrong, but the renditions of miniature armies battling over and around railroad tracks, fence lines, and farmhouses — each numbered and keyed to a descriptive text block — seized my imagination and whetted my appetite for more. I wanted to visit a battlefield, and Gettysburg seemed a natural place to start. I carried those already dog-eared volumes with me, and one site that I was particularly interested in seeing was that jumble of massive boulders called Devil's Den.

Like most kids who visit Gettysburg, I scrambled over, around, and between those fantastic rocks, and in my mind's eye conjured up an image — no doubt entirely incorrect — of the fighting that had occurred there a century before. I recall being intrigued by the site of photographer Alexander Gardner's famous image of the slain Confederate "sharpshooter" and took a snapshot from the same angle as the 1863 photograph. I was also rather awed by a grizzled fellow in Civil War costume who was regaling the tourists alongside the monument to Captain James Smith's 4th New York Independent Battery, and I took his photo too. He was wearing a blue work shirt with red chevrons, red-striped dungarees, and a cavalry saber sheathed in a chrome-plated scabbard. I later realized that his uniform left a good deal to be desired in the authenticity department, but at the time he made quite an impression.

Four years after that first visit to Gettysburg, having read several of Catton's books along with Nolan's *Iron Brigade,* Kyd Douglas's memoirs, and just about everything else I could get my hands on, I purchased my first regimental history. On a dusty, crowded shelf on an upper floor of Argosy Books in Manhattan, I discovered Charles H. Weygant's *History of the 124th Regiment N.Y.S.V.* The book was in beautiful shape, and that 1877 first edition — for which I paid $15 — remains one of my favorite regimentals. Weygant served with the 124th as company officer and eventually a unit commander and shed his blood with his comrades from Orange County. His narrative is extremely well written, frequently autobiographical, and it brought home to me the sense of the regiment as something of an extended family — brothers in arms enduring the fiery crucible of battle.

The commander of the 124th New York — Col. Augustus van Horne Ellis — became something of a hero to me as I read the regimental history. The former ship's captain was brave, proud, stern, profane, earnest, and every inch a soldier. When I found a photograph of Ellis, his appearance matched Weygant's description of him: "as trim as an arrow, and so straight that he seemed to bend backward." It was Ellis who dubbed the 124th the "Orange Blossoms" — an ironically pastoral nickname for warriors, but one that reflected a certain wry humor on their commander's part.

I was enthralled by Weygant's account of the Orange Blossoms' fight on July 2, 1863. Their desperate grapple with the Texas brigade on the slope of Houck's Ridge came to life in Weygant's words — Maj. James Cromwell urged to dismount but responding, "The men must see us today," then falling in the vanguard of the New Yorkers' counterattack; Col. Ellis leading another charge, sword upraised, only to be toppled from his horse with a fatal wound; the bodies of the slain officers borne to the rear and laid atop a boulder as the battle raged on. It was stirring stuff for a young and impressionable Civil War buff.

The next time I visited Gettysburg I walked the slope of the Triangular Field, stood at Smith's guns, and gazed upon the granite statue of Col. Ellis with a deeper appreciation of what that field and those memorials represented. Of how every rock and fold of ground bore a connection to the heroic tragedy that had unfolded there. And in the hundreds of times I've been to Gettysburg in the decades since, I usually make a point of stopping at the monument to the 124th New York and walking over to that clearing near Devil's Den where many of them gave their lives. I am told that some people visit the Triangular Field in search of ghosts and apparitions. I've never seen a spirit there myself (not being attuned to the spectral wavelength, I suppose) but I certainly have felt something deeply spiritual there. And it may be that the little fat kid with the crew cut felt something of the same there, on that hot summer day in 1964.

Brian Pohanka was a researcher, writer, editor, and consultant for Time-Life Books' Civil War *series and series consultant for the A&E/History Channel series* Civil War Journal. *He is active in battlefield-preservation issues and serves as captain in the 5th New York ("Duryée's Zouaves") living history organization. He is author or editor of numerous articles and books, including* An Illustrated History of the Civil War *(2000) and* Don Troiani's Civil War *(1995).*

The Fight for Little Round Top

by Thomas A. Desjardin

Taking in the landscape at the southern end of the Gettysburg battlefield, it's not hard to be in awe of many things. The physical geology of the Round Tops and Devil's Den and the creek that once carved the valley between them, for example, are enough to leave anyone wondering how such features came to be. I remember one visitor on a tour asking, "Who put those rocks here?" and how that simple question led to a lengthy discussion of nonglacial geology, diabase boulders, and erosion. I also remember that the small crowd surrounding us seemed held in rapt attention to this side subject, which seemed about as far from the battle of Gettysburg — the presumed object of their visit — as one could get. "Wow!" I thought. "Is there anything about this place that doesn't fascinate the millions who come to see it?" The answer, after years of my intense scrutiny, is no, not really.

The sunsets are spectacular, the view immense, but the more time I spend at the Round Tops, the more I realize that what makes them such a special place is the people. Most prominently, the people who struggled so fiercely for the right to stand on them in July 1863, but also those who have visited and marveled at them since.

Largely, the smaller hill's fame lies in the number of commanders killed there. Col. Patrick O'Rorke, Col. Strong Vincent, Acting Brig. Gen. Stephen H. Weed, 1st Lt. Charles Hazlett — all dead where only five Union regiments fought. My own people settled in Maine in 1636, and that long connection to the state inevitably draws me to the southern slope of Little Round Top, to the place where men from towns and families just like mine fought, killed, and died to hold the lower slope. It is nearly impossible to spend any time on the famous hill without admiring Joshua Chamberlain, the professor-turned-soldier whose 20th Maine Infantry held the left of the Union line on that pivotal July 2. But I often find an even greater fascination with the men who served in the ranks. Most of them made enormous sacrifices and then returned to quiet farms, rocky soil, and the struggle that was everyday life in the nineteenth century. These were men with names like Elisha, Alonzo, and Obediah, but also Sam, John, and Tom. They came from the well-to-do families of Searsport and Portland, but also from the poorer classes in Plymouth, Cornville, and Durham. They stayed not even three full days at Gettysburg; if they survived, they spent the remainder of their lives retelling the story to friends, relatives, and the local newspaper.

Ever since, people of all classes from all sorts of places have traveled to see the Gettysburg hills they have heard and read so much about. These pilgrims are as varied as the men who fought there, and more so. Despite fairer victories on other fields, even the descendants of the Confederates who fought here marvel at the place where their forebears met defeat. Young and old, men and women, native and foreign, they each bring with them and take away a different meaning from the place. It is hard to be there and not feel some larger sense of being.

In 1912, Chamberlain made his last visit to the hill that had dramatically altered his life a half-century before. As he sat along his old regimental line, he had an almost ethereal experience as the power of the place and what had happened there rose around him. Many years before, he had helped define the meaning of this kind of pilgrimage, which so many millions have since made, when he wrote:

And reverent men and women from afar, and generations that know us and we know not of, heart-drawn to see where and by whom great things were suffered and done for them, shall come to this deathless field, to ponder and dream; and lo! The shadow of a mighty presence shall wrap them in its bosom, and the power of the vision pass into their souls.

Tom Desjardin was born and raised in Maine, where he received his Ph.D. in American History, and he has lived and studied in Gettysburg since 1995. His book Stand Firm Ye Boys from Maine *was published in 2000 by Oxford University Press; he is now working on another book,* American Valhalla: Gettysburg in Myth and Memory, *due in 2002.*

Rose's Whirlpool of Death

by John S. Heiser

It's a quiet pasture, a sidelight of the auto tour. Vehicles pass slowly through it, pause briefly at the field exhibit, then continue up Sickles Avenue past the monument to the Irish Brigade, with its bronze Celtic cross and wolfhound. Most cruise through this part of the field without understanding it, and without a doubt it is one of the more confusing aspects of the battle. The chain of events was just as perplexing for the participants, who likened the scene to a whirlpool. Everyone who marched into the Rose Farm was drawn into the swirl of battle around the Wheatfield.

When George Rose sowed wheat in his prime growing field that spring, he had no idea the significance his planting would have. Ideal for wheat, the field sloped to the south, it drained well, and it had excellent exposure to the summer sun. At the southern end, where the field remained moist, Rose fenced in a small meadow for summer grazing. Rocks and boulders plowed from the field made up a strong stone wall on the southeast side of the meadow, into which Rose tied in a stout rail "zigzag" fence. Rose's woods of chestnut, maple, and oak framed the 19-plus acres to provide firewood and lumber, as well as a barrier against westerly winds that could sweep the field dry. His labors paid off, and the wheat grew rich and thick. Sunlight glistened off the lush grain, turning it a golden brown in the last week of June. Though George Rose had planned to gather in his yield within the next few weeks, circumstance dictated a different fate for his crop. Doubtless the rich field was admired by many of the Union soldiers who marched past it on the morning of July 2. Many a farmer-turned-soldier eyed that field, perhaps recalling the days when he had planted the same crop on his own land, but the occupation of war took precedence.

Soon after one o'clock, Brig. Gen. Philippe de Trobriand's brigade tore down the rail fence on the north side of the field and marched into the center of it, followed by Battery D, 1st New York Light Artillery, tramping over Rose's precious wheat. Horse teams strained to pull their loads into the field, the drivers wheeling the limbers about so that the gunners could unhitch the 12-ponder bronze guns from the limbers. Set up on the high center of the field, the shining bronze guns commanded a sweeping view of the field and trees around it. The infantrymen stood in the knee-high wheat, which swayed from a gentle breeze. The only noises were the sounds of birds and horses, the low murmurs of the men as they spoke among themselves, and the rustle of the wheat stalks as they brushed trouser legs. Three hours later, a crimson sunset cut through the haze of battle smoke to reveal not a grain of wheat standing. Rose's harvest was not wheat, but death. The once golden field was smashed as with a giant roller, the wheat stalks red and broken. Bodies in blue and gray faded to black as the battered trees around the field shaded it from the last rays of sun.

Rose's field is silent now, marked with stone instead of wheat. The veterans may be gone, but their monuments speak volumes. Gray granite memorials rise where they stood during those brief moments that warm July afternoon. The 17th Maine's stone wall still stands today, restacked by the hands of Civilian Conservation Corps workers in the 1930s. The rocky knoll defended by Barnes's men and the Irish Brigade is still covered with the large boulders that once offered shelter. Rose Run still flows by the field's edge, no longer running red from the countless wounded Southerners who crawled into it to quench their thirst and evade the hail of lead above them. Descendants of the trees that shaded the combatants still frame the Wheatfield, now home for wildlife. Rose and his family are long gone as well, the remains of their rich farm now a quiet memorial to the armies that fought here.

And on a quiet summer's afternoon, if you stand in the shade of Rose's trees, I swear that you can hear the soft rustle of wheat stalks brushing against a soldier's boots.

A North Carolina native, John Heiser graduated from Western Carolina University and worked as a historian at Fredericksburg and Spotsylvania National Military Park before joining the staff at the Gettysburg park in 1980. Among John's many tasks is editing and maintaining the park's superb Web site. He is also celebrated as a military cartographer, famous for creating the detailed maps for Gettysburg *magazine. John is also active in World War II history.*

CONFEDERATES ATTACK CULP'S HILL

★ JULY 3, 1863 ★

Culp's Hill from the Baltimore Pike
View east
July 1863

The third day's battle commenced early. At daybreak, Maj. Gen. Edward "Alleghany" Johnson's reinforced division attacked again at Culp's Hill. This time, Yankee batteries opened fire for 15 minutes at dawn, attempting to push back the encroaching Confederate line. But the effort proved insufficient. After the bombardment, Johnson moved forward with Brig. Gen. John M. Jones's, Col. Jesse M. Williams's, and Brig. Gen. George H. Steuart's brigades, focusing their assaults toward Brig. Gen. George S. Greene's line, which extended from the summit of Culp's Hill down to lower Culp's Hill. The tremendous booming of cannon and fusillade of Minié bullets zipping through the thickets blended with the occasional thud of projectiles striking a tree or thumping into a human body, with attendant cries and screams. Men moved at the double quick to fill the flowing lines of battle; sometimes a shell or ball struck squarely into a tree, sending a shower of debris flying down onto them.

Encountering brisk return fire, Johnson's attack stalled. Union defenders crawled along the ground, peeking out from boulders and sending heavy fire into the approaching Southern ranks. The 1st Maryland Potomac Home Brigade (Col. William P. Maulsby), which was part of Brig. Gen. Henry H. Lockwood's brigade, attacked from the Baltimore Pike, moving swiftly into the area of Spangler's Spring and toward the 2d Virginia Infantry (Col. John Q. A. Nadenbousch), a regiment of Brig. Gen. James A. Walker's Stonewall Brigade. Unsupported in the rear, however, the Marylanders withdrew after a short fight. The heavily pressed 2d Virginia, on the left of the Confederate battle line, was finally relieved by the brigade of Brig. Gen. William "Extra Billy" Smith.

**Brig. Gen.
Alpheus S. Williams**

Often lagging behind in terms of promotion and assignment because he was a volunteer rather than a regular army officer, Williams was a well-educated man who served as both a corps and division commander prior to Gettysburg. He led the 12th Corps at Gettysburg when Maj. Gen. Henry W. Slocum briefly acted as a wing commander.

Col. Charles Candy

Prominent in the 12th Corps action on Culp's Hill was the brigade of Candy's Ohioans and Pennsylvanians. The volunteer soldier served for a time as colonel of the 66th Ohio Infantry before leading a brigade.

Brig. Gen. Junius Daniel

North Carolina–born Daniel graduated low in his West Point class and was a planter prior to the war. He commanded a brigade at Gettysburg, taking an active role in the assaults on Culp's Hill.

**Maj. Gen.
Edward Johnson**

Johnson's division of Ewell's corps attacked briskly into the Union defenses of Culp's Hill on the morning of July 3. Heavy small-arms fire and the booming Federal cannon, whose rocketing projectiles struck the Confederate lines and splintered trees, helped to stall Johnson's assault. Two more attacks by Johnson on this day ultimately failed.

**Maj. Gen.
Isaac R. Trimble**

Virginian Trimble was an artillerist and engineer who moved to Maryland before the war. He became a Confederate general officer shortly after the war commenced. Trimble served as an aide to Ewell, boisterously pressing for an early attack of the Culp's and Cemetery Hill areas, and on July 3 he participated in the Pickett-Pettigrew-Trimble Charge, commanding Maj. Gen. William Dorsey Pender's old division, in which he lost his left leg and was captured.

Johnson was not easily turned back from his goal. Unwilling to accept defeat, he attacked again. As mid-morning approached, the 2d Virginia and the 1st North Carolina Infantry (Lt. Col. Hamilton A. Brown) spread out and acted as skirmishers in the area east of Rock Creek, south of the Zepheniah Taney (or Tawney) House. As Walker's Stonewall Brigade moved out of the battle line, searching for more ammunition, Col. Edward A. O'Neal's brigade moved forward, replacing Williams's exhausted men, opposite Greene's center.

Throughout savage fighting, Federal positions also shifted. The brigades of Col. Charles Candy and Brig. Gen. Henry H. Lockwood marched forward to support Greene in the Culp's Hill breastworks. Meanwhile, on the lower part of the hill, Brig. Gen. John W. Geary left two key regiments in place along Spangler's Lane to face a possible Confederate strike; they were the 5th Ohio Infantry (Col. John H. Patrick) and the 147th Pennsylvania Infantry (Lt. Col. Ario Pardee, Jr.). Moving in from the right, the 20th Connecticut Infantry (Lt. Col. William B. Wooster) began a slow-paced skirmishing action that would last for several hours. On the Confederate side, O'Neal's and Steuart's boys struck hard into Greene's right but, after considerable gunfire and casualties, failed to dislodge the bluebellies.

By late morning, a third Confederate attack into Culp's Hill was developing. Having failed to take the summit of the hill, so ably defended by Greene, the attack point now shifted to the open field (soon to be called Pardee's) near the top of Lower Culp's Hill. Steuart's brigade moved into position there, with Walker relieving O'Neal and moving toward Greene's center. The brigade of Brig. Gen. Junius Daniel also readied for an assault, directed at the area between the summit and the lower hill.

189

Culp's Hill from the Baltimore Pike
June 8, 1997

**Culp's Hill from the Baltimore Pike
View east
July 1863**

Avery's July 2 attack by his North
Carolinians on East Cemetery Hill
proceeded directly toward the camera
position of this view. Culp's Hill looms
in the background. The white tent at
right belongs to Capt. Gilbert H.
Reynolds's Battery of the 1st New York
Artillery, a unit assigned to the 1st Corps.
Gun emplacements mark the foreground
of the image. According to William
Frassanito, the authorship of the photo,
though uncertain, may be attributed to
Frederick Gutekunst of Philadelphia.

Pvt. John Wesley Culp

A second cousin of Henry Culp, John
Wesley Culp enlisted as a Confederate
private soldier of the 2d Virginia Infantry
and fought against his Pennsylvania
relatives at Gettysburg. He was killed on
the morning of July 2 while skirmishing in
the area, near but not on — as is often
reported — his family's ancestral land.

One of the celebrated actions in the battle now unfolded, one that was frequently mentioned in later accounts of the action on Culp's Hill. A prominent stone wall had been constructed along the northeastern side of the open field at Lower Culp's Hill, and a vicious fight erupted throughout this field. During the engagement, Pardee directed his 147th Pennsylvania Infantry to recapture the stone wall, which they did, to subsequently employ as a natural rifle pit. Securing the wall would be critical to holding the position; this action encouraged later historians to call the area "Pardee Field" in honor of the 23-year-old Pennsylvania engineer who led his men that day.

Brig. Gen. Alexander Shaler's brigade joined the fight in Pardee Field midway through, and the 122d New York Infantry (Col. Silas Titus) fought stubbornly in the line for a time. Meanwhile, the detached 20th Connecticut Infantry, skirmishing west of Spangler's Spring, tangled with the 10th Virginia Infantry (Col. Edward T. H. Warren). Resisted by the Pennsylvanians and other troops, the Pardee Field attack of Steuart's brigade failed. Oddly, one of the incidents of the moment that soldiers recalled later focused on the 2d Maryland Battalion's mascot. During the charge of Steuart's men, a dog raced forward from the Confederate line. "At first — some of the men said, he barked in valorous glee," wrote Union Brig. Gen. Thomas L. Kane later, "but I myself first saw him on three legs between our own and the men in Gray on the ground as though looking for a dead master, or seeking on which side he might find an explanation of the Tragedy he witnessed, intelligible to his canine apprehension. He licked someone's hand, they said, after he was perfectly riddled." Kane had the dog buried after the battle as "the only Christian minded being on either side."

On the Union far right, amid continuous fire by the 12th Corps artillery, Slocum dispatched the brigade of Brig. Gen. Thomas H. Neill to hold the right of the Federal line, prompted Neill to post 4 regiments on Wolf's Hill near the J. Taney House. A brief, violent skirmish erupted with the 2d Virginia Infantry. By now the Federal resistance was becoming more determined, and the Confederates met withering musketry fire that made attacking into the Union position fruitless. After receiving a stinging fire and suffering considerable casualties, the Virginians withdrew. Near the summit of Culp's Hill and the area of Pardee Field, Confederate attacks melted away in the midst of strong Union counterfire. On Powers's Hill, well to the southwest, Slocum established headquarters and ordered the 77th New York Infantry (Lt. Col. Winsor B. French) to guard the Union guns on the hill.

Henry Culp House, North of Culp's Hill
June 7, 1997

At the eastern end of Middle Street stands the Culp Farm, which served as a large Confederate hospital during the battle. The body of Col. Isaac E. Avery, who was fatally shot in the neck in the July 2 assault on East Cemetery Hill, was brought to this house.

Henry Spangler House, Baltimore Pike
April 25, 1995

Owned by Abraham Spangler in 1863, this house was occupied at the time of the battle by Henry and his wife, Sarah. Built in the mid-18th century and enlarged in 1819, the house served as a 12th Corps field hospital. Eighty-three soldiers were buried on the property and later reinterred elsewhere.

Artillery on Benner's Hill
April 25, 1995

Ewell positioned Confederate batteries of Maj. Joseph W. Latimer's Battalion on Benner's Hill on July 2 to support his long-awaited attack on nearby Culp's Hill. They received devastating Union counterbattery fire in return from the area of Evergreen Cemetery.

Johnson's third attack on Culp's Hill had failed. In the aftermath, Federal regiments in the area launched a counterattack through Spangler's Spring. Col. Silas Colgrove ordered the 27th Indiana Infantry (Lt. Col. John R. Fesler) and the 2d Massachusetts Infantry (Lt. Col. Charles R. Mudge) to assault the Confederate left. Steuart's Confederates retreated to the southern slope of lower Culp's Hill. From McAllister's Woods, Colgrove moved his Indiana and Massachusetts men through Spangler's Meadow, past Spangler's Spring, and into the southern end of the Confederate line along the edge of Culp's Hill. Receiving heavy fire from the Confederate brigade of Extra Billy Smith, the 2d Massachusetts Infantry slid westward from Spangler's Spring. After skirmishing briskly with Smith, the 27th Indiana Infantry also fell back across the meadow and disengaged. Though this counterattack failed, so had the Confederate attacks on Culp's Hill; Lt. Gen. Richard S. Ewell's movements at Gettysburg were disastrous to the Confederate cause, piling up immense casualties and resulting in no tactical or strategic gains whatsoever.

Lee now faced a deteriorating set of choices. His only fresh units were Maj. Gen. George E. Pickett's division of Longstreet's corps and Jeb Stuart's cavalry, which had finally arrived on the battlefield by the afternoon of July 2, too late to help out substantially. Accounts of the celebrated exchange between Lee and Stuart vary wildly, many having been concocted long after the war, but certainly Lee must have been disappointed with Stuart's ride around the Union army, and with his absence, despite the latitude Lee himself had granted to Stuart for making those decisions. By one account, Lee snapped at Stuart, claiming that the 125 captured wagons "are an impediment to me now" and declaring that he needed Stuart's help and would not discuss the matter any further with the cavalryman.

Longstreet had not given up his favorite logic, either. Again on July 3 he urged Lee to move around the Union left, endanger or cut Meade's communications, and force the Union army to attack the Confederates. If the Confederates moved toward Washington or Baltimore, Longstreet reasoned, Meade would be sent scrambling to intervene and perhaps would have to fight on poor tactical ground. Lee would not accept this choice, however; he could not bear to break off the Gettysburg engagement and appear to be retreating. This point is often discussed as one of the great mysteries of Civil War history, but it's rather straightforward if one recalls Lee's strategic goals for the Gettysburg campaign and how, as yet, none of them had been met. The key word for Lee, strategically — and general officers thought in strategic terms — was *desperation*. A battle needed to be won on Northern soil to reaffirm the hallmarks of Confederate success, including the Northern peace movements and the possibility of foreign recognition, and it needed to be won now. And Lee, based on the near success his men had had the previous evening fighting as three of Anderon's brigades crossed the Emmitsburg Road and closed on the Union center, firmly believed it could be won at Gettysburg.

Culp's Hill
July 3, 1863, Daybreak

Confederates attacked Culp's Hill at dawn on July 3 by sending Maj. Gen. Edward Johnson's reinforced division against the fortified Union positions. After an artillery fight, the brigades of Brig. Gens. George H. Steuart, John M. Jones, and Col. Jesse M. Williams (Nicholls's brigade) attacked into the line of Brig. Gen. George S. Greene. This attack sputtered after heavy fighting, but it would be repeated again and again later in the morning.

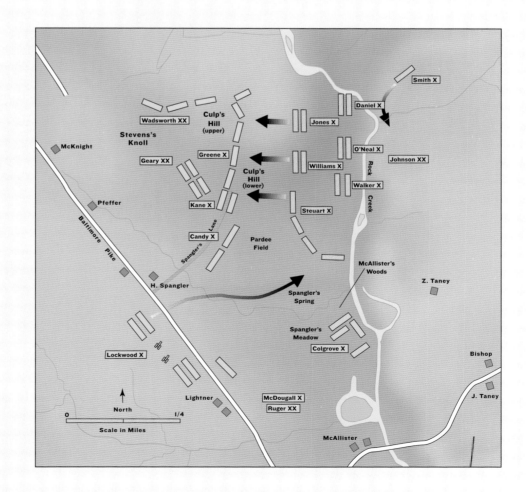

Culp's Hill from Cemetery Hill
Charles and Isaac Tyson
View east-southeast
August 1863

The Tysons' similar view of Culp's Hill
reveals a higher-resolution image of the
landscape, although it is positioned and
aimed slightly differently. It superbly
shows the stone wall that came under
attack on July 2 as waves of
Confederates rushed toward the camera
position. Avery's assault here encountered nine companies of the 41st New
York Infantry, led by Lt. Col. Detleo von
Einsiedel.

Culp's Hill from Cemetery Hill
August 21, 2000

Rock Creek near Culp's Hill
Charles and Isaac Tyson
ca. 1865

Some two years after the battle, the Tyson brothers captured the approximate position where Col. Jesse M. Williams's brigade (Nicholls's brigade) crossed Rock Creek on July 2 en route to attacking Culp's Hill.

Rock Creek near Culp's Hill
Charles and Isaac Tyson
ca. 1865

Another Tyson brothers view along Rock Creek shows similar ground and water over which the soldiers of "Alleghany" Johnson's reinforced division marched on their way toward one of several attempts to capture Culp's Hill.

195

Panorama of Culp's Hill from the Summit
April 25, 1995

This view shows the topographic
importance of Culp's Hill as a formidable
position and suggests the difficulty the
Confederates had in attacking it. In the
background of the central portion are
the Round Tops; near the bottom center
is the George S. Greene Monument.

196

Brady Assistant on Culp's Hill
Mathew B. Brady
View east
ca. July 15, 1863

Trees battered by small-arms fire pepper the fore- and mid-ground of this view in which a Brady assistant reclines, imitating a dead soldier, midway up Culp's Hill. Brady's photographs were the first to show features on Culp's Hill. On this eastern slope, Brady's image reveals the side of the trees struck by Federal fire as the Union lines defended the position. The light-colored ground at right and running through a portion of the image appears to mark a pathway through the woods.

Brady Assistants on Culp's Hill
Mathew B. Brady
View southeast
ca. July 15, 1863

**Position of Brady Assistants
on Culp's Hill**
June 8, 1997

Taken from a position west of that of
the image on page 197, this photograph
features two of Brady's assistants, this
time peering out over the breastworks
constructed on the right of the Union
line. The position here is very close
to the modern road; the portion of
Brig. Gen. George S. Greene's line here
sheltered the 78th New York Infantry
(Lt. Col. Herbert von Hammerstein)
and 102d New York Infantry
(Col. James C. Lane).

Sharpshooter's Boulder on Culp's Hill
Mathew B. Brady
View southeast
ca. July 15, 1863

Sharpshooter's Boulder on Culp's Hill
June 8, 1997

The same Brady assistant who was photographed reclining amid bullet-scarred
trees on the Culp's Hill line here poses in
front of a boulder used for cover by
sharpshooters. The assistant is now
wearing a white linen duster. The area
here was attacked briskly by units that
included Col. Jesse Williams's
Louisianans; the defenders included the
60th New York Infantry (Col. Abel
Godard) and the 102d New York Infantry.

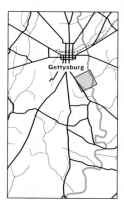

Johnson Attacks Culp's Hill a Second Time
July 3, 1863, about 8 A.M.

Continuing the movement toward Culp's Hill from the previous evening, Maj. Gen. Edward Johnson sent his three brigades across Rock Creek and formed them for an assault against the Yankees. The brigades of Brig. Gen. Junius Daniel and Col. Edward A. O'Neal also participated.

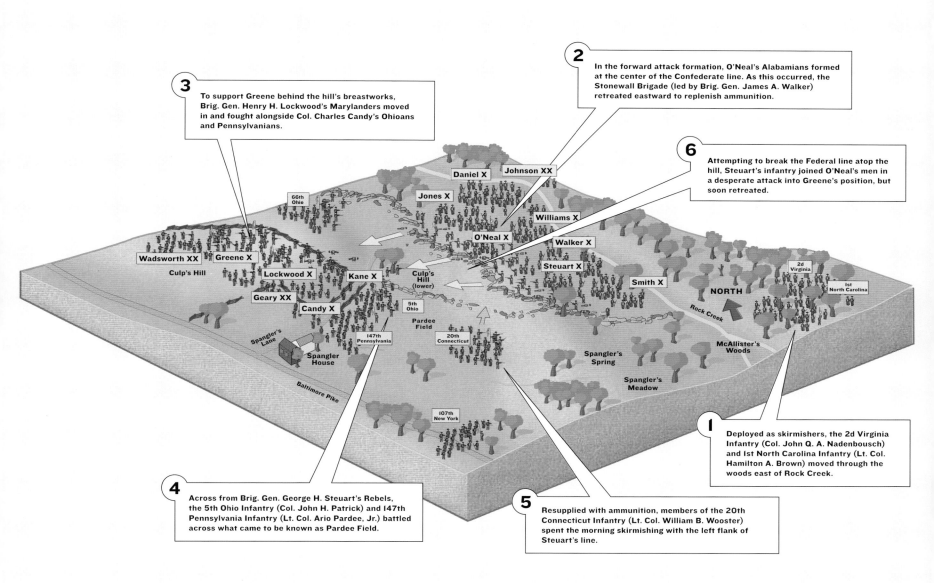

3 To support Greene behind the hill's breastworks, Brig. Gen. Henry H. Lockwood's Marylanders moved in and fought alongside Col. Charles Candy's Ohioans and Pennsylvanians.

2 In the forward attack formation, O'Neal's Alabamians formed at the center of the Confederate line. As this occurred, the Stonewall Brigade (led by Brig. Gen. James A. Walker) retreated eastward to replenish ammunition.

6 Attempting to break the Federal line atop the hill, Steuart's infantry joined O'Neal's men in a desperate attack into Greene's position, but soon retreated.

4 Across from Brig. Gen. George H. Steuart's Rebels, the 5th Ohio Infantry (Col. John H. Patrick) and 147th Pennsylvania Infantry (Lt. Col. Ario Pardee, Jr.) battled across what came to be known as Pardee Field.

5 Resupplied with ammunition, members of the 20th Connecticut Infantry (Lt. Col. William B. Wooster) spent the morning skirmishing with the left flank of Steuart's line.

1 Deployed as skirmishers, the 2d Virginia Infantry (Col. John Q. A. Nadenbousch) and 1st North Carolina Infantry (Lt. Col. Hamilton A. Brown) moved through the woods east of Rock Creek.

Final Attack on Culp's Hill
July 3, 1863, Late Morning

The last attack on Culp's Hill unfolded as Brig. Gen. George H. Steuart charged into Pardee Field and the "Stonewall Brigade," led by Brig. Gen. James A. Walker, attacked uphill into Brig. Gen. George S. Greene's fortified line. The Union brigades of Brig. Gen. Thomas L. Kane and Col. Charles Candy defended the area between the upper and lower crests. Despite spirited assaults, the Confederate onslaught failed.

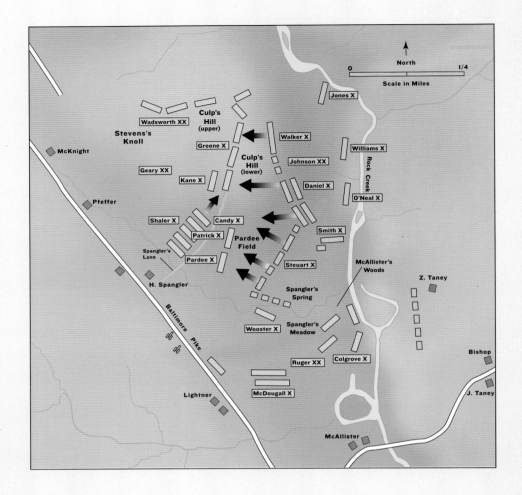

The morning of July 3 offered no significant help for Lee or his strategic goals; in fact, he had simply lost more men for no gain. The Rebel commander had attacked both Union flanks unsuccessfully on July 2 and the right again on the morning of July 3. The most promising attack had occurred as Brig. Gen. Ambrose Wright's men had assaulted the Union center on Cemetery Ridge late on the evening of the second day, but the success was only momentary. For Lee, the solution seemed to be to attack the center again. Ignoring Longstreet's counsel, Lee ordered a frontal attack on the Union center, beginning at the Confederate lines along Seminary Ridge and attacking nearly a mile eastward toward Cemetery Ridge.

CHAPTER 6 : CONFEDERATES ATTACK CULP'S HILL

**Tree Damaged by Shell Fire and Boulder
Used for Shelter, Culp's Hill**
Charles and Isaac Tyson
View north
ca. 1865

The boulder perched behind this splintered trunk of a tree was incorporated into the defensive line constructed by soldiers of the 60th New York Infantry along their Culp's Hill position.

Position of Greene's Line Boulder
June 8, 1997

201

Brig. Gen. John W. Geary

Atop Culp's Hill, Geary held fast with his "White Star" division of the 12th Corps against many Confederate attacks that aimed to capture the hill. After the war, he became governor of Pennsylvania.

**John W. Geary
Monument, Culp's Hill**
April 25, 1995

A Pennsylvania volunteer soldier and former mayor of San Francisco and territorial governor of Kansas, Geary led a brigade through much of the war before being assigned as a division commander late in 1862. Geary's monument was erected in 1914 along the Culp's Hill Union lines.

**Brig. Gen.
George S. Greene**

Greene was a Rhode Island native who graduated high in his West Point class and worked as a railroad and civil engineer in New York before the war. His son, Samuel Dana Greene, was the executive officer of the USS *Monitor*, who took over for its blinded commander, Lt. John Worden, during the ship's legendary March 9, 1862 fight with CSS *Virginia* at Hampton Roads.

**George S. Greene
Monument, Culp's Hill**
April 25, 1995

One of the nearly forgotten heroes of Gettysburg, Greene held the summit of Culp's Hill against repeated Confederate attacks with a brigade of Geary's division. His monument, near the hill's summit, was dedicated in 1907.

JULY 3, 1863

**1st Maryland Eastern Shore Infantry
Monument, Culp's Hill**
April 25, 1995

Among the latecomers to the Culp's Hill
line was the 1st Maryland Eastern Shore
Infantry, led by Col. James Wallace. The
regiment arrived on the field on July 3
and helped to defend the Union line,
erecting a monument to its service in
1888.

**Trees Battered by Shell and Small-Arms
Fire, Culp's Hill**
Mathew B. Brady?
ca. July 15, 1863?

Trees and brush damaged by small-arms
and artillery fire fascinated early photographers who braved Culp's Hill. Though
Brady was the earliest to record such
scenes, others photographed them
through the 1860s.

**Trees Damaged by Small-Arms and Shell
Fire, Culp's Hill**
ca. 1865

An unidentified view, perhaps early postwar, of Culp's Hill woods shattered by
shell and small-arms fire.

Culp's Hill Woods
Charles and Isaac Tyson
ca. 1865

In one of several postbattle views of
Culp's Hill woods taken by the Tyson
brothers, many shell-damaged trees
remain visible two years after Gettysburg.
Even after the War Department cleaned
up the battlefield of major artifacts such
as salvageable guns, the number of artifacts still visible on the ground after
war's end was staggering.

Culp's Hill Woods
Charles and Isaac Tyson
ca. 1865

Dark patches along the tree trunks of
several hardy individuals standing on
Culp's Hill suggest a long-term effect
of battle on nature: apart from the
physical damage of bullets striking and
splintering wood at the time of battle,
the lead balls lodged inside the trees
slowly poisoned the cells surrounding
them for years to come.

Tree Damaged by Shell Fire, Culp's Hill
Charles and Isaac Tyson
ca. 1865

This view shows a tree that may have
been the recipient of an artillery hit,
which knocked it over. The majority of
damage came from bullets, however, and
two dozen or more trees standing at the
time of the battle — "witness trees" —
probably still contain lead balls, as with
the "God Tree" (see "The God Tree," on
page 204).

202

Spangler's Meadow
Charles and Isaac Tyson
View south
ca. 1866

Greene's New York troops held the Culp's
Hill line against Johnson's attack of July
2, but the onrushing Confederates did
capture the vacant works on the lower
crest south of Greene's line. Early on the
following morning, Johnson attacked
again and received stinging counterassaults from the Union defenders. Through
Spangler's Meadow, south of Culp's Hill,
Col. Silas Colgrove sent two units of his
brigade — the 2d Massachusetts Infantry
(Lt. Col. Charles R. Mudge) and 27th
Indiana Infantry (Lt. Col. John R. Fesler)
in a futile charge.

Spangler's Meadow
June 8, 1997

Spangler's Meadow
Charles and Isaac Tyson
View north
ca. 1866

This view shows the wood line briefly captured by the 2d Massachusetts during its unsuccessful charge. The area where the Tyson camera was poised is now heavily overgrown with woods, and thus the boulders, in the present area of Spangler's Spring, appear closer in the modern companion image below.

Spangler's Meadow
August 22, 2000

Spangler's Spring
April 25, 1995

Near Spangler's Meadow stand the boulders and a little spring fittingly termed Spangler's Spring. Numerous stories of wounded soldiers crawling to the spring and sharing water in the midst of the three-day battle are probably spurious.

CHAPTER 6 : CONFEDERATES ATTACK CULP'S HILL

By late morning, when Lee hoped to initiate the attack, he found Longstreet planning for a movement around the right. A defining moment occurred between the commander of the Army of Northern Virginia and his chief subordinate, as Longstreet proclaimed words to the effect of, "General, I have been a soldier all my life. I have been with soldiers engaged in fights by couples, by squads, companies, regiments, divisions, and armies, and should know, as well as anyone, what soldiers can do. It is my opinion that no fifteen thousand men ever arranged for battle can take that position."

Lee would not hear of it, though. "The enemy is there, and I am going to strike him," he replied. As Longstreet recalled, "Nothing was left but to proceed." Lee would be in for more unpleasantness, however. He could not know that the relatively weak Union center attacked by Wright had been reinforced on the night of July 2 by Federal troops that had been sent away from the line earlier in the evening, and that 1st and 3d Corps veterans had been placed in support as reinforcements for other threatened sectors. Such a Union center would comprise a formidable position to attack.

207

**Spangler's Meadow from
the Baltimore Pike
Charles and Isaac Tyson
View northeast
ca. 1866**

**Another Tyson view reveals Spangler's
Meadow in the foreground and, in the
far background, land belonging to
the Zachariah Taney Farm. Colgrove's
advance into the field began along the
distant wood line in this image.**

THE BLOODY REPULSE
OF PICKETT'S
CHARGE

★ JULY 3, 1863 ★

Leister House
View northwest
July 6, 1863

**Gardner photographed the house
three days after the battle, showing
considerable debris along the Taneytown
Road and the Leister Barn at left.**

The second half of day three at Gettysburg culminated in a vicious, bloody climax. The decisive battle would not occur on Culp's Hill, after all: that engagement ended by late morning. As the Culp's Hill threat began to subside, Meade's artillery chief, Brig. Gen. Henry J. Hunt, commenced an inspection tour of the Federal cannon posted along Cemetery Ridge. As Hunt observed the status of his guns and ammunition, he watched with amazement as Confederate guns were established along a long line extending from a point just south of the town, southward along Seminary Ridge, to near the Peach Orchard. The Union artillerist pondered the meaning of these large Confederate concentrations. By 11 A.M. he had to wonder whether the maneuver aimed to protect against a Union attack or simply to reinforce the main battle line and liberate men who could support Ewell's attack. A third, seemingly unlikely, scenario must have sprung to mind: Was the artillery being massed to prepare for a major Confederate attack on the Union center? Perhaps Confederate gunners wished to engage in an artillery duel, forcing Union cannoneers to deplete themselves of ammunition before the Rebel infantry marched forward. If that were the intention, Hunt determined to hold ammunition in reserve so that he would be able to open fire as troops approached within close range.

Leister House
View northwest
June 8, 1997

Hunt termed the array of Confederate guns "an unbroken mass" that covered a vast amount of ground; he believed they constituted "a magnificent display." The Federal commander now took advantage of a lull over the field. Invited by Brig. Gen. John Gibbon to sit and rest after a long morning of observing the battle's evolution, sometime between 11 A.M. and noon George Meade placed himself on a cracker box near the Leister House. Others of the Federal high command were there: Hancock, Newton, Pleasonton, and many 2d Corps staff officers. The group dined on stewed chickens and discussed the opportunities for action in the afternoon.

At the Confederate headquarters, Lee did not issue the anticipated orders to advance all through the morning. Finally, around 1 P.M., he sent an order to begin the artillery barrage that would precede the planned Confederate attack. Some 160 Confederate guns commenced firing. After the massed guns had fired, Confederate Brig. Gen. Evander M. Law concluded, "The cannonade in the center . . . presented one of the most magnificent battle-scenes witnessed during the war. Looking up the valley toward Gettysburg, the hills on either side were capped with crowns of flame and smoke, as 300 guns, about equally divided between the two ridges, vomited their iron hail upon each other."

JULY 3, 1863

211

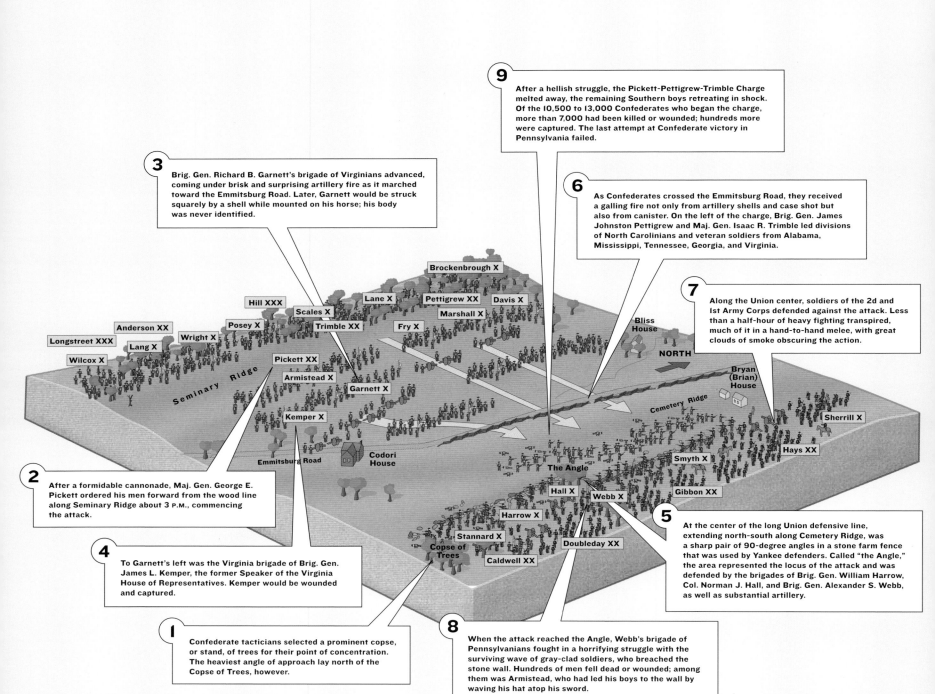

The Pickett-Pettigrew-Trimble Charge
July 3, 1863, Mid-Afternoon

Believing the Union center vulnerable (it had actually been reinforced), Gen. Robert E. Lee determined to make one more strike at the Yankee battle line. A massive artillery bombardment preceded the charge, which melted away in failure after some of the war's most intense hand-to-hand fighting.

Gettysburg

9 After a hellish struggle, the Pickett-Pettigrew-Trimble Charge melted away, the remaining Southern boys retreating in shock. Of the 10,500 to 13,000 Confederates who began the charge, more than 7,000 had been killed or wounded; hundreds more were captured. The last attempt at Confederate victory in Pennsylvania failed.

3 Brig. Gen. Richard B. Garnett's brigade of Virginians advanced, coming under brisk and surprising artillery fire as it marched toward the Emmitsburg Road. Later, Garnett would be struck squarely by a shell while mounted on his horse; his body was never identified.

6 As Confederates crossed the Emmitsburg Road, they received a galling fire not only from artillery shells and case shot but also from canister. On the left of the charge, Brig. Gen. James Johnston Pettigrew and Maj. Gen. Isaac R. Trimble led divisions of North Carolinians and veteran soldiers from Alabama, Mississippi, Tennessee, Georgia, and Virginia.

7 Along the Union center, soldiers of the 2d and 1st Army Corps defended against the attack. Less than a half-hour of heavy fighting transpired, much of it in a hand-to-hand melee, with great clouds of smoke obscuring the action.

2 After a formidable cannonade, Maj. Gen. George E. Pickett ordered his men forward from the wood line along Seminary Ridge about 3 P.M., commencing the attack.

4 To Garnett's left was the Virginia brigade of Brig. Gen. James L. Kemper, the former Speaker of the Virginia House of Representatives. Kemper would be wounded and captured.

5 At the center of the long Union defensive line, extending north-south along Cemetery Ridge, was a sharp pair of 90-degree angles in a stone farm fence that was used by Yankee defenders. Called "the Angle," the area represented the locus of the attack and was defended by the brigades of Brig. Gen. William Harrow, Col. Norman J. Hall, and Brig. Gen. Alexander S. Webb, as well as substantial artillery.

1 Confederate tacticians selected a prominent copse, or stand, of trees for their point of concentration. The heaviest angle of approach lay north of the Copse of Trees, however.

8 When the attack reached the Angle, Webb's brigade of Pennsylvanians fought in a horrifying struggle with the surviving wave of gray-clad soldiers, who breached the stone wall. Hundreds of men fell dead or wounded; among them was Armistead, who had led his boys to the wall by waving his hat atop his sword.

Brockenbrough X
Lane X
Pettigrew XX
Davis X
Hill XXX
Scales X
Marshall X
Longstreet XXX
Anderson XX
Posey X
Trimble XX
Fry X
Lang X
Wright X
Bliss House
Wilcox X
Seminary Ridge
Pickett XX
Armistead X
Garnett X
NORTH
Bryan (Brian) House
Kemper X
Cemetery Ridge
Sherrill X
Hays XX
Codori House
Emmitsburg Road
The Angle
Smyth X
Gibbon XX
Hall X
Webb X
Harrow X
Doubleday XX
Stannard X
Copse of Trees
Caldwell XX

**Lydia A. Leister House,
George Meade's Headquarters
View North**
July 6, 1863

When George Meade finally arrived on
the battlefield early on the morning of
July 2, he selected the Leister House on
the Taneytown Road as a headquarters
and used the structure on and off
through the end of the action. Here he
held the critical council of war on the
evening of July 2. Many images were
taken of Meade's headquarters; the first
were made by Gardner three days after
the battle. Gardner captured dead horses,
shattered trees, fences knocked apart,
and battle debris over the landscape.

Leister House
June 8, 1997

To the soldiers in the Union lines, the sudden cannonade seemed like a thunder-clap. Meade rode off to Powers's Hill to consult with Slocum and then moved on to East Cemetery Hill, cautioning Maj. Thomas W. Osborn's gunners not to exhaust their ammunition during the artillery fight. To the Union gunner Col. Charles Wainwright, the noise from the barrage was "as continuous and loud as that from the falls of Niagara." Maj. Gen. Oliver O. Howard, commanding the 11th Corps on East Cemetery Hill, recalled, "Shells burst in the air, on the ground, at our right and left, and in front, killing men and horses, exploding caissons, overturning tombstones, and smashing fences. The troops hugged their cover, when they had any, as well as they could. One regiment of Steinwehr's was fearfully cut to pieces by a shell. Several officers passing a certain path within a stone's-throw of my position were either killed or wounded. . . . As there seemed to be actually no place of safety, my staff officers sat by me nearly in front of four [ten-pound] Parrott guns that played over our heads, almost every available space being covered by artillery."

Hunt could not hold back forever, despite his concerns over conserving ammunition. Federal guns answered with a tremendous blast of their own. During this phase of the battle, citizens of the Pennsylvania countryside as far away as Pittsburgh claimed to have heard low rumbles. The Federal ring of cannon consisted of 175 field pieces in line, including 132 posted between Little Round Top and Cemetery Hill. Hunt also had 95 pieces waiting in reserve that could be brought up to the front lines. This complex of Yankee artillery was separated into three components: the south Cemetery Ridge line (or McGilvery's line), which commanded Plum Run Valley; the Cemetery Ridge line (Hazard's line), commanding the area at the Union center and from south of the Codori Farm north to the Bliss Farm; and the Cemetery Hill line (Osborn's line), which was commanded by Osborn and Wainwright and swept the position from northern Seminary Ridge to the Codori Farm.

As the artillery duel continued, with blasts of debris occasionally flying upward along the field, Hunt, Howard, Osborn, and Maj. Gen. Carl Schurz stood talking on East Cemetery Hill. Osborn proposed suddenly ceasing fire to suggest to the Southern gunners that the Union line was running low on ammunition, hoping that Lee might take the bait and attack with infantry. "Hunt said that he thought I was correct," wrote Osborn, "and if Howard agreed to it, he would give the order. Howard thought the suggestion a good one and said that he would like to see the experiment tried. . . . [Hunt] then gave the order to stop firing and said that he would ride down the line and stop all the batteries."

213

JULY 3, 1863

Leister House
View northeast
November 20, 1863

Gardner's stereo view of the house, the view he had planned to make when he also photographed Benjamin B. French, was taken from the same camera position. The Catherine Guinn House, on the opposite side of the Taneytown Road, is visible on the right background. The mound of dirt in front of the house in the November 1863 images may mark the position of a burial trench for dead horses.

Leister House
View northwest
ca. 1863–1865

A postbattle wartime view of the house taken by an unidentified photographer shows artillery or small-arms damage on the eastern side of the structure and an apparently cleaned up Taneytown Road and stone fence.

The scheme worked. Shortly after the Union guns stopped firing, ranks of Confederate infantry assembled in front of the Seminary Ridge wood line. The celebrated attack that became known as Pickett's Charge, and more recently as the Pickett-Pettigrew-Trimble Charge, commenced.

The charging troops were from James Longstreet's and A. P. Hill's corps, amounting to some 10,500 to 13,000 men. To the north, west of the Bliss Farm, the division of Henry Heth formed (a part of which had opened the battle on July 1), now commanded by Brig. Gen. James Johnston Pettigrew. (Heth had been wounded on the first day when a Minié bullet struck him in the head. Fortunately a folded paper placed behind the sweatband of an oversized hat cushioned the blow and he received a severe concussion.) Pettigrew was beloved in the Army of Northern Virginia. A highly educated North Carolinian and the nephew of the Charleston Unionist James L. Petigru, Pettigrew was a scholar and author. His brigades, right to left, were led by Cols. Birkett D. Fry (Archer's brigade), Col. James K. Marshall, Brig. Gen. Joseph R. Davis, and Col. John M. Brockenbrough. Assembled to the rear of Pettigrew's division were two brigades commanded by Maj. Gen. Isaac R. Trimble, the testy Marylander who had so criticized Ewell for his lackadaisical effort at Culp's and Cemetery Hills. (Ewell not only received criticism on this day, but to add insult to injury, was also shot in his wooden leg.) Trimble was assigned to command William Dorsey Pender's division after Pender was struck in the thigh by a shell fragment on the second day. (Pender appeared to improve for a time before his leg was amputated on July 18, and he died several hours later.) Trimble's brigades were led by Col. Milton J. Ferguson and Brig. Gen. James H. Lane. To the south, Longstreet's corps consisted of Pickett's division in the center of the attack force and Maj. Gen. Richard H. Anderson's division on the southern end. Anderson's men, the brigades of Brig. Gen. Cadmus M. Wilcox and Col. David Lang (Perry's brigade), would support the right flank. The attack in the center would come from Maj. Gen. George E. Pickett's brigades of Brig. Gens. Lewis A. Armistead (in the center, west of the Codori Farm), Richard B. Garnett (north of the Spangler House), and James L. Kemper (south of the Spangler House).

CHAPTER 7 : THE BLOODY REPULSE OF PICKETT'S CHARGE

**William H. Tipton with the Tyson Brothers'
Darkroom Wagon at the Lydia A. Leister House
View northwest**
ca. 1863

**Tipton, the Gettysburg photographer who would
become associated with Gettysburg imagery during
the late 19th century, was a 12-year-old apprentice
to the Tyson brothers in 1863. He ultimately took
over the Tyson gallery and collected and produced
a vast archive of Gettysburg images now housed in
the National Archives.**

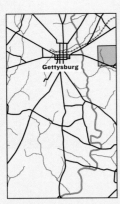

The Cavalry Clash East of Gettysburg
July 3, 1863, Mid-Afternoon

After Jeb Stuart's lackluster ride around the Union army and a subsequent campaign largely spent on the sidelines for both cavalry arms, the Federal and Confederate horse soldiers finally found each other as the Pickett-Pettigrew-Trimble Charge commenced on the main battlefield.

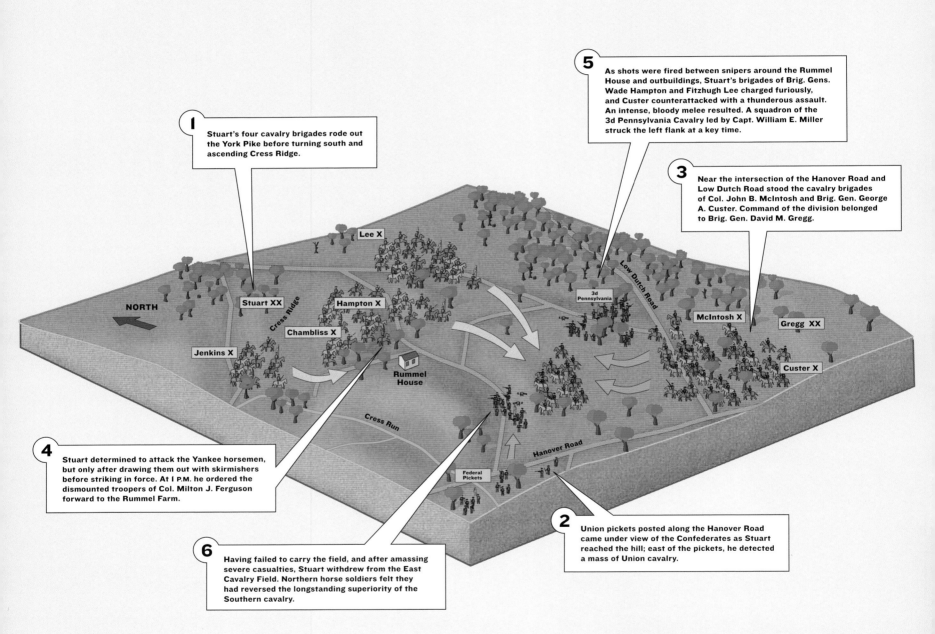

1 Stuart's four cavalry brigades rode out the York Pike before turning south and ascending Cress Ridge.

2 Union pickets posted along the Hanover Road came under view of the Confederates as Stuart reached the hill; east of the pickets, he detected a mass of Union cavalry.

3 Near the intersection of the Hanover Road and Low Dutch Road stood the cavalry brigades of Col. John B. McIntosh and Brig. Gen. George A. Custer. Command of the division belonged to Brig. Gen. David M. Gregg.

4 Stuart determined to attack the Yankee horsemen, but only after drawing them out with skirmishers before striking in force. At 1 P.M. he ordered the dismounted troopers of Col. Milton J. Ferguson forward to the Rummel Farm.

5 As shots were fired between snipers around the Rummel House and outbuildings, Stuart's brigades of Brig. Gens. Wade Hampton and Fitzhugh Lee charged furiously, and Custer counterattacked with a thunderous assault. An intense, bloody melee resulted. A squadron of the 3d Pennsylvania Cavalry led by Capt. William E. Miller struck the left flank at a key time.

6 Having failed to carry the field, and after amassing severe casualties, Stuart withdrew from the East Cavalry Field. Northern horse soldiers felt they had reversed the longstanding superiority of the Southern cavalry.

NORTH

Lee X
Stuart XX
Cress Ridge
Hampton X
Chambliss X
Jenkins X
Rummel House
Cress Run
Federal Pickets
3d Pennsylvania
Low Dutch Road
McIntosh X
Gregg XX
Custer X
Hanover Road

Leister House with Benjamin B. French
View northeast
November 20, 1863

Gardner returned to Gettysburg during the period of the Gettysburg Address in November and again photographed at the Leister House. Here, a day after Lincoln's famous speech, he captured Benjamin B. French, commissioner of public buildings in Washington, who had accompanied Lincoln's party on the train to Gettysburg.

Nicholas Codori House
April 25, 1995

Pickett probably watched the charge unfold, fail, and reel backward in retreat from the vicinity of the Codori House on the Emmitsburg Road.

Nicholas Codori Barn
April 25, 1995

The Codori Barn witnessed numerous casualties on the day of the charge. Years later, farmers plowed up many pieces of human remains associated with the battle, which had been buried and the locations forgotten before they could be reinterred. On the Codori Farm in June 1886, the tenant farmer uncovered the bones of a soldier with a piece of skull pierced by a bullet; a percussion cap box was recovered with the bones.

General Headquarters, Army of the Potomac Monument, near Leister House
April 25, 1995

The upturned cannon signifying Leister House as the headquarters site was placed in 1913.

Mary M. Pfeffer House
View north
ca. July 15, 1863

The Pfeffer house, a prominent structure on the Baltimore Pike, may have served as Meade's headquarters after the battle. The house was occupied in 1863 by a widow, Mary Pfeffer, and it stood northeast of the Leister and Guinn Houses, just south of Stevens's Knoll. In modern times the structure fell into a state of disrepair; its ruin is now overgrown by brush.

Col. Edward Porter Alexander

A Georgian and expert artillerist, Porter Alexander became Longstreet's chief of artillery for the Pickett-Pettigrew-Trimble Charge bombardment on July 3. At 1:35 P.M. on that day he sent Pickett the famous note asking for a commencement of the attack: "For God's sake come quick. The 18 guns are gone. Come quick or I can't support you."

Brig. Gen. Henry J. Hunt

The artillerist Hunt, a native Michigander, fought well in the Mexican War before serving as a regular army man in the Civil War. As Meade's chief of artillery, he coordinated the sporadic bombardment that preceded the Pickett-Pettigrew-Trimble Charge to make Confederate gunners believe he was running low on ammunition.

Maj. Gen. George E. Pickett

The bold Virginian Pickett graduated last in his West Point class and went on through Mexican War service before serving in the Civil War as an artillery officer and then brigade commander. Leading his division of Virginians at Gettysburg, he pushed for making the famous charge that now bears his name. After it failed, he shifted blame onto Lee, saying after the war that the old man (Lee) had had Pickett's division slaughtered.

218

Abraham Bryan (Brian) House
View west
ca. July 15, 1863

Abraham Bryan (alternatively spelled Brian or Brien) was a free black who lived in a small farmhouse on the southern edge of Ziegler's Grove, west of the Leister and Guinn Houses. Bryan's house would be placed right in the storm of the Pickett-Pettigrew-Trimble Charge, just north of the Angle. This view reveals extensive damage to the structure from artillery and small arms.

Bryan House
May 7, 1996

The unfortunate soldiers on the receiving end of this massive Confederate attack comprised the center of Hancock's 2d Corps. Gibbon's division was in fact the center itself, with the brigades of Brig. Gen. William Harrow, Col. Norman J. Hall, and Brig. Gen. Alexander S. Webb stretched along the stone wall that stood on a north-south axis along Cemetery Ridge. The troops of Webb and Hall occupied ground adjacent to the Copse of Trees that had served as an attack point the previous evening and would serve as the target of convergence again. North of the copse, the stone fence abruptly turned eastward and then again to the north, making a pair of corners that would come to be known as the Angle. North of this position were posted brigades from Brig. Gen. Alexander Hays's division, those of Col. Thomas A. Smyth and Col. Eliakim Sherrill. South of Harrow's brigade were the brigades of the 1st Corps, Doubleday's division, most prominently that of Brig. Gen. George J. Stannard.

The assaulting Confederates faced a monstrous challenge. They would need to cover a mile and a quarter of ground under heavy cannon fire simply to reach the Union center. Stand at the copse today and consider the attack as it unfolded: Although the ground between the woods along Seminary Ridge and the Copse of Trees appears relatively flat, the terrain is actually slightly rolling in nature, which gave Union observers along the line a good view of the approaching parade lines of Confederate infantrymen. The final moments of the Confederate artillery barrage had been intense for Col. Edward Porter Alexander, who had lost guns and was himself running low on ammunition. At 1:35 P.M. he sent Pickett a note that read, "For God's sake come quick. The 18 guns are gone. Come quick or I can't support you." A few minutes later Longstreet rode up and, after asking Porter Alexander to delay Pickett and replenish his ammunition before the assault, was startled by the response. Alexander told Longstreet that very little ammunition was left, even in the trains, and that an attack had to come now or never. Longstreet replied, "I don't want to make this attack — I believe it will fail — I do not see how it can succeed — I would not make it even now, but that General Lee has ordered and expects it."

219

Bryan House
View west-northwest
ca. July 15, 1863

Another angle on the house shows the debris scattered on this ground of the Pickett-Pettigrew-Trimble Charge and an apparent square artillery strike in the brick chimney on the house's eastern end.

Abraham Bryan Barn
View northeast
ca. 1863–1865

Bryan's Barn, just west of the little house, apparently fared poorly during the battle as well, but this view may have been made long after the action ceased.

220

George Pickett did not lack enthusiasm for the assault that would bear his name. "Up, men, and to your posts! Don't forget today that you are from old Virginia!" he yelled along the line about 3 P.M. as his men formed and began to march. Not long after it commenced, however, the attack was bogged down when the Federals, who had held back their cannonade, let loose. The attack became a bloody disaster. "When half the valley had been traversed by the leading column," wrote Pvt. Randolph A. Shotwell of the 8th Virginia Infantry, "there came such a storm of grape and canister as seemed to take away the breath, causing whole regiments to stoop like men running in a violent sleet. Shower upon shower of the fatal shot rattle through the ranks, or scream through the air overhead till one wonders that a single human being can escape. But there is no pause, scarcely a waiver; on, on on! Within six hundred yards of the Yankee breastworks!"

The resurgent Union guns raked into the oncoming Confederates with fury, many cannon issuing an enfilading fire that slew whole rows of soldiers with a single shell. The Confederate ranks closed up and proceeded toward the Union line gallantly, despite the incessant booming and smoke-filled pall that hung over them on this hot, sunny day. After crossing the fence along the Emmitsburg Road, Southern boys were struck by canister rounds, striking and maiming immense numbers of men. As the Rebels drew closer, Federal soldiers behind the stone wall cried out "Fredericksburg! Fredericksburg!" hoping to exact revenge and cast off their uncomfortable memories. "The moment I saw them I knew we should give them Fredericksburg," asserted Henry Livermore Abbott of the 20th Massachusetts Infantry. "So did every body. We let the regiment in front of us get within 100 feet of us, & then bowled them over like nine pins, picking out the color first. In two minutes there were only groups of two or three men running around wildly, like chickens with their heads off. . . . The rebels behaved with as much pluck as any men in the world could; they stood there, against the fence, until they were nearly all shot down."

Bloody chaos reigned over the battlefield. The brigades of Garnett and Kemper struck the Union center (with Armistead just behind) near the Angle and Copse of Trees, and Stannard's Vermonters attacked northward from their position. A crazed melee of hand-to-hand fighting ensued. Musket stocks were smashed into heads and torsos as a few hundred of Pickett's men momentarily fought along the stone wall, surging over the crest of the line amid a fusillade of cannon fire and crackles of musketry, with the whole scene of grisly carnage wrapped in an almost impenetrable blanket of thick white smoke. As Union Lt. Col. Edmund Rice recalled, "Voices were lost in the uproar; so I turned partly toward them, raised my sword to attract their attention, and motioned to advance. They surged forward, and just then, as I was stepping backward with my face toward the men, urging them on, I felt a sharp blow as a shot struck me, then another; I whirled round, my sword torn from my hand by a bullet or shell splinter. My visor saved my face, but the shock stunned me."

The soldiers of Garnett's and Armistead's brigades who made it through battled gruesomely with Yankees at the Angle, skirmishing with Union soldiers who received support from fresh troops in the rear. Yankees from the 69th Pennsylvania Infantry (Col. Dennis O'Kane), 71st Pennsylvania Infantry (Col. Richard P. Smith), and 72d Pennsylvania Infantry (Col. DeWitt C. Baxter) aided in the vicious fight. Col. Frank A. Haskell of Union Brig. Gen. John Gibbon's staff remembered the hellish final moments of the charge: "The line springs — the crest of the solid ground with a great roar, heaves forward its maddened load, men, arms, smoke, fire, a fighting mass. It rolls to the wall — flash meets flash, the wall is crossed — a moment ensues of

Bryan House
View northwest
ca. July 15, 1863

Another Brady plate
of the house taken from
a slightly different angle
reveals extensive damage
to the house, a decayed
dead horse in the fore-
ground, battle debris
littered around the
structure, and an assis-
tant once again posing
as a deceased victim of
the battle.

Bryan House
August 22, 2000

**Cannon Struck by a Round,
Seminary Ridge**
September 7, 1998

Many cannon on the field at Gettysburg
are authentic Civil War guns, though few
are known specifically to have been used
at Gettysburg. One bronze Confederate
gun on the Seminary Woods line shows
evidence of a direct hit on the muzzle that
must have made a terrific ringing roar.
The gun was manufactured at the
Confederate States Arsenal in Columbus,
Georgia, in 1863.

**Copse of Trees, near the Angle,
Cemetery Ridge**
September 7, 1998

The copse, now surrounded by monuments marking the center of the Union
line, was designated by Confederate tacticians as the point of convergence for the
Pickett-Pettigrew-Trimble Charge.

222

thrusts, yells, blows, shots, and indistinguishable conflict, followed by a shout univer-
sal that makes the welkin ring again, and the last and bloodiest fight of the great
battle of Gettysburg is ended and won."

After an hour of desperate, brutal combat, the Pickett-Pettigrew-Trimble Charge
melted away. The wave of Confederate attackers had been stunned and turned back,
with all of its participants either wounded, killed, captured, or slowly retreating back
to the Confederate lines, many walking backward, facing the enemy so they wouldn't
be shot in the back. Kemper's brigade took a heavy blow from the counterattack by
the 13th Vermont Infantry (Col. Francis V. Randall) and 16th Vermont Infantry (Col.
Wheelock G. Veazey).

Among the enormous number of Confederate casualties was Kemper, age 40,
a former Speaker of the House of the Virginia legislature. He fell from his horse,
gravely wounded, when a ball struck him in the thigh, passed through his body,
and lodged near his spine. Captured by Federal troops, he was retaken by the
Confederates and talked briefly with Robert E. Lee, telling his commander he was
mortally wounded. He was captured again by Federals during the Confederate
retreat, but he survived imprisonment and was exchanged after two months.

Others were not so fortunate. Virginian Richard Brooke Garnett, cousin of the
first Confederate general officer to die in the war (Robert Selden Garnett, killed in
western Virginia in the summer of 1861), had mounted his bay horse because he

Early Postwar View of the Pickett-Pettigrew-Trimble Charge Field
W. H. Tipton and Co.?
View west?
ca. 1870s

No close-up wartime views of the Pickett-Pettigrew-Trimble Charge are known to exist; the area appears only as a distant background landscape in a portion of Brady's famous image marked by a prominent boulder on the summit of Little Round Top. By the 1870s, however, a number of photographers had created photographs of the ground over which the valiant Confederate attack failed.

was too sick to walk and was killed as he approached the stone wall. Witnesses recalled seeing both horse and rider vanish in a blast of cannon fire. The ferocity of the battle was confirmed by the fact that Garnett's body was never identified. His sword, curiously, did show up in a Baltimore pawn shop many years later and was purchased by ex-Confederate Brig. Gen. George H. Steuart.

Brig. Gen. Lewis A. Armistead, age 46, was mortally wounded in the charge. He was the son of U.S. Bvt. Brig. Gen. Walker K. Armistead, who had distinguished himself in the War of 1812. Dismissed from West Point in 1836 for breaking a dinner plate over Cadet Jubal A. Early's head, Lewis Armistead nevertheless had amassed an impressive record as a soldier. Armistead led his men in gray with a yell on that third day: "Give them the cold steel!" He placed his hat on his sword as he marched his men forward, and as he led them over the stone wall at the Angle, he was struck in the chest and arm. He fell at the base of a Union cannon and died two days later at the nearby George Spangler Farm. Trimble, too, was wounded and captured, but he survived. Pickett, watching in horror in the rear, possibly beside the farm buildings on the Codori property, was criticized by many for not materially participating in the attack, but that would have been highly unusual for a division commander, because it almost certainly would have cost Pickett his life.

CHAPTER 7 : THE BLOODY REPULSE OF PICKETT'S CHARGE

**Dead Confederate Soldiers
Ready for Burial
Alexander Gardner
July 5–6, 1863**

Gardner's photograph shows a number
of South Carolina soldiers readied for
burial. They were probably members
of the 3d South Carolina Infantry
(Maj. Robert C. Maffett), one of the
units of Kershaw's brigade that fought
on Rose Farm.

**Confederate Soldiers in the Burial
Process
Timothy O'Sullivan
July 5–6, 1863**

An unfinished Confederate burial along
the Rose Lane, probably also consisting of
members of the 3d South Carolina
Infantry. The faint headboard inscriptions
"TWS / E / 3" and "WC / 3" are visible,
suggesting to William Frassanito the 3d
South Carolina identification.

As a final, senseless act at Gettysburg, around 5:30 P.M. near Big Round Top, Acting Union Brig. Gen. Elon J. Farnsworth's cavalry brigade was ordered by the reckless Brig. Gen. Judson Kilpatrick to form and charge the Confederate right. Michigan-born Farnsworth, age 25, had enlisted in the 8th Illinois Cavalry and risen to the command of a brigade. Farnsworth strongly protested his orders as suicidal, but Kilpatrick would not relent. Kilpatrick later recalled that the charge set off "through a piece of woods, and drove the enemy from one position to another until a heavy stone wall was reached, behind which the enemy was gathered in great numbers." The charge failed miserably, and Farnsworth was shot five times and killed. Reports of his drawing a pistol and committing suicide rather than subjecting himself to capture, however, are almost certainly postwar propaganda. Although often described as a brigadier general, Farnsworth's appointment as such was never confirmed.

The largest and gravest battle of the war, Gettysburg had produced staggering losses. Of the 93,534 engaged in the Army of the Potomac, the losses were 3,149 killed, 14,503 wounded, and 5,161 missing; Confederate casualties among the 70,274 engaged were 4,637 killed, 12,391 wounded, and 5,846 missing. About 163,808 men had come together by accident and made war on the hills of Pennsylvania during three sweltering hot July days; afterward, about 45,687 were dead, wounded, or missing — 28 percent of those who fought in the battle and more than the total number of American casualties in the Revolutionary War, War of 1812, and Mexican War combined.

The disappointment on the Confederate side must have been great, especially in Lee's mind. Gettysburg was a strategic loss for Lee, and because the South never recovered fully from its losses sustained there, and many Civil War buffs believe it such a crucial battle, it is often termed the "high water mark of the Confederacy." Satisfied with Lee's strategic failure, Meade determined not to attack on July 4, despite the urgings of the wounded Hancock to do so, using the 6th Corps, which had been held in reserve, along with elements of the 5th and 12th Corps. Lee's line, established on the night of July 3, stretched from Oak Hill to the Peach Orchard; despite the mauling of his army, Lee established his aggressive nature again by staying in place on July 4, awaiting a possible Federal attack. As rains set in, transforming into a heavy downpour on the night of the United States's 87th anniversary, the Army of Northern Virginia commenced a retreat from Pennsylvania, sending the supply and ammunition trains by way of Cashtown and Chambersburg and the bulk of the army through Fairfield. Amid a depressing, cold rain, the campaign was drawing to a close.

227

A Lasting Memory

by Wayne E. Motts

"I cannot believe that soldiers would cross this field under all that fire." During my eleven years of guiding on the Gettysburg battlefield, nearly every visitor to the famed fields of Pickett's Charge has made the same comment. What led a soldier in the Army of Northern Virginia to obey Lee's orders and attack the strong Union position on Cemetery Ridge at the battle on July 3, 1863? Although the question of how these men could bring themselves to face near-certain annihilation is on every visitor's mind, seldom do people ask about those who survived the slaughter.

Countless books and monographs attempt to document nearly every aspect of this renowned assault. Regiment and battery positions are placed on maps — as well as in various narratives — with precision. The strengths and losses of both sides are counted to the man. Mapmakers authoritatively plot numbers and types of artillery pieces. Despite all this effort to settle the "real truth" of the battle for Cemetery Ridge, it is impossible to ascertain all the particulars related to Pickett's Charge.

One underlying "truth," if truth can be found, is that every soldier, North or South, blue or gray, who survived the third day at Gettysburg would forever be held a prisoner by the memories of the struggle. Thousands were physically wounded, but all — regardless of their allegiance — were profoundly changed psychologically by their experiences. One hour, of one day, of one year comprised their entire lives; these men would carry to their graves the graphic, intense reminders of their part in the war's greatest contest.

It took me years to realize the true significance of interpreting Pickett's Charge. Although I collected dozens of statistics, compiled detailed maps to the regimental level, struggled to place every artillery battery in its true position during the attack, mapped the deployment of Lee's Confederates and Meade's Union defenders, I did not recognize until recently what was truly important in documenting the history of July 3, 1863: the men themselves. Not just where they served on the field and how they moved, but how those who survived lived with the memory of what they experienced.

As a result, my tour of this field has changed dramatically. I have walked the field of Pickett's Charge hundreds of times, from every conceivable position, Union and Confederate, and referenced where things occurred. Now, each time I start a tour near the Virginia Memorial and end at the famous "Angle," I never fail to tell the story of the living as well as the dead.

It is impossible to tour the historic field of Pickett's Charge without first thinking of all those killed or mortally wounded. The sacrifice of these men should not and will not be forgotten. In many ways, however, those who survived to fight another day suffered immeasurably more and for a longer period of time than the soldiers who died — and this story too should not be overlooked.

Various participants' accounts reveal how deep and lasting the pain of Pickett's Charge was to the men who were left standing at 4 P.M. Henry L. Abbott of the 20th Massachusetts Infantry survived July 3, 1863, but later fell at the Wilderness.

**Robert E. Lee–Virginia Monument,
Seminary Ridge**
April 25, 1995

Virginia's monument, often more associated with the bronze equestrian statue
of Lee than with the state, marks a central position along the Confederate battle
line on Seminary Ridge. Near this position
Lee watched the charge, and his men
assembled in the woods over a long front
prior to the attack.

229

Virginia Monument, Detail
April 25, 1995

One of the finest examples of bronze
statuary at Gettysburg adorns the
eastern face of the Lee-Virginia
Monument. The tribute to Virginia's
sons was erected in 1917.

The Angle, Cemetery Ridge
April 25, 1995

Union batteries stood in force, ready to fire shells and then canister, at the Angle, the name of which derived from a series of bends in the stone wall. It was used as a defensive position by the Union troops and was the central focus of the Pickett-Pettigrew-Trimble Charge. The Southern boys were directed to converge on the Copse of Trees, visible at left; this image looks toward the southwest from the position of the Federal batteries.

"When our great victory was over," he wrote, "the exultation of victory was so great one didn't think of our fearful losses, but now I can't help feeling a great weight on my heart."

Capt. Henry Owen of Pickett's division, who attacked near Abbott's regiment, wrote to his wife nearly six months after the charge describing a dream of the battle he could not shake. Union staff officer Frank A. Haskell took a moment to reflect near the famous Copse of Trees shortly after the end of the fight: "Near me, saddest sight, of the many of such a field, and not in keeping with all this noise, were mingled, alone the thick dead of Maine, and Minnesota, and Michigan, and Massachusetts, and the Empire and Keystone states, who, not yet cold, with blood still oozing from their death wounds, had given their lives for their country upon this stormy field."

George Nethery of the 14th Virginia Infantry was severely wounded during Pickett's Charge but recovered and survived the war. More than 20 years later, when he was asked to come back to Gettysburg during a reunion of Pickett's division, he refused: "I had been to that place one time [and] that was enough."

These reminiscences serve to remind us of the war's human dimension. Although the physical wounds of those hurt in the attack healed, the painful recollections that lingered remain key to our understanding of how the war affected the very fabric of our nation.

A native Ohioan, Wayne Motts graduated from Ohio State University and moved to Gettysburg in 1990 to pursue his career as a historian. He has earned his master's degree from Shippensburg University, acted as a licensed battlefield guide, and now serves as research historian for the renowned military artist Dale Gallon. Wayne is author of many articles and several books, including "Trust in God and Fear Nothing": Lewis A. Armistead, C.S.A. *(1994). He serves as a contributing editor of* North & South *magazine.*

High Water Mark Monument, Cemetery Ridge
April 25, 1995

After Gettysburg, soldiers of the Confederate armies always longed for the days before the Pickett-Pettigrew-Trimble Charge, a time when hope for Confederate victory seemed brighter. Though Gettysburg's strategic importance has been debated for decades, certainly the Rebel efforts in Pennsylvania (and on July 4 at Vicksburg) represent a high water mark for the Confederate war effort. The monument erected at the Copse of Trees in 1892 memorializes this.

231

High Water Mark Monument, Detail, Cemetery Ridge
September 7, 1998

A bronze book inscribed with the commands of the Confederacy that participated in the charge sits atop the monument.

"Come On, You Wolverines!"

by Jeffry D. Wert

Across the pastures, the fields of grain, and woodlots, a quietness has settled in for a long time. Few visitors come to pause and to understand; few residents have intruded upon the land and the silence. It is a place where one can walk, often alone, with history as a companion. It is a place where horses' hooves once thundered, where sabers clanged, where gunfire exploded, and where men bled amid the smoke and the hellish noise of combat.

It is a place too often bypassed, but for me, it is a place that often beckons with its silence, its beauty, its past.

For more than 135 years the land has withstood time's passage. Trees still crowd the broad spine of Cress Ridge, and beneath it, Little's Run still carves a shallow ditch through the fields. Although the fences that once defined farms of the Rummel, Lott, Spangler, and Howard families are long gone, some of the original buildings still stand, and traces of old lanes can still be followed. To the south, Hanover Road, and to the east, Low Dutch Road, paved and widened, frame the fields that for several hours on July 3, 1863, served as a battleground for warriors on horseback.

On a day overflowing with drama, this place, roughly four miles east of Gettysburg's town square, bore testimony to an emerging reality, a herald for the conflict's final moments. Here, Federal cavalrymen, as they had weeks earlier at Brandy Station, Aldie, Middleburg, and Upperville, affirmed that the domination of Jeb Stuart's vaunted Confederate cavaliers was near its end. Here, the blue-jacketed troopers withstood the thrusts of their gray-clad opponents and held the ground, protecting their army's right flank.

The battle unfolded slowly on that "hot day all around," in the words of a Northern trooper. During the noontime hours, the Rummel barn and outbuildings and Little's Run marked the contested ground as dismounted Virginians skirmished with New Jerseyans, Michiganders, and Pennsylvanians. Behind these men, artillery crews worked cannon. It was a billowing fight, with gains and losses measured in yards.

About three o'clock, however, Stuart decided to settle the issue with a mounted attack. He chose his old command, the 1st Virginia Cavalry, and these veterans moved down the slope of Cress Ridge toward the dismounted Federals and braces of cannon. As the Virginians came on, the Union skirmishers scattered, clearing a path to the guns for the Rebels. But ahead, dark against the summer's foliage, the 7th Michigan Cavalry, mounted in a column, approached at a gallop. In its front rode a new brigade commander, 23-year-old George Armstrong Custer. Dressed in a black uniform of velveteen, Custer led the counterattack, shouting, "Come on, you Wolverines!"

The forces met head-on in a crash of men and horses. Some of the Michiganders lanced through a gap and drove toward Cress Ridge. Stuart met them with additional units and sent the Federals south toward Hanover Road. But Stuart was not finished. Before long, another body of Confederates, more in number and led by Wade Hampton, cleared the trees on Cress Ridge.

"On came the rebel cavalry, yelling like demons," wrote a watching Union officer. The Federal artillerists unleashed double charges of canister, and from a hollow beyond Hanover Road, the 1st Michigan Cavalry advanced to meet the attack. For a second time, Custer rode in front, and for a second time shouted, "Come on, you Wolverines!"

The columns barreled into each other, with "a crash, like the falling of timber," wrote the Union officer. The struggle was a maelstrom as "wild furious men" triggered pistols into one anothers' faces and swung sabers. More Federals knifed into the flanks of the Southern column. It lasted only minutes before the Confederates retreated to Cress Ridge. The Federals pursued a short distance and then withdrew. Neither side wanted more, so it ended.

Today, a handful of markers, cannon, and monuments either designate positions or honor units. In the center of the battlefield, where the Michigan men stopped the Confederate onslaught, a granite obelisk to these Northerners dominates the ground. These things of stone and metal are silent in a place of silence. The past echoes to us, often with the clang of discordant sounds, but here, perhaps at times, a clear voice may be heard, calling, "Come on, you Wolverines!"

Jeffry D. Wert is a native Pennsylvanian who first visted Gettysburg at age 14. He is a high-school history teacher and accomplished Civil War author whose many books include Gettysburg: Day Three *(2001),* General James Longstreet: The Confederacy's Most Controversial Soldier *(1994),* A Brotherhood of Valor: The Common Soldiers of the Stonewall Brigade, C.S.A., and the Iron Brigade, U.S.A. *(1999), and* Mosby's Rangers *(1991).*

**Brig. Gen.
Alexander Hays**

Commanding one of the 2d Corps divisions, Pennsylvanian Hays, a West Point alumnus, former gold miner, engineer, iron manufacturer, and Mexican War soldier, steadfastly held a portion of the Union center. After Hancock's wounding on July 3, Hays briefly led the 2d Corps. He would die in the Wilderness the following spring.

**Brig. Gen.
Lewis A. Armistead**

Armistead was the son of Bvt. Brig. Gen. Walker K. Armistead, U.S.A. A North Carolinian by birth, he served during the Mexican War before leading Virginia troops in the Civil War. Armistead died two days after the charge in the nearby George Spangler House.

**Brig. Gen.
James L. Kemper**

Another high-grade victim of the charge was Kemper, a volunteer soldier who had been Speaker of the Virginia House of Representatives before the war. Kemper led one of Pickett's brigades; in the assault, his brigade fought stubbornly against Vermont troops stationed along the Federal line. Kemper fell from his horse, badly wounded, shot in the thigh by a ball that traversed his body and lodged near his spine. He was subsequently captured, his wound thought to be mortal, then rescued by Confederates, only to be captured again. He was exchanged two months later and lived through the war.

**Brig. Gen.
George J. Stannard**

Stannard was a farmer, teacher, and foundry clerk before turning soldier in the militia. He was wounded in the right thigh while leading his Vermonters into their northward attack during the Pickett-Pettigrew-Trimble Charge.

234

**Brig. Gen.
John Gibbon**

Gibbon led the famed "Iron Brigade" of the West before rising to divisional command. He was wounded in the left arm and shoulder during the charge on July 3; subsequently, he rose to corps command in the Army of the James and was present at Appomattox.

**Brig. Gen.
Alexander S. Webb**

Webb's career included relatively high success at West Point before service as an artillery officer in the U.S. Army. He acted as an aide to the artillerist William F. Barry early in the war and evolved into a staff specialist, serving as chief of staff to the elite 5th Corps of the Army of the Potomac by late in 1862. He won the Medal of Honor for his actions at Gettysburg.

**Acting Brig. Gen.
Elon J. Farnsworth**

Farnsworth, age 25 and a native Michigander, was ordered by Brig. Gen. Judson Kilpatrick on July 3 to make an ill-conceived cavalry charge on the Confederates. It failed miserably and resulted in Farnsworth's death.

**Maj.
William Wells**

One of the few heroes of Farnsworth's charge, Wells received the Medal of Honor for his gallantry in regrouping the 150 survivors of the 225 men who made the charge. Wells's monument was erected in 1913.

**Brig. Gen.
H. Judson Kilpatrick**

The man who ordered Farnsworth's desperate charge was known as "Kill-Cavalry" because of his reckless spirit. He survived the war to serve as U.S. minister to Chile.

**Brig. Gen.
George A. Custer**

Custer, who of course achieved immortal notoriety for being slaughtered at Little Bighorn, served well during the Gettysburg campaign as a cavalry brigade commander under Kilpatrick, distinguishing himself in the East Cavalry Field fight.

**Brig. Gen.
David M. Gregg**

Pennsylvanian Gregg was a highly capable division commander and guided his men well on the afternoon of July 3. He was renowned for wearing one of the heaviest beards in the Army of the Potomac, one which seemed to droop down to nearly the tops of his high cavalry boots.

**Brig. Gen.
Wade Hampton III**

A distinguished and wealthy South Carolinian, Hampton commanded a brigade in Jeb Stuart's cavalry division. He was an attorney and state legislator who was one of the richest landowners in South Carolina.

235

**Brig. Gen.
Fitzhugh Lee**

Robert E. Lee's nephew led another of Stuart's cavalry brigades. Although he graduated low in his West Point class, Lee went on to fight Indians and then sided with Virginia at the war's commencement. He was an able, if not spectacular, horse soldier.

**Brig. Gen.
Beverly H. Robertson**

Another of Stuart's cavalry brigades was led by Robertson, a Virginian who had served in the dragoons and cavalry of the U.S. Army on the prewar frontier. He was dismissed for disloyalty in early 1861 and quickly received a Confederate commission.

**Pvt.
Benjamin F. Lincoln**

Ironically, one of the Confederate cavalrymen at Gettysburg, Pvt. Benjamin F. Lincoln of the 10th Virginia Cavalry (Col. James L. Davis), was the Union president's cousin. Lincoln survived the battle.

**Pvt.
George D. Barnes**

The Pickett-Pettigrew-Trimble Charge utterly failed, and nearly all of the 10,500 to 13,000 men who participated in it were killed, injured, or captured, or retreated slowly back to the Confederate lines. Young Barnes of the 9th Virginia Infantry (Maj. John C. Owens) was struck in the knee in front of the stone wall near the Angle and subsequently captured.

Winfield Scott Hancock Wounding Monument, Cemetery Ridge
May 7, 1996

Hancock, arguably the architect of Union success at Gettysburg, was struck in the right thigh while sitting atop his horse. The shot carried wooden and metallic pieces of his saddle pommel into his muscles, necessitating a slow, painful recovery. Before his serious wounding he was alleged to have said, in response to pleas for him to seek shelter in the rear, "There are times when a corps commander's life does not count."

72d Pennsylvania Infantry Monument, Cemetery Ridge
April 25, 1995

Among the defenders of the Union center during the charge was the 72d Pennsylvania Infantry (Col. Dewitt C. Baxter). The regiment's monument, showing a bronze soldier attacking with clubbed musket, is one of the most dramatic on the field. It was constructed in 1891.

20th Massachusetts Infantry Monument, Cemetery Ridge
April 25, 1995

South of the 72d Pennsylvania, along the Union defensive line, was stationed the 20th Massachusetts Infantry (Col. Paul J. Revere). The regiment's leader was the grandson of the Revolutionary War patriot Paul Revere; he was mortally wounded on the fight of July 2. During the charge, the 20th Massachusetts fought hand to hand with the assaulting Rebels. Their monument, erected in 1886, features an 18-ton conglomerate rock that once stood in a park in Roxbury, Massachusetts, where many of the regiment's members had played as boys.

Lewis A. Armistead Mortal Wounding Monument, Cemetery Ridge
April 25, 1995

Among the numerous fatalities from Pickett's Charge was Brig. Gen. Lewis A. Armistead, who led a brigade in Pickett's division. Ironically, Armistead had been close friends with Winfield Scott Hancock prior to the war. He was struck in the chest and arm as he led his men right up to and over the stone wall at the Angle.

236

Jacob Hummelbaugh House
April 25, 1995

The Hummelbaugh House, which stands near the Taneytown Road just south and east of the center of the charge field, served as a hospital following the climactic action. Confederate Brig. Gen. William Barksdale was brought to this house after his mortal wounding on July 2. Union cavalry commander Alfred Pleasonton used the house as a headquarters for two days following the battle.

Alonzo H. Cushing Death Monument, Cemetery Ridge
January 18, 1991

Young Cushing, one of the most promising regular army artillerists, was a native Wisconsinite. As he manned his battery of the 4th U.S. Artillery, facing down a hand-to-hand melee of oncoming Rebels, Cushing was struck in the face and died at his guns. His monument was erected in 1887.

Pennsylvania Monument, Cemetery Ridge
April 25, 1995

The grandest monument on the field, the domed Pennsylvania Monument contains the names of more than 34,000 Pennsylvanians who fought at Gettysburg. Erected in 1910, the memorial holds bronze statues of Pennsylvania high commanders at the battle: Meade, Reynolds, Hancock, Birney, Pleasonton, and Gregg. Also appearing are statues of Abraham Lincoln and Pennsylvania's wartime governor, Andrew Curtin.

Vermont Monument, Cemetery Ridge
April 25, 1995

Constructed in 1889, Vermont's state memorial honors the Vermonters who fought at Gettysburg and particularly the units that defended against the charge on July 3. The massive Corinthian column supports a statue of George J. Stannard, who commanded the 1st Corp's Vermont brigade. Stannard is depicted as missing his right arm, which he lost at Fort Harrison, Virginia, in the autumn of 1864.

John Gibbon Monument, Cemetery Ridge
April 25, 1995

Philadelphian John Gibbon graduated midway up in his West Point class before compiling an admirable career as a soldier. On Gettysburg's third day, he commanded one of Hancock's divisions, the one stretching over the Union center and including the Angle. His monument was a latecomer, having been unveiled in 1988.

Alexander S. Webb Monument, Cemetery Ridge
April 25, 1995

Webb, a New Yorker, led the brigade of Pennsylvanians centered on the Copse of Trees and Angle, which fought savagely to defend the central attack during the charge. His monument was erected in 1915.

George G. Meade Monument, Cemetery Ridge
April 25, 1995

The equestrian statue of Meade, the hot-tempered "goggle-eyed snapping turtle," according to a staff officer's diary, who led the Army of the Potomac to success at Gettysburg and beyond, was erected near the Angle in 1896.

North Carolina Monument, Seminary Ridge
September 7, 1988

The Tarheel State's memorial to its fallen sons was created in 1929 by Gutzon Borglum, the sculptor behind the Mt. Rushmore presidential monument. A group of infantrymen belonging to Pettigrew's portion of the July 3 charge are depicted.

237

Tennessee Monument, Seminary Ridge
June 6, 1997

A short distance south of the North Carolina Monument stands the 1982 Tennessee State Monument, a sharp contrast to its neighbor. The Tennessee units honored belonged to Archer's brigade of Heth's division and saw action on July 1.

Gregg Cavalry Monument, East Cavalry Battlefield
April 25, 1995

As the Pickett-Pettigrew-Trimble Charge occurred on the main field, cavalry actions flared three miles east of the town. Stuart's 6,000 Southern horsemen were intercepted by David M. Gregg's Union cavalry, and a spirited fight unfolded. The Gregg Cavalry Monument was constructed in 1884.

JULY 3, 1863

Pickett-Pettigrew-Trimble Charge Field
September 7, 1998

This image shows a modern view of the charge field from the perspective of the Confederate attackers. One can imagine the terror encountered by the Southern soldiers as they traversed this enormous field under heavy artillery attack, past the Codori Barn (right-center horizon) and toward the Copse of Trees (center horizon). A murderous enfilade fire of shot and shell opened up on them from East Cemetery Hill, to the north, to Little Round Top, to the south. Fortunately, the intrusive "National Tower" tourist attraction (left horizon) no longer exists, having been felled by demolition charges on July 4, 2000.

More Marching and Fighting Tomorrow

by Peter Sutter

On the evening of July 2, 1863, Maj. Gen. George E. Pickett's Confederate division bivouacked near a stone bridge four miles from the Gettysburg battlefield. The approximately 6,800 soldiers had marched some 500 miles on their way toward glory. They were young soldiers, the average age about 22 years, and many were in their late teens. The unit was not battle tested; on detached duty for the last campaign, they had missed the great victories of the spring of 1863 and wanted to join their brothers in a great defeat of the Union army.

The previous day had seen Pickett and his division some 30 miles away, at Chambersburg. A long forced march over a rocky turnpike, with the boys carrying rations and ammunition enough for battle, took its toll. By the time the division reached Gettysburg, fatigue was all over it. Although Pickett's men were overwhelmed by heat and exhaustion, there would be little time to recover or rest. Their orders were to prepare for marching early the following morning. The dull thud of booming cannon and dim crackles of musketry fire, coupled with the spectrum of noises of a bivouacked army, made a difficult evening. All the while, rumors were circulating that a big Federal assault would take place in the wee hours of the morning.

The exuberance of youth, the desire to participate in a victorious battle, and feeling of loyalty to their state of Virginia gave Pickett's troops their resolve. It would be much in need as the events of July 3 unfolded. The evening before marching into battle, the boys wrote letters home, collected their thoughts, ate what they could, and tried to sleep. Adrenaline coursing through their veins must have made sleep very difficult. At 3 a.m. the sound of reveille signaled Pickett's division to a new day. After breakfast and roll call, the soldiers began their march toward Gettysburg.

They marched down Knoxlyn Road, then east on Hereter's Mill Road, then south on a farming road, across Willoughby's Run, and finally east toward Spangler's Woods. The last part of the march employed a portion of Seminary Ridge to shield the soldiers from view by the Union army and brought the division into position for a planned assault. Lee's plan called for an early attack, but a number of factors caused delays. The troops sat and waited.

Sometime after positioning the artillery and assembling the remnants of all available ammunition, orders passed along to fire the guns. The cannon began pelting on the Union line at approximately 1 p.m. on July 3. This monstrous barrage continued in earnest as the Union Army answered with dozens of field guns along Cemetery Ridge. The Union artillery slowed its fire; the cannon fired intermittently, with long periods of silence between each blast. The time for the assault was at hand. The Union artillery was low on ammunition, or so it seemed. The Confederate artillery was also running low on shot. The gallant troops in Pickett's division knew what to expect. They prepared themselves for the glory of destiny. They marched forward against the heavy blasts of Federal cannon, into the pages of legend.

Peter Sutter was born in Washington, D.C., and raised in Alexandria, Virginia, among constant reminders of the Civil War. He visited many battlefields throughout his childhood, growing interested in the war at an early age. Gettysburg is his favorite place. He is a member of Milwaukee's Civil War Round Table, an avid photographer, and a technology consultant.

CHAPTER 8

RETREAT TO THE POTOMAC

★ JULY 4–JULY 14, 1863 ★

Maj. Gen. George G. Meade

Though criticized at the time and by later
historians for not pursuing the retreating
Confederates vigorously enough,
Meade served as a solid commander of
the Army of the Potomac at Gettysburg,
particularly since he had just received
the command days before the battle.
He continued to lead the North's premier
eastern army until the Confederate
surrender at Appomattox.

George Meade has been soundly criticized since the battle of Gettysburg ended for not pursuing the Confederates vigorously during the days that followed. Meade might have ended the war in mid-1863, some historians have claimed, by smashing into Lee's army as it scurried away. Indeed, at the time, many officers and government officials were angry at Meade for allowing the Rebels to "escape" back into the South. "We are tired of scientific leaders and regard strategy as it is called — a humbug. Next thing to cowardice. What we want is a leader who will go ahead," wrote Alexander Hays of his army commander's failure to pursue the Confederates more vigorously. "We have done an incredible amount of labour, if we have accomplished but little," penned John Sedgwick. Lincoln was very upset during the final days of the Gettysburg campaign, believing that Meade had lost an opportunity to deal a crushing blow to the Southern army. But viewed dispassionately, in hindsight, both armies had been seriously bludgeoned and were hardly capable of continued fighting after the three-day affair in the Pennsylvania hills. Lee had lost nearly one man out of every three, and Meade one out of four. Ammunition and supplies were almost entirely depleted from both armies. The dismal weather on Independence Day did not bolster any idea of pursuit along the bogged-down roads. (It is curious to note that, as many soldiers commented, heavy rains almost invariably followed major battles, and indeed waterlogged, bloated bodies are visible in many of the postbattle photographs of Gettysburg victims.) Although Lee had been soundly defeated at Gettysburg, marking his poorest performance on the field, he did not yield the initiative to Meade. The Federal commander reorganized and took stock of his army on July 4; he halfheartedly organized a reconnaissance for the following day, but by then Lee's army had slipped away.

Skirmishing erupted on July 6 at Hagerstown and Williamsport, Maryland, but Meade did not throw troops into pursuit. Lee faced significant danger by relying for his route of retreat on a single pontoon bridge across the Potomac River at Falling Waters, Maryland. Without this bridge over the river, which was now rising with the rains, Lee's men would be trapped against the Potomac. Indeed, when they reached the river (Lee arrived at Williamsport, along the river, on July 7), they saw the bridge was gone: Union cavalry commanded by Maj. Gen. William H. French had been ordered to destroy it on July 3.

For Lee, the march itself did not go well. Straggling and desertion were rampant, reducing the army's strength to about 35,000. With rising concern bordering on alarm, Lee had his hungry, soaked, and demoralized men entrench along the river as engineer troops dismantled warehouses and barns, gathering material to use in constructing a new bridge. Lee wrote Ewell from Hagerstown, anticipating a possible attack: "Strengthen your line, rectifying your position as circumstances require, & do every thing in your power to ensure success."

Bedazzled by the loss of men at Gettysburg, still organizing his command of the army, Meade approached the retreating Confederates cautiously and on July 12 held another council of war. Conservatism prevailed, and Meade determined not to attack the retreating Southern troops. Contrary advice reached him from several sides: general-in-chief Halleck had telegraphed Meade that same day, warning him: "Call no council of war. It is proverbial that councils of war never fight. . . . Do not let the enemy escape." Lincoln was almost fanatical about not allowing the Rebels to escape. But officers along with Meade, those who knew the exhausted condition of the army, had more conservative views on continuing to fight. Meade was not the only one under attack: Halleck, too, was feeling the heat for his perceived inaction and incompetence. In Washington, Navy Secretary Gideon Welles wrote: "He has suggested nothing, decided nothing, done nothing but scold and smoke and scratch his elbows. It is possible the energies of the nation should be wasted by the incapacity of such a man?" On the night of July 13 and early the following morning, before Meade could bring himself to attack, Lee began crossing his army into West Virginia. Brig. Gen. John Buford's cavalry detected the move on July 14 and fought an action at Falling Waters that captured 500 prisoners and inflicted a number of casualties, including mortally wounding the beloved Brig. Gen. James Johnston Pettigrew, who was struck by a pistol shot in the left abdomen; he died three days later.

Capt. Wayland F. Dunaway of the 40th Virginia Infantry was one of the officers captured at Falling Waters. His account of the trip to a Yankee prison reflects surprisingly jovial relations between the two sides, who had so recently tried to annihilate each other. As the prisoners were in transit, Yankees guarded them and offered plentiful food and drink each night. "The supper being ended, a polite negro who looked like an Old Virginia darky, and who acted in the two-fold capacity of cook and butler, cleared away the dishes and supplied their place with cigars and bottles of liquor of several varieties," reflected Dunaway. "More than once or twice the bottles passed from hand to hand. . . . In the midst of this hilarious scene our Yankee host proposed a health to President Lincoln, which we of the Gray declined to drink; whereupon I offered to substitute a joint health to Abe Lincoln and Jeff. Davis, which they of the Blue rejected. I then proposed the toast, 'The early termination of the war to the satisfaction of all concerned,' and that was cordially drunk by all."

A skirmish erupted near the old Antietam battlefield at Shepherdstown, West Virginia, as Lee's army began to move back up the Shenandoah Valley. "I said 'Boys drop that Rebel flag,'" wrote Union soldier Samuel E. Cormany of the fight. "We fired — the flag fell. Another reb picked it up — another little volley and dropped it again — another picked it up, and stepped behind a lone tree — held it out, i.e., the flagpole rested on the ground — the arm extending from the tree — held the pole erect. Again our little group fired 'for that arm' and the flag fell."

The mood of soldiers on both sides seemed to have lightened — any time away from the terrorizing moments of battle would seem to do that. But Lincoln and Lee were still morose. "I was deeply mortified by the escape of Lee across the Potomac," Lincoln informed Maj. Gen. Oliver O. Howard a week after Falling Waters, "because the substantial destruction of his army would have ended the war, and because I believed, such destruction was perfectly easy — believed that Gen. Meade and his noble army had expended all the skill, and toil, and blood, up to the ripe harvest, and then let the crop go to waste. . . . A few days having passed, I am now profoundly grateful for what was done, without criticism for what was not done. Gen. Meade has my confidence as a brave and skillful officer, and a true man."

243

244

Lee's retreat
July 13, 1863

Following the disastrous Pickett-Pettigrew-Trimble Charge and a day of reorganization, Lee sent his troops southward on a retreat, held up by rain-swollen roads and rivers. After a rear-guard action at Falling Waters (in which Brig. Gen. James Johnston Pettigrew was mortally wounded), the Southern Army fled back across the Potomac to carry on the war for two more bloody years.

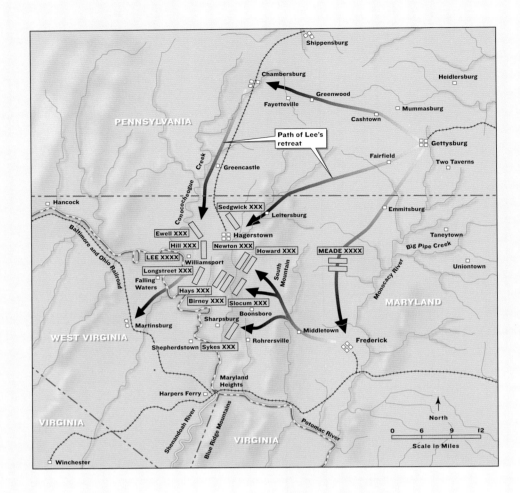

Lee, shamed by his performance, offered to resign. By August 8 he wrote Jefferson Davis, "I . . . request Your Excellency to take measures to supply my place. . . . I cannot even accomplish what I myself desire. How can I fulfill the expectations of others? In addition I sensibly feel the growing failure of my bodily strength. . . . Everything, therefore, points to the advantages to be derived from a new commander, and I the more anxiously urge the matter upon Your Excellency from my belief that a younger and abler man than myself can readily be attained."

Davis believed Lee's resignation was the last thing the Confederacy needed. "Were you capable of stooping to it, you could easily surround yourself with those who would fill the press with your laudations, and seek to exalt you for what you had not done, rather than detract from the achievements which will make you and your army the subject of history and object of the world's admiration for generations to come," he wrote Lee three days later. "To ask me to substitute you by some one in my judgment more fit to command, or who would possess more of the confidence of the army, or of the reflecting men in the country, is to demand from me an impossibility."

Davis rightfully had faith in Lee, but others lacked faith in Davis. "Mr. Davis's friends say that he is honest, pure, patriotic but no administrator — the worst judge of men in the world, apt to take up with a man of feeble intellect or character, and when he has done so, holds on with unreasoning tenacity," wrote Robert G. H. Kean, chief of the Confederate Bureau of War. "It is the same way with ideas. The fatal notion of making each military Department a separate nation for military purposes without subordination, co-operation, or concert — the same on which in point the President and General [George W.] Randolph split — has lost us the Mississippi."

Back on the Gettysburg field, the visual scene remaining was horrific. "Our brigade moved to the front in order to feel and develop the enemy," wrote Capt. Francis A. Donaldson of the 118th Pennsylvania Infantry. "On reaching the slope and foot of the hill — what a sight presented itself. The ground was literally covered with shattered and shot torn limbs of trees, whilst there was scarcely room to move without treading upon the dead body of an enemy. As far as the eye could see the dead lay in all manner of shapes, some upon their faces, others upon their backs, others still kneeling behind the rocks where they had taken shelter, some of them with their muskets still poised and supported by the rocks in readiness to fire."

"I spent the night in the middle of the battlefield with the dead and wounded that still remained," recorded Col. Philippe de Trobriand. "This morning, I saw all around me, the most terrible piles of bodies that I never saw before. In some places and in front [of] our batteries they were piled up." After walking across the battlefield, Pvt. Wilbur Fisk described the scene: "Their bodies were swollen, black, and hideously unnatural. Their eyes glared from their sockets, their tongues protruded from their mouths, and in almost every case, clots of blood and mangled flesh showed how they had died, and rendered a sight ghastly beyond description. My God, could it be possible that such were lively and active like other people so shortly previous, with friends, parents, brothers and sisters to lament their loss. It certainly was so, but it was hard to realize it."

Those who had survived the battle had a spectrum of discomforting problems to contend with. "As I thought you would be uneasy about me I have concluded to drop you a few lines to let you know that I am well and standing the marching very well," Pvt. John Caldwell of the 33d North Carolina had written his father on June 22. "We have just halted from a march of sixteen miles and wading both the forks of the Shenandoah. . . . Don't be uneasy about me." The next communication the family received was a letter from Col. Clarke M. Avery, the boy's commanding officer, who wrote on July 18, "I delayed until this time in writing you with the fond hope that I could write you certainly with regard to the fate of your gallant son in the late fight at Gettysburg. . . . On the 3d day we were ordered to storm the heights. We advanced to within forty yards of the Enemys work and it was here that my little friend Jonny fell. . . . A wounded Lt. who was near Jonny (but was unable to walk off the field) thinks he was shot in the breast. . . . Accept for yourself and Mrs. Caldwell my warmest sympathy in account of this distressing casualty."

Pvt. Addison R. Tinsley wrote Charlotte Branch, informing her of her son's wounding at Gettysburg. 1st Lt. Sanford Branch was a Georgia boy who fell and was left in a Yankee field hospital. "You have ere this received I hope the list of casualties in the [Oglethorpe Light Infantry] which at Sandy's request was forwarded . . . to be transmitted to you by telegraph, also a despatch from him in my name as follows, 'Saw Sandy today, doing well, considered out of danger.' I left him about noon today, he was much better than yesterday & cheerful, seemed to feel no danger & requested that I should write you. The surgeon considers him a great deal better, & out of danger. The wound is in the left breast, through the lung. It is of course a severe & dangerous one, but not considered by any means a fatal one." Unlike many, Branch survived Federal imprisonment and the war.

245

Assisted by the poor communication, rumors, and notoriously unreliable newspaper accounts of the day, woundings often produced rumors of the deaths of officers who were alive. "Gen. Frémont desires me to ask if you will refer to the proper communication for information as to time, place, and manner of death of the late Genl. Gabriel R. Paul," Col. Albert Tracy wrote Brig. Gen. Seth Williams, Meade's assistant adjutant general, on July 7. "Also as to where his remains can be obtained. This request is made on application of the brother of Genl. Paul, Mr. E. W. Paul of St. Louis, Missouri." Imagine the Paul family's discovery that their general was not dead after all. In the South, wishful thinking pervaded many early accounts of the battle and campaign. "You have full account of Gen Lees glorious exploits in the North," wrote Confederate Capt. Thomas Henderson. "We have dispatch to day that he has whipped Genl Meade at Gettysburg & taken 40,000 prisoners. Most too many to be true, I have no doubt he has whipped him & may get Baltimore & threaten Washington, but avails but little if [Vicksburg] has fallen."

After Gettysburg, as with the wake of any battle, bickering and posturing surfaced among officers. On the battlefield, after being assigned command of the 1st Corps and then losing the assignment to the trusted officer Maj. Gen. John Newton, Abner Doubleday wasted no time seeking what he believed to be his. "I have the honor to apply for the command of one of the Corps which are now vacant, it being the position to which I think myself entitled by my rank," he wrote Seth Williams on July 3, from the battlefield. Then, with Lee's army escaping, Doubleday argumentatively wrote Williams again two days later. "The order placing Genl. Newton in command of the 1st Corps was at once obeyed by me under the impression he was my senior officer. Will you please tell me whether he is my senior or my junior as there seems to be some doubt on the subject, and I would like to have the question settled at once. Should he prove to be my junior, I desire either to be placed in command according to my rank or be relieved from duty, and ordered to report elsewhere." On the same day, after determining for himself that he was senior to Newton, Doubleday again pestered Meade's adjutant. "Having ascertained officially that Maj. Gen. Newton commanding 1st Army Corps, is my junior, his appointment dating from the 30th of March 1863, while mine dates from the 29th of November 1862, I have the honor to report to Headquarters of the Army for duty." Distrusted by Meade and nicknamed "Forty-eight Hours" because of his slowness to act on the field, Doubleday held only desk commands around the city of Washington for the rest of the war.

If the commanding general liked an officer, the officer was likely to do well even without making applications for promotion. Meade wrote to Halleck on September 1, "I wish to place on record, my earnest personal desire, that as soon as it is practicable, the commission of Maj. Gen. be conferred on Brig. Genls. Buford & Gibbon for distinguished & meritorious services at the battle of Gettysburgh." Gibbon's star rose rapidly during the war; only Buford's untimely death prevented greater glory for him. Still, disappointment pervaded the Lincoln administration even if an odd mixture of celebration and gloom gripped the civilians. "The Army of the Potomac is near enough to Washington, it is true, to be continually interfered with by the authorities here," observed newspaper reporter and politician Noah Brooks in the capital city, reflecting on the army's lack of success relative to the western armies. "And it is also near enough to permit its Colonels, brigadiers, and Major Generals to be rushing in at every frequent breathing spell in pursuit of promotion, changes, and various other favors for themselves, friends, and favorites; therefore, it is no slander to say that the army is one vast hot-bed of bickerings, heart-burnings, and jealousies."

Some, including Brig. Gen. Thomas A. Rowley, were wounded but hurt even more by their foolish actions, such as drinking on the field. "Genl. Rowley . . . failed to obey an order of Major Genl. Doubleday comdg. 1st Corps to relieve the 1st Brigade 1st Division then in his front," accused Brig. Gen. Lysander Cutler, alleging that Rowley had been drunk on the battlefield and demonstrated cowardice in the face of the enemy. Rowley was court-martialed, found guilty, dismissed from service, and then reinstated a year later, when experienced officers, though they might drink, were becoming scarce.

Recent historians have demonstrated that at least to a degree, the Confederate army did not panic following Gettysburg. Even if that is true, much of the Southern press was disgusted with the turn of events. "It is impossible for an invasion to have been more foolish and disastrous," editorialized the *Charleston Mercury*. Other Confederates, even some principally involved in the campaign, seemed lighthearted about the whole affair. If Jeb Stuart was admonished by Lee during the late stages of the battle, he certainly didn't show it in writing his wife, Flora Cooke Stuart, 10 days later. "I am all right thus far, and all the staff have thus far escaped," wrote Jeb. "I had a grand time in Penna. and we return without defeat to recuperate and reinforce. . . . I crossed near Drainesville [*sic*] and went close to Georgetown and Washtn. cutting 4 important railroads and joining our army in time for the battle of Gettysburg, with 900 prisoners and 200 wagons and splendid teams. . . . I have been blessed with great success in this campaign and the accidents and loss in the way of captures are in no way chargeable to my command." Stuart actually seemed to believe the whole operation a grand success. "We must invade again," he continued. "It is the only way to peace. . . . If they had only sent 10,000 reinforcements and *plenty of ammunition* to join him here, our recrossing would have been under banners of peace."

Invasion's End on Falling Waters Road

by Ted Alexander

Brig. Gen. James Johnston Pettigrew

One of the ablest and most highly educated officers of the Army of Northern Virginia, Pettigrew led a division in the famous charge on Gettysburg's third day. The commander was much beloved by his men. On July 14, during the retreat, he was mortally wounded at Falling Waters, Maryland. Pettigrew died three days later in Virginia.

"I want a chance to make one saber charge," Capt. Peter Weber remarked to fellow officer J. H. Kyd as they traveled with the 6th Michigan Cavalry. Riding along the dust-filled roads through Maryland prior to the battle of Gettysburg, the Michiganders could barely envision what lay ahead. Although he was only 23, Weber was a born leader. He had started the war as a private soldier in the 3d Michigan Infantry but soon served as battalion adjutant with the 2d Michigan Cavalry. In 1862 Weber went home to help form the 6th regiment of cavalry. In the Gettysburg campaign the 6th was part of the Michigan Brigade under the newly commissioned Brig. Gen. George A. Custer. Weber and his horse soldiers served credibly, scouting and skirmishing with the enemy. During the campaign, Weber was commissioned a major. At the end of the campaign, on the wet, muddy morning of July 14, Weber would indeed get his chance to lead a saber charge.

Following the brutal destruction of men and supplies at Gettysburg, a long and bloody road lay ahead between the battlefield and the Potomac River. For 11 days the armies jockeyed for position as Lee extricated his battered army. Much of this skirmishing was a cavalry campaign, as the opposing horsemen sparred at locations in Pennsylvania and Maryland such as Monterey Pass, Smithsburg, Hagerstown, Funkstown, Boonsboro, and Williamsport. On July 4 a detachment of Union cavalry had destroyed Lee's pontoon bridge at Falling Waters. Meanwhile, heavy rains had swollen the river to flood stage, forcing Lee to dig in on a line more than 10 miles long from the Williamsport area to Hagerstown.

While his cavalry thrust and parried with the retreating Confederates, Meade marched the bulk of his force via Frederick, Maryland, across the Catoctin and South mountain ranges. By July 12 most of the Army of the Potomac was configured in a line paralleling the historic Hagerstown-Sharpsburg Pike, facing Lee's entrenched Rebels.

Had Meade forcefully attacked Lee along this line, it might have been crushing for the Southerners. But Meade met with his corps commanders and determined not to attack, at least not right away; thus, the Federal commander bought Lee the time to slip the Army of Northern Virginia across the Potomac. On the evening of July 13 the Confederates began crossing the river at two points. Most of them crossed on the newly rebuilt pontoon bridge at Falling Waters; Ewell's Corps and most of Stuart's cavalry waded the river at the ford upstream from Williamsport.

On the damp morning of July 14, Union Brig. Gen. John Buford's mounted division moved from the east to attack the Confederate rear guard. Acting without orders, an impatient Judson Kilpatrick took his command, including the Michigan Brigade, out of Hagerstown and raced toward the Potomac. Kilpatrick's horsemen reached Williamsport just as the last elements of Ewell's Corps waded into the river.

When Kilpatrick received word that more Confederates were crossing five miles downstream at Falling Waters, he turned his column in that direction, in what one cavalryman described as a "wild ride." The Michigan Brigade took the lead. Maj. Weber and two troops, B and F, of the 6th regiment, led the way. The cavalry moved along the

Falling Waters Road in a wooded area in front of Maj. Gen. Henry Heth's position; Heth's division served as Lee's rear guard on this morning. On seeing the well-entrenched Confederate line, Custer ordered Weber and the advanced guard to dismount, form a skirmish line, and probe the Rebel position. Kilpatrick countermanded Custer's instructions and ordered Weber to remount and attack. Weber had fewer than 60 men for the assignment, but, eager for glory, he didn't question Kilpatrick's order.

At first the Confederates believed the Michigan horsemen to be Confederate cavalry assisting the rear guard. They soon realized, however, that the horse soldiers were Yankees. In his report of the action, Kilpatrick termed Weber's attack "the most gallant ever made." One Confederate participant termed it "a charge of dare-devils." Although they penetrated the Confederate line, causing some startled Southerners to throw down arms, the Michigan horsemen were soon in trouble. As Weber's outnumbered men rode up the line, they were cut to pieces. In a flash, 18 Wolverines fell, including Weber, shot in the head. Fourteen more were wounded and most of the rest captured. Confederate losses were negligible, except for a sad casualty of the melee, Brig. Gen. James Johnston Pettigrew, the brilliant coleader of Gettysburg's famous charge.

The fighting along Falling Waters Road transformed into an engagement lasting more than two hours as Kilpatrick thrust more men into a dismounted skirmish line. Though armed with Spencer repeaters, the Federals were repulsed by a Rebel counterattack that was in turn pushed back by Kilpatrick's reinforced line. Meanwhile, part of William Dorsey Pender's Division, now led by Brig. Gen. James H. Lane, returned to support Heth. Buford's troopers came to the aid of Kilpatrick. Eventually the Southerners faced Yankee cavalry along several lines; Heth's soldiers retreated to the river, fighting all the way. On the broken, wooded ground between the river and Heth's front line, a number of Confederate units were separated from the main battle line. Accordingly, many a weary Rebel soldier fell into Union hands. For example, the 34th North Carolina Infantry lost nearly 200 prisoners of their 300 engaged. Altogether, some 1,000 Confederates were captured that day.

That afternoon the Confederates exchanged parting shots with the Union cavalry before crossing the river and finding safety on Virginia's shore. Although the Federal pursuit would continue for several weeks, the Gettysburg campaign essentially ended on July 14 at Falling Waters. Ironically, some of the same commands that opened the battle of Gettysburg on July 1, those of Buford and Heth, ended the campaign north of the Potomac some two weeks later.

**Donnelly House,
Falling Waters, Maryland**
August 26, 2000

In this stately house's garden, one of the premier leaders of the Army of Northern Virginia met his end during the retreat from Gettysburg.

ONE
DAY IN
NOVEMBER

★ NOVEMBER 19, 1863 ★

The Gettysburg Address Ceremony
View southwest
November 19, 1863

252

Eighteen weeks after the battle of Gettysburg it was not at all clear to anyone what the struggle in Pennsylvania would ultimately mean to the American nation. It wasn't clear that there would be an American nation. Perhaps the death and waste of men killing each other would come to no purpose, the American states spiraling away into a European-like fragmentation, and the march of slavery, and the accursed evil of the Constitution, would carry on after all. Such pivotal times in world history offer the chance for actors in the drama to step in to define the moment, to give the momentous events meaning beyond the moment. But this happens only rarely. In the case of Gettysburg and the American Civil War, it did occur. Abraham Lincoln had been invited to Gettysburg to deliver "a few appropriate remarks," as he put it, at the dedication of the new Federal cemetery, where the bodies of Union men and boys lay entombed in the soft Pennsylvania clay just four and a half months after the cannon and muskets ceased to fire across that very spot. Remarkably, Lincoln's invitation had essentially been an afterthought: the main speaker of the day would be the leading orator of the American nation, Edward Everett, age 69, an eminent Unitarian clergyman and statesman. Known by all, Everett had seemingly done it all. He was the first professor of Greek at Harvard; he had been a member of the U.S. House of Representatives from Massachusetts, governor of Massachusetts, minister to Great Britain, president of Harvard, Secretary of State under Millard Fillmore, a U.S. senator, and a presidential candidate.

CHAPTER 9 : ONE DAY IN NOVEMBER

Gettysburg Address Procession
Charles and Isaac Tyson
View north
November 19, 1863

Presumably taken a short time after
the view on page 254, this Tyson brothers image shows the procession itself
moving toward the camera position,
which stood near the intersection of
the Baltimore Pike and the Emmitsburg
Road. Although impossible to confirm,
Abraham Lincoln may be in this scene
of the procession.

The Gettysburg Address Ceremony
Alexander Gardner
View northeast
November 19, 1863

Crowds assembled for the dedication of
the Soldiers' National Cemetery mill
about prior to the Everett and Lincoln
addresses. The Evergreen Cemetery
Gatehouse is visible on the left horizon.
The area of the speakers' stand is on the
right edge of the photograph.

View of the Ceremony Ground
August 21, 2000

NOVEMBER 19, 1863

Gettysburg Address Procession
Charles and Isaac Tyson
View north
November 19, 1863

Prior to the dedication ceremony at
the Soldiers' National Cemetery on
November 19, the Tyson brothers
recorded the scene as Lincoln, Everett,
and other dignitaries prepared to ride
from the town to the cemetery. The
structure at left is the John Rupp House.

Site of the Gettysburg Address
Procession
June 8, 1997

NOVEMBER 19, 1863

Railroad Depot, Gettysburg
May 8, 1996

In November 1863, Abraham Lincoln came to Gettysburg to dedicate the Soldiers' National Cemetery with a two-minute address. He would follow Edward Everett, the primary speaker, who would talk for almost two hours. Lincoln traveled from Washington to Gettysburg by train, disembarking at the town's Railroad Depot, a building that still stands.

The Gettysburg Address Ceremony
P. S. Weaver?
View southwest
November 19, 1863

An unknown photographer's view prior to the ceremony (the image is probably the product of Weaver, according to William Frassanito). It was taken from a position just behind the Evergreen Gatehouse. The area of the speakers' stand is now on the left horizon.

View of the Ceremony Ground
June 8, 1997

In November 1863 the town of Gettysburg was still recovering from the physical damage of the battle, still filing claims to rebuild damaged property and dealing with dead and wounded neighbors and friends. A crowd of at least 15,000 mostly local and regional citizens gathered to witness a parade march from the shell-shocked town up to Cemetery Hill, where a crowd of several thousands would listen to the dedicatory speeches in the new cemetery, constructed adjacent to Evergreen Cemetery.

Lincoln wrote the draft of his speech in Washington (it was not penned on an envelope en route, as the oft-repeated myth would have it) and traveled by train from Washington through Baltimore and on to Hanover Junction in southern Pennsylvania, where the train turned westward toward Gettysburg. Lincoln brought an impressive party of fellow travelers from the capital city. Three cabinet members, William Henry Seward, Montgomery Blair, and John P. Usher, came along. The French minister to the United States, Henri Mercier, accompanied the party as a special guest. Presidential secretaries John G. Nicolay and John M. Hay attended, as did chief marshal Ward Hill Lamon (Lincoln's "bodyguard") and his assistant, Benjamin B. French. Pennsylvania governor Andrew G. Curtin was on hand. General officers were too: Darius N. Couch, Julius Stahel, and Robert C. Schenck were among them. Lincoln and some of his associates stayed at the home of David Wills on Gettysburg's town square ("The Diamond"). Wills, a prominent attorney in town, had helped to organize the event and the creation of the cemetery.

CHAPTER 9 : ONE DAY IN NOVEMBER

The Gettysburg Address Ceremony
View east
November 19, 1863

Another view of the crowd made by an unknown photographer shows a view uphill, away from town, toward the speakers' stand. The Evergreen Gatehouse is visible on the left center horizon, the speakers' stand on the right horizon.

View of the Ceremony Ground
June 8, 1997

The Gettysburg Address Ceremony
View east
November 19, 1863

A rarely published view of the ceremony crowd by an unknown photographer reveals stacks of arms and soldiers amid the crowd.

257

The Gettysburg Address Ceremony
View southeast
November 19, 1863

The most celebrated view of the
dedication ceremony is this one,
probably by Bachrach, an employee of
the Baltimore firm of William H. Weaver.
Taken from downhill, looking eastward
up toward the cemetery, it depicts the
speakers' stand on the left center horizon. Enlargements (see the following
images) reveal Lincoln himself.

258

View of the Ceremony Ground
June 8, 1997

Detail of Bachrach View Showing Speakers' Stand
View southeast
November 19, 1863

A closer view of the crowd around the speakers' stand reveals a throng of dignitaries; Lincoln is at left, bending with his head prominently visible. Studies by Josephine Cobb of the National Archives and by other scholars have proposed identifications for a number of those pictured: Seated on the stand are Pennsylvania governor Andrew Curtin and his young son (right of center). To their left is Secretary of the Interior John P. Usher. To Curtin's right, standing and balding, is Benjamin B. French. To his right, with a partial face recorded on film, may be Gettysburg attorney David Wills. Lincoln's address was so brief that, apparently caught unprepared, the photographer exposed this image at the address's conclusion.

Detail of Bachrach View Showing Abraham Lincoln
View southeast
November 19, 1863

A further enlargement of the Bachrach image clearly shows Lincoln in the frame's center. To his immediate right are his secretaries, John Nicolay and, behind Nicolay, with his lower face obscured, John Hay. The prominent, tall man with top hat to Lincoln's left is Ward Hill Lamon, the "bodyguard" of the president's, who also introduced him. Between Lincoln and Lamon (with a smeared facial image turned sideways) may be William H. Seward. Behind Lamon and to his left is the balding figure of Everett, his face partially smeared.

259

Edward Everett

Former congressman, minister to the Court of St. James, president of Harvard University, secretary of state, teacher, and Unitarian clergyman, Everett represented the pinnacle of American intellectualism in the mid-19th century. He was 69 years old in 1863, and his address at the Gettysburg ceremony, though well crafted and meaningful, plodded on for almost two hours before the beleaguered crowd.

Abraham Lincoln

Lincoln was 54 when he came to Gettysburg, a veteran of two and a half years of presidential experience during the most tumultuous era in American history. His brief address, which many thought inadequate at the time, would stand as one of the great statements of democratic thought in world history. This image of the president was made II days before the Gettysburg dedication ceremonies, at the Washington gallery of Alexander Gardner.

On the appointed day, Thursday, November 19, the parade and dedication absorbed the small community. On horseback, Lincoln rode in the procession that moved slowly toward the hill and burying ground. Some 3,629 Union soldiers would lie interred within what would eventually be termed Soldiers' National Cemetery, and later Gettysburg National Cemetery, adjacent to the town's own cemetery, Evergreen. Despite the cold weather and incontinence caused by failing kidneys, Everett managed to rise to the speakers' platform, erected where all could see the event, and deliver his lengthy address. Everett's speech droned on for 117 minutes, filled with wordy, purple declarations aimed at the heavens, at Americans, or at the dead.

After nearly two hours of Everett, the crowd was more than ready for the president. Lincoln's rise and subsequent speech was so brief, lasting only two minutes, that a photographer on hand had just barely made an image of Lincoln and the surrounding group of dignitaries by the time the commander-in-chief sat down. Lincoln's "few appropriate remarks," saved in five separate versions with minor variations (possibly it was the so-called second draft used for the speech), were

Four score and seven years ago our fathers brought forth, upon this continent, a new nation, conceived in Liberty, and dedicated to the proposition that all men are created equal.

Now we are engaged in a great civil war, testing whether that nation, or any nation, so conceived, and so dedicated, can long endure. We are met here on a great battle-field of that war. We have come to dedicate a portion of it as a final resting place for those who here gave their lives that that nation might live. It is altogether fitting and proper that we should do this.

But, in a larger sense we cannot dedicate — we cannot consecrate — we cannot hallow this ground. The brave men, living and dead, who struggled here, have consecrated it far above our poor power to add or detract. The world will little note, nor long remember, what we say here, but can never forget what they did here. It is for us, the living, rather to be dedicated here to the unfinished work which they have, thus far, so nobly carried on. It is rather for us to be here dedicated to the great task remaining before us — that from these honored dead we take increased devotion to that cause for which they here gave the last full measure of devotion — that we here highly resolve that these dead shall not have died in vain; that this nation shall have a new birth of freedom; and that this government of the people, by the people, for the people, shall not perish from the earth.

CHAPTER 9 : ONE DAY IN NOVEMBER

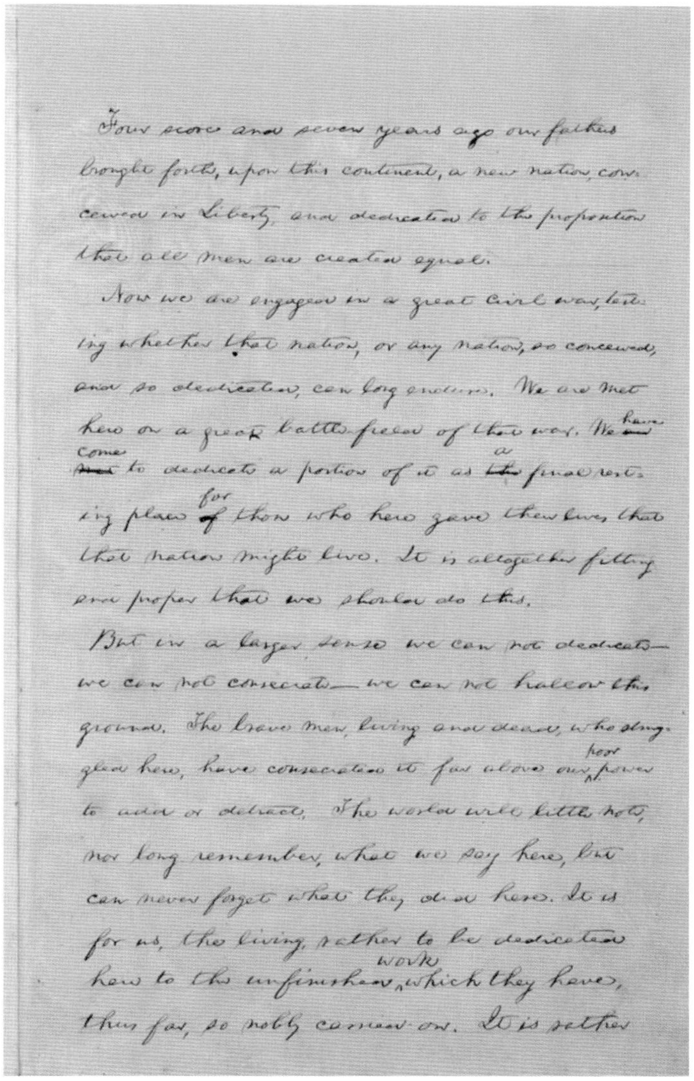

Gettysburg Address, "Hay Copy"

At least seven important versions of the Gettysburg Address are known to exist. In addition to five (or six) copies in Lincoln's hand, two early shorthand reporters' versions exist from journalists on the scene at the dedication. (Scholars are still undecided about the authenticity of a single-page copy of a portion of the address apparently in Lincoln's hand discovered in 1991; that copy, inscribed to David Wills by Lincoln, does appear tantalizingly authentic, which if true would bring the total to eight copies.) The so-called Hay Copy appears to have been written in Washington, and it ended up in possession of John Hay; it may have been Lincoln's file copy.

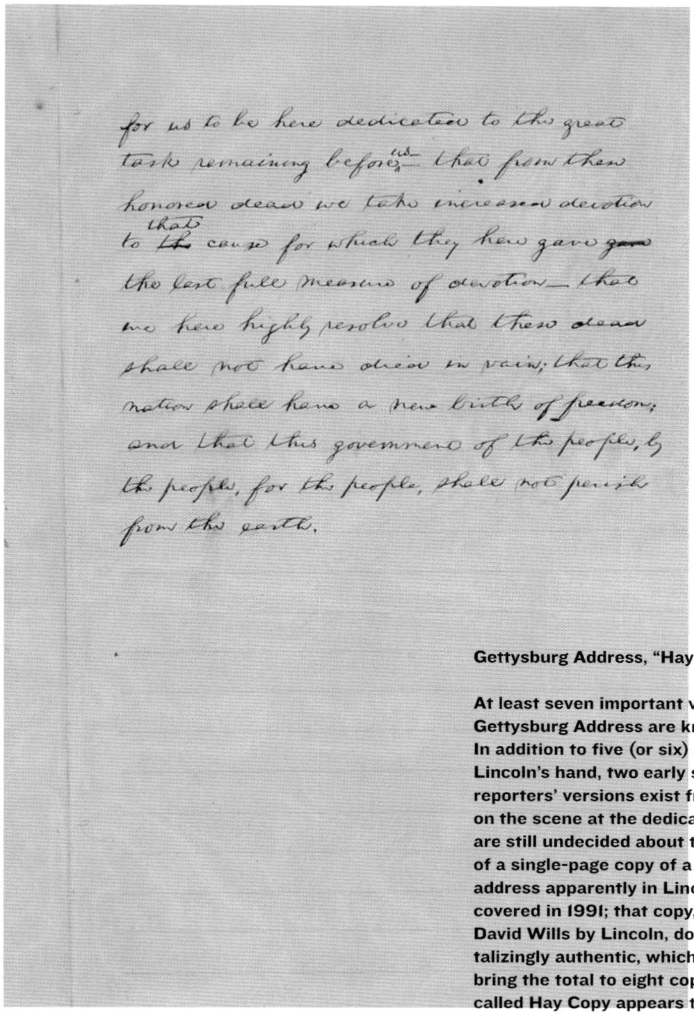

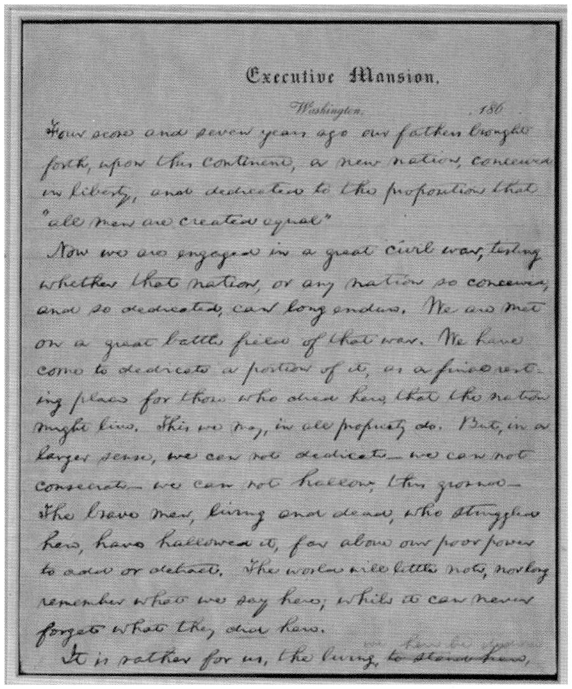

Gettysburg Address, "Nicolay Copy"

The so-called Nicolay Copy, written partly in pen and finished in pencil, appears to be the earliest copy of the address; it was written in Washington and may have been the "reading copy" used at the ceremony. It passed into the hands of John Nicolay, then to Hay after Nicolay's death, and then to the Library of Congress, where both early copies now reside.

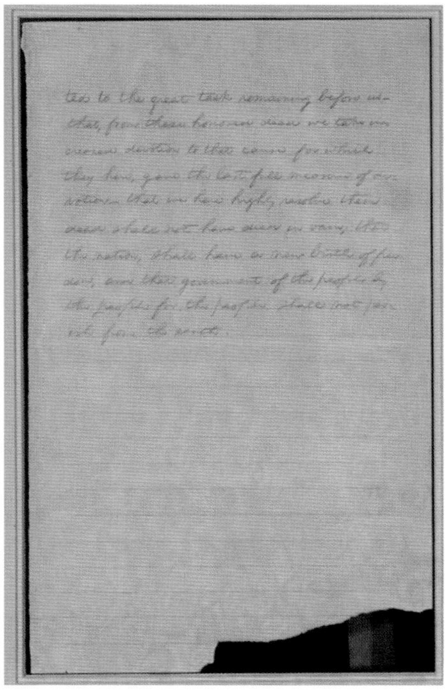

263

NOVEMBER 19, 1863

David Wills House
August 18, 1992

Today the Wills House
contains a museum in
remembrance of
Lincoln's visit.

David Wills

Wills sealed his place in
history by hosting
Lincoln. From a second-
story window in the
Wills house, Lincoln
spoke to a crowd the
night before the address.
After a few words,
Lincoln begged off from
speaking any longer, say-
ing that he "should not
say any foolish things,"
to a response of appre-
ciative laughter from the
onlookers.

David Wills Grave,
Evergreen Cemetery
June 7, 1997

Wills's grave marks the
final resting place of the
man who, among local
citizens, accomplished
the most to preserve and
protect the memory of
the fallen soldiers.

David Wills House
View southeast
ca. 1865

Wills, a prominent Gettysburg attorney,
helped to form the Gettysburg Battlefield
Memorial Association shortly after the
battle and was a driving force behind
establishing the National Cemetery. He
invited Lincoln to stay at his roomy house
on Gettysburg's town square ("The
Diamond") on the president's visit for
the dedication ceremony, and Lincoln
accepted.

Brown Family Vault, Evergreen Cemetery
April 25, 1995

Extensive analysis in the late 1970s by Kathy Georg Harrison and Thomas J. Harrison using the dedication photographs demonstrated that the position of the speakers' stand — of the site of Lincoln's address — was not where it had been presumed to be for more than a century. The presumption was that the site of the Soldiers' National Monument marked the site of the address. Not so. The Harrisons demonstrated the site was higher up the hill, within the boundaries of the present Evergreen Cemetery, near the position of the modern Brown Family vault.

Soldiers' National Monument, Gettysburg National Cemetery
April 25, 1995

Though it may not mark the actual position of the address, the Soldiers' National Monument, erected in an elaborate ceremony in 1869, provides a place for tens of thousands of visitors each year to remember Lincoln's words as they visit the National Cemetery.

John F. Reynolds Monument, Gettysburg National Cemetery
April 25, 1995

The first monument to an individual erected on the Gettysburg field was Reynolds's standing bronze, placed in the National Cemetery in 1871.

New York Monument, Gettysburg National Cemetery
April 25, 1995

One of the most prominent state memorials on the field is that of New York, which was erected in the grounds of the National Cemetery in 1893.

Presbyterian Church, Gettysburg
May 8, 1996

Before returning to Washington, Lincoln met with the oldest hero of Gettysburg, John Burns, at the Wills House. They then walked southward along Baltimore Street to the Presbyterian church, where Lincoln and Burns sat beside each other in a pew. They listened to Col. Charles Anderson, brother of Fort Sumter hero Robert Anderson, deliver a speech about the treacherous nature of the Rebels. At the time, Anderson was Lt. Governor–elect of Ohio. Then Lincoln and Burns parted ways, and the president began his journey back to Washington.

Mary Virginia "Jennie" Wade Grave, Evergreen Cemetery
April 25, 1995

Evergreen Cemetery contains the graves of numerous famous names from the town of Gettysburg — Weikerts, Trostles, Codoris, Culps, Sheads, Bushmans, Benners, and Lightners. Among the most celebrated is the grave of Jennie Wade, the civilian casualty of the battle who was struck by stray fire while baking bread.

John L. Burns Grave, Evergreen Cemetery
April 25, 1995

Burns, who died in 1872, rests with his wife in the local cemetery.

Edward McPherson Grave, Evergreen Cemetery
June 7, 1997

The owner of the farm tract near where the battle commenced, a volunteer aide to John Reynolds, lies peacefully in the cemetery.

U.S. 2d Corps Hospital
Frederick Gutekunst
ca. July 9–11, 1863

The Philadelphia photographer produced this view of the Union 2d Corps hospital along Rock Creek shortly after the battle. It was probably taken when the hospital was situated on the Jacob Schwartz Farm, between July 5 and 23.

Michael Frey Farm, Taneytown Road
May 8, 1996

Dozens of houses and farmsteads served as hospital sites in the wake of the battle. On the east side of the Taneytown Road some 175 yards south of the Granite Schoolhouse Road, Michael Frey's farm served as a Union 2d and/or 3d Corps hospital. The structure also probably briefly served as headquarters for Brig. Gen. Robert O. Tyler, who commanded the Union reserve artillery.

Peter Frey Farm, Taneytown Road
May 8, 1996

North of the Michael Frey Farm and east of the Angle stands the Peter Frey Farm, used on the second and third days of battle as an aid station and hospital. This structure was probably the one where Col. George L. Willard, commander of a brigade in the 2d Corps, was taken after being mortally wounded.

CHAPTER 9 : ONE DAY IN NOVEMBER

Capt. Andrew Ackerman

A survey of the dozens of hospital sites in the days following the battle began to convey the extreme horror of the Gettysburg casualties to Federal military officials. Each of the 45,687 casualties became human, significant once again, as fathers, mothers, sisters, wives, and cousins discovered their boy or husband or kin was dead, ailing, or missing. Ackerman, of the 11th New Jersey Infantry, was killed on July 2 along the Emmitsburg Road.

Albert H. Clark and Jonathan Clark

The Clark boys were killed, along with their father, as members of the 42d Mississippi Infantry on July 1.

Pvt. Joseph K. Ewing

A member of the 4th Virginia Infantry, Ewing was killed on July 3 in one of the Culp's Hill assaults.

Capt. Henry Fuller

An officer of the 64th New York Infantry, Fuller was struck in the eye and fell dead in the Wheatfield on July 2.

Pvt. Francis M. Griswold

One of the defenders of Little Round Top as part of the 44th New York Infantry, Griswold was shot in the head and died on July 2.

Capt. Reuben V. Kidd

One of the brave attackers of Little Round Top, Kidd survived as a soldier of the 4th Alabama Infantry, only to be killed 10 weeks later at Chickamauga.

Pvt. Thomas C. Sheppard

A soldier of the 1st South Carolina Infantry, Sheppard was killed on July 1.

Col. George H. Ward

Commanding the 15th Massachusetts Infantry in the bloody fighting of July 2, Ward was struck in the head and died defending against the attack of Brig. Gen. Ambrose Wright's brigade.

Capt. John C. Ward

On the battle's final day, this officer of the 11th Virginia Infantry was captured.

NOVEMBER 19, 1863

Panoramic View of Camp Letterman
Charles and Isaac Tyson
ca. September 1863

A panoramic view of the camp taken two
months after the battle shows the kind of
tent city that doctors, surgeons, and
nurses occupied along with several thousand patients. The camp was erected
largely on the George Wolf Farm along
the York Pike (the first part on what was
originally called the "Hospital Woods"); it
opened on July 22 and quickly swelled in
size and activity.

Maj. Jonathan Letterman

Amid the terrible loss of life and
heavy casualties following the battle,
Letterman established an efficient
system of generalized hospital and
surgical care at Gettysburg. As medical
director of the Army of the Potomac,
the officer had already done more
than the surgeon general of either
side to progress medical treatment
and sanitation in the field. The primary
hospital established at Gettysburg,
which served the wounded — some
of whom needed weeks of treatment
— for several months, was established
east of the town and would bear
Letterman's name.

Amputation Scene at Camp Letterman
P. S. Weaver
October 1863

It's not known whether this scene
was authentic or staged for the
camera, but in either case it's the
most frequently published view of
a Civil War amputation scene.

Camp Letterman Scene
ca. autumn 1863

In this scene, made in the Hospital
Woods and showing U.S. Sanitary
Commission workers, "Mrs. Holstein's
Tent" is depicted with Dr. Gordon
Winslow, superintendent of the commis-
sion, at right. The others, left to right,
are identified as **Mr. Holstein, Steward
King, Mrs. Bartsman (seated), Anna
M. Holstein, Dr. May,** and **Mrs. May.**

The Kitchen at Camp Letterman
ca. autumn 1863

The kitchen in the Hospital Woods was undoubtedly one of the busiest spots in the Gettysburg area during the weeks following the battle.

U.S. Sanitary Commission Headquarters, Camp Letterman
Charles and Isaac Tyson
August 1863

Among those pictured at the Sanitary Commission headquarters are Superintendent Gordon Winslow (seated, with white beard), and individuals identified as (left to right) Mrs. Winslow, "Surgeon Chamberlain" (seated on table), "Surgeon Brakey," and "Mrs. Sampson" (seated).

U.S. Sanitary Commission Headquarters, Camp Letterman
ca. autumn 1863

A variant view of the Sanitary Commission headquarters shows a United States flag and a vacated tent.

"Capt. Huff's Camp" at Stevens's Knoll
Alexander Gardner
View east
ca. July 4, 1865

For an obscure reason, Gardner exposed
two images at "Capt. Huff's Camp," as he
labeled them, capturing the location at
Stevens's Knoll, close to the present-day
monument to Henry W. Slocum, where
Huff, the officer in charge of commissary
stores for the cornerstone ceremony, was
encamped.

Position of Capt. Huff's Camp
August 21, 2000

Capt. Huff's Camp at Stevens's Knoll
Alexander Gardner
View west
ca. July 4, 1865

A second image of Capt. Huff's camp
reveals a number of soldiers and servants
lounging with cooking pans in the foreground and a wagon with horses in the
background.

Position of Capt. Huff's Camp
August 21, 2000

Camp of the 50th Pennsylvania Infantry,
Culp's Hill
Alexander Gardner
ca. July 4, 1865

On July 4, 1865, a ceremony was held
to lay the cornerstone for the Soldiers'
National Monument in the cemetery.
On that occasion Gardner came to
Gettysburg to photograph the event;
he also made several images in and
around Culp's Hill. His photograph
of the 50th Pennsylvania Infantry in
camp shows the unit that, although
it was not present at the battle two
years before, was dispatched to
oversee the cornerstone ceremony.

Col. Charles H. T. Collis

Even those who were absent from Gettysburg could not escape its spell as a major turning point of the war. Collis (at left, with an unidentified officer), colonel of the 114th Pennsylvania Infantry, termed "Collis's Zouaves," was absent; his unit was led at Gettysburg by Lt. Col. Frederick F. Cavada. Yet after the war Collis could not help moving to Gettysburg and collecting a museum's worth of battlefield relics.

Daniel E. Sickles, Joseph B. Carr, and Charles K. Graham at Gettysburg in 1893

After the war ended, old warriors often visited the battlefield of Gettysburg to remember the great events of the past. Ulysses S. Grant visited the field in 1867. Many of the participants returned, and huge reunions were held on the 50th and even 75th anniversaries of the battle. Troublesome Dan Sickles, who had jeopardized his 3d Corps at the battle only to be carried off after being struck by a cannonball (or possibly a caseshot), responded to comments about his missing monument by alleging, "The whole damn battlefield is my monument." Here Sickles (center) returns 30 years after the battle with former Union generals Carr (left) and Graham, who had served at Gettysburg as a division and brigade commander for Sickles, respectively.

Charles H. T. Collis Grave, Gettysburg National Cemetery
April 25, 1995

After his death in 1902, Collis, a Medal of Honor recipient for Fredericksburg, was buried in Gettysburg National Cemetery.

By the end of 1863, with a bitter war and a partisan political year ahead of him, Lincoln seemed to experience something of a revival in his confidence in the American people as well as the American government, army, and navy. "The President tonight had a dream," wrote John Hay, the day before Christmas Eve. "He was in a party of plain people and as it became known who he was they began to comment on his appearance. One of them said, 'He is a very common-looking man.' The President replied 'The Lord prefers Common-looking people: that is the reason he makes so many of them.'"

The year had begun with a disastrous state of affairs for the American nation as Confederate military victories in the east and west seemed to suggest no end to the violence, and perhaps even the success of a driving peace movement in the North that would help to split the Union and continue slavery in the Southern states. The victories at Gettysburg and, nearly simultaneously, Vicksburg, turned that momentum away, righting the ship of the Federal Union. Lincoln's definition of Gettysburg and what it meant to the United States guided the Union philosophy over the remaining two years of conflict. The battle would help to spark the military conquest of the Rebel states and the reunification of the divided Union. That is why Gettysburg, like no other battle of the war, continued to resurface in the letters, journals, and memories of the soldiers, the civilians, and the descendants of the soldiers, blue and gray, who fought there.

**Grave of an Unknown U.S. Soldier,
Gettysburg National Cemetery**
April 25, 1995

Many of the greatest heroes left no voices from the past, no identities for history. They lie unknown in their graves, nameless victims of a struggle that preserved the nation.

The Monuments

by John Y. Simon

President Abraham Lincoln declared that we "cannot hallow this ground" while in the very process of forever hallowing a battlefield in his address dedicating the Gettysburg cemetery. Instead, said Lincoln, "the brave men, living and dead, who struggled here" had consecrated that ground. Those men, Lincoln need not have added, had all fought for the Union. Their opponents, excluded from the national cemetery, had opposed the "proposition that all men are created equal." Time has softened the impact of a field dedicated to preserving the memory of a battle that saved the nation. Few visit the battlefield today with Lincoln's implicit sense of Union righteousness.

After a battle, how did soldiers know which side had won? For commanders through men in the ranks, the most common indication was possession of the field. Even before officers wrote reports or counted casualties, or journalists could publish assessments, occupation of the ground declared the outcome. An army that withdrew conceded defeat. Confederates left Gettysburg to Union armies apparently too stunned by the magnitude of the conflict to mount an effective pursuit of the foe.

The Gettysburg battlefield was horrifying. Soldiers and civilians first buried their dead, then those of the enemy. Dead horses and mules still littered the field. When Lincoln arrived months later he saw coffins stacked for the reburial of men quickly thrust into shallow and inadequate graves.

Gradually the entire field assumed the aspect of a giant cemetery, with monuments revealing as much about those who built them as about those who fought. Even scenes of bitterest fighting played a role as the nation traveled a road to reunion. During the 1880s veterans of both armies first gathered on battlefields for joint reunions. In 1895, the federal government took over the battlefield, then threatened by an electric railway. Only then did the idea of marking and memorializing the Confederate position gain favor. In 1913, marking the fiftieth anniversary of the battle, President Woodrow Wilson rejoiced that North and South were "enemies no longer, generous friends rather, our battles long past, the quarrel forgotten — except that we shall not forget the splendid valour, the manly devotion of the men then arrayed against one another."

In 1938, veterans North and South came to Gettysburg for a 75th anniversary reunion, and President Franklin D. Roosevelt dedicated an eternal light peace memorial. "Lincoln spoke in solace to all who fought upon this field," said Roosevelt, quite inaccurately. Rhetoric replaced reality as Roosevelt spoke soothingly. "Men who wore the blue and men who wore the gray are here together — brought together by the memories of old divided loyalties, but they meet here in united loyalty to a united cause which the unfolding years have made it easier to see." In that spirit of reconciliation, perhaps Roosevelt lost the quintessential meaning of the struggle, and his words recall mournfully Lincoln's plea "that these dead shall not have died in vain." A statue installed in 1956 represented a veteran believed to be the last surviving soldier of the Grand Army of the Republic. Sentimentality ultimately replaced patriotism as a determinant of honor.

Monuments, statues, and markers represent attempts to impose order and meaning on landscape. First at Gettysburg came the markers, drawing upon soldiers' memories to establish troop positions. Veterans had information too valuable to disappear. Then came memorialization, conscious attempts to shape the meaning that the field would hold for succeeding generations. Amid bitter infighting among Confederate veterans about assigning blame for defeat, James Longstreet lacked a monument at Gettysburg until 1998. Then he received the dubious honor of a poorly proportioned statue, crafted in an outdated style.

Gettysburg today is neither the Gettysburg of the past nor that of the future. Each generation brings to the field its own imperatives; the artistry of the past attempts to shape modern experience without fully succeeding. In the first years of the 20th century, reunion supplanted union as the battlefield theme. Easily forgotten words of 20th-century presidents serve only to emphasize the timeless depth of Lincoln's definition of the Civil War. Across the fields, monuments and statues beseech the visitor to remember what some would prefer to forget.

John Y. Simon received a B.A. at Swarthmore College in 1955 and a Ph.D. in history at Harvard University in 1961. He taught at Ohio State University, began editing The Papers of Ulysses S. Grant *in 1962, and in 1964 moved to Southern Illinois University in Carbondale, where he is professor of history as well as editor of the Grant papers, with 24 published volumes. He is a founder of the Association for Documentary Editing and a spokesperson for the craft. He frequently writes on Civil War topics.*

Notes

Introduction

10. *It was early on the morning* William Frassanito, *Early Photography at Gettysburg*, 83.
10. *On his way back* Ibid., 84.
10. *"They were lying"* Gregory A. Coco, *A Strange and Blighted Land*, 46.
10. *South of town* Ibid.
10. *"In the front room"* Ibid., 58–59.
11. *The battle produced* John W. Busey and David G. Martin, *Regimental Strengths and Losses at Gettysburg*, 312.
11. *"It is all my fault"* Lesley J. Gordon, *General George E. Pickett in Life and Legend*, 116.
12. *The spy, a mysterious individual* Tony Trimble, "Harrison: Spying for Longstreet at Gettysburg," in *Gettysburg*, no. 17 (1997):17–19.
12. *Whether or not Heth's Confederates* David G. Martin, *Gettysburg, July 1*, 63–64.

Chapter I. Lee's Army Moves North

16. *As the year began* John H. Eicher and David J. Eicher, *Civil War High Commands*.
19. *"We should neglect"* Robert E. Lee, *The Wartime Papers of R. E. Lee*, 507–9.
20. *Lincoln, maturing* Abraham Lincoln, *The Collected Works of Abraham Lincoln*, vol. 4, 273.
25. *At 3 A.M. on June 28* Edwin B. Coddington, *The Gettysburg Campaign*, 209.
25. *Among the other candidates* Ibid., 37.
26. *"By direction of the President"* George G. Meade, General Orders No. 66, Headquarters, Army of the Potomac, June 28, 1863, from the George G. Meade Papers, Record Group 94, Adjutant General's Office Records, Generals' Papers, NARA, Washington.
26. *On that day* Jacob Hoke, *The Great Invasion of 1863*, 123.
26. *He became the first soldier* Wilbur Sturtevant Nye, *Here Come the Rebels!*, 245–46.
28. *"Some of the arches"* Ibid., 293.
29. *"I spent some time"* L. M. Blackford, to his father, near Chambersburg, Pennsylvania, June 28, 1863, from the L. M. Blackford Papers, University of Virginia Valley of the Shadow Project Archive, Charlottesville.
29. *"If you find"* U.S. War Department, *The War of the Rebellion: Official Records of the Union and Confederate Armies*, series 1, vol. 27, pt. 3, 913. (hereafter termed *O.R.*)
30. *Meade's orders received* Ibid., series 1, vol. 27, 1, 61.
30. *Additionally, he commanded* Eicher and Eicher, *Civil War High Commands*.
30. *In the afternoon of June 30* U.S. War Department, *O.R.*, series 1, vol. 27, pt. 3, 458–59.
33. *The stories of Confederate expeditions* Ibid., series 1, vol. 27, 2, 637–39.

Chapter 2. Shots Crackle along Willoughby's Run

40. *By 7:30 A.M.* Martin, *Gettysburg*, 63–64.
42. *This ridge held* Frassanito, *Early Photography*, 58–59.
44. *"We were being hurried"* Martin, *Gettysburg*, 100.
50. *The Confederate high command* Eicher and Eicher, *Civil War High Commands*.
50. *His body was taken* Jack D. Welsh, *Medical Histories of Union Generals*, 275.
50. *"He had taken"* Joseph G. Rosengarten, "General Reynolds' Last Battle," in Alexander K. McClure, ed., *The Annals of the War Written by Leading Participants North and South*, 63.

52. *"The line of the [regiment]"* James L. McLean, *Cutler's Brigade at Gettysburg*, 81.
52. *"My color guards"* Lance J. Herdegen and William J. K. Beaudot, *In the Bloody Railroad Cut at Gettysburg*, 201.
56. *One of the great stories* Frassanito, *Early Photography*, 84–87.
59. *"When we were in point blank range"* Robert K. Krick, "Failures of Brigade Leadership," in Gary W. Gallagher, ed., *The First Day at Gettysburg*, 133.
59. *The Union brigade* Welsh, *Medical Histories of Union Generals*, 253–54; Eicher and Eicher, *Civil War High Commands*.
63. *Years later, Gordon* Martin, *Gettysburg*, 291–296.

Chapter 3. A Dizzying Retreat through Town

66. *"I got up and went"* Martin, *Gettysburg*, 314.
69. *Inside the McClellan House* Frassanito, *Early Photography*, 119–123.
69. *There he hid* Martin, *Gettysburg*, 331–32.
69. *By 4:30 P.M.* U.S. War Department, *O.R.*, series 1, vol. 27, pt. 2, 313–325.
71. *According to Lt. Col. H. C. Jones* Martin, *Gettysburg*, 514.
72. *Hancock arrived* Ibid., 483.
72. *Howard allegedly replied* Ibid., 483–487.
74. *"They seemed to fear"* Ibid., 524.
81. *Ewell was also* Ibid., 555.
81. *In another of the multitudes* Jubal A. Early, *Autobiographical Sketch and Narrative of the War between the States*, 271.
82. *Arriving after his journey* Harry W. Pfanz, *Gettysburg: The Second Day*, 42.
82. *The night remained hot* Penrose G. Mark, *Red, White, and Blue Badge*, 216.

Chapter 4. James Longstreet Prepares for Attack

100. *He is known* Welsh, *Medical Histories of Confederate Generals*, 134–36.
101. *Subsequently, Lee and Trimble* Pfanz, *Gettysburg: The Second Day*, 111.
101. *Lee next returned* Ibid., 112.
101. *Longstreet told Hood* Ibid.
102. *Indeed, the written order* Coddington, *The Gettysburg Campaign*, 377.
105. *"The enemy was massed"* Richard A. Sauers, *A Caspian Sea of Ink: The Meade-Sickles Controversy*, 35.

Chapter 5. Union Forces Seize the High Ground

112. *"With this wound"* John Bell Hood, from a letter written from Hood to James Longstreet, June 28, 1875, *Southern Historical Society Papers*, vol. 4, 150 (1877).
113. *With their case shot* Pfanz, *Gettysburg: The Second Day*, 186.
113. *The fighting at the Devil's Den* Ibid., 187.
113. *At one point* Ibid., 187, 191.
113. *Among the dead* Eicher and Eicher, *Civil War High Commands*.
120. *"Soon we found"* Thomas A. Desjardin, *Stand Firm Ye Boys from Maine*, 54.
123. *"At this moment"* Ibid., 68.
123. *"It was imperative"* Oliver W. Norton, *The Attack and Defense of Little Round Top*, 214–15.
123. *"Suddenly, in the midst"* Ellis Spear, *The Civil War Recollections of General Ellis Spear*, 34–35.
123. *Col. Strong Vincent* Welsh, *Medical Histories of Union Generals*, 353.
123. *After the battle* Fred T. Locke, to Seth Williams, Headquarters, 5th Corps, August 7, 1863, from the Strong Vincent Papers, Record Group 94, Adjutant General's Office Records, Generals' Papers, NARA, Washington.
123. *"I'm as dead"* Welsh, *Medical Histories of Union Generals*, 362–63.
123. *Other youthful Unionists* Pfanz, *Gettysburg: The Second Day*, 240.
123. *Paddy O'Rorke* Brian A. Bennett, *The Beau Ideal of a Soldier and a Gentleman*, 124.